Integrated Literacy Instruction in the Middle Grades

Integrated Literacy Instruction in the Middle Grades

Channeling Young Adolescents' Spontaneous Overflow of Energy

Pamela Sissi Carroll
Florida State University

Boston ▪ New York ▪ San Francisco
Mexico City ▪ Montreal ▪ Toronto ▪ London ▪ Madrid ▪ Munich ▪ Paris
Hong Kong ▪ Singapore ▪ Tokyo ▪ Cape Town ▪ Sydney

Series Editor: *Aurora Martínez Ramos*
Editorial Assistant: *Erin Beatty*
Marketing Manager: *Elizabeth Fogarty*
Senior Editorial-Production Administrator: *Anna Socrates*
Editorial-Production Service: *Susan McNally*
Manufacturing Buyer: *Andrew Turso*
Composition and Prepress Buyer: *Linda Cox*
Cover Administrator: *Joel Gendron*
Electronic Composition: *Publishers' Design and Production Services, Inc.*

For related titles and support materials, visit our online catalog at www.ablongman.com.

Between the time Website information is gathered and published, some sites may have closed. Also, the transcription of URLs can result in typographical errors. The publisher would appreciate notification where these errors occur so that they may be corrected in subsequent editions.

Library of Congress Cataloging-in-Publication Data

Carroll, Pamela S.
    Integrated literacy instruction in the middle grades : channeling young adolescents' spontaneous overflow of energy / Pamela Sissi Carroll.
        p.   cm.
    Includes bibliographical references.
    ISBN 0-205-37554-5
    1. Language arts (Middle school)—United States.   I. Title.

    LB1631.C443   2004
    428'.0071'2—dc21   2003050029

Printed in the United States of America

10   9   8   7   6   5   4   3   2   1   08   07   06   04   03

For Joe

CONTENTS

5 Overflowing with Ideas: Writing as Students, Writing as People   121

8   Integrated Literacy across the Curriculum   210

PREFACE

This book is about how prospective and practicing teachers of middle grades language arts can tap into young adolescents' spontaneous overflow of energy and channel that energy toward literacy learning. The goals that are promoted throughout the book focus on helping our young adolescents become effective and critical "languagers," people who receive and generate language to make sense of and know their world. I introduce and reinforce the use of an integrated literacy pedagogy as the theoretical basis on which the book is grounded. The integrated literacy pedagogy combines the following: attention to students as humans with both individual and group identities; attention to students as humans who come to us with differing skills and experiences, interests and anxieties; attention to the need for a broad and expanding dynamic definition of literacy so that what students learn in our classes today will continue to be useful tomorrow; and attention to the balance between our own intuitions and observations as teachers who spend time with our students and the professional standards that guide our decisions regarding curricula and activities.

During the 1980s, when I worked as a teacher of eighth graders at Elizabeth Cobb Middle School in Tallahassee, Florida, I became enchanted with young adolescents. The eighth graders I met were still likely to respond to my statements and queries with wonderment. They wanted to know, to learn, to grow. Unfortunately, I did not have the confidence during my first few years of teaching to be flexible. I did not stray from my teacher's texts or the state and county standards. I was reluctant to encourage participation from my students, because I feared hearing thoughts that I had not anticipated—thoughts that might challenge my authority and knowledge while I stood in front of class. I did not create enough opportunities for my students to choose topics, books, assignments. I restricted my definition of literacy to print texts. I gave tests that covered facts but that did not promote learning. I expected my middle school students to act like adults, since many of them looked grown up.

I still feel apologetic that I did so many things wrong those first few years. However, because I can't apologize to all of the students I taught (or tried to teach) in the 1980s, I have worked instead, over the past 15 years, to begin to articulate what it means to teach young adolescents in middle grades language arts classes. While teaching a specific course, "Teaching English/Language Arts in the Middle School," for over 12 years at Florida State University, I have had the opportunity to collect and cogitate on ideas about the complicated and sometimes exhausting demands of teaching language arts. Finally, and with an enormous amount of help from classroom teachers and university colleagues—whose ideas I have mined shamelessly—I decided that it was time to put my ideas into a methods book for prospective and practicing teachers of middle grades language arts.

In this book, I move from Chapter 1, which is an overview of the four core beliefs of the integrated literacy pedagogy, to Chapter 2, which is a quick look at the realities that today's young adolescents face. From there, the emphasis becomes more specific to the language arts classroom teacher's subject matter. Students are always at the center of the discussions, and the chapters focus on the primary aspects of literacy instruction: reading instruction (Chapter 3), literature instruction (Chapter 4), writing instruction (Chapter 5), oral language instruction (Chapter 6), popular media instruction (Chapter 7), and interdisciplinary instruction (Chapter 8).

    Throughout the book, you will find descriptions of how the chapters reflect the integrated literacy pedagogy, followed by an overview of the chapter plan, or organization. There are scenarios from classrooms, discussions of contemporary theory about the specific subject, and examples of how to move from theory into practice through sample lesson sets. The voices of many talented classroom teachers are sprinkled throughout the book, too, bringing the necessary perspective of teachers who are engaged in literacy instruction as language arts teachers every day. Photographs give us a glimpse into today's middle school classrooms. Chapters 3 through 8 address integration and connections to professional standards: Each includes a list of integrated language activities that are suggested in the chapter, notes on help for English language learners, and a list of the National Council of Teachers of English/International Reading Association Standards for English Language Arts that are addressed within the chapter.

    My hope is that you will find this book useful if you are beginning your adventure as a teacher of language arts. For those of you in teacher education programs, I have included detailed descriptions of the lesson ideas that I introduce. Feel free to modify the ideas to fit your needs. I hope, too, that you will find this book useful if you are an experienced teacher of language arts. Because of its focus on a student-sensitive pedagogy that relies on broad definitions of literacy, I hope that you find some fresh perspectives, some new ways of thinking about what you have learned to expect and what you practice in your classroom. I hope that your teaching will be enriched by the ideas in this book.

Acknowledgments

I would like to thank the teachers of middle school students with whom I work regularly, because they have given me the gift of access not only to their classrooms but also to their thoughts about what today's teachers of middle grades language arts need to know.

    This book would not have been possible without the many contributions of the following wonderful teachers: Jan Graham, Mary Carpenter, Kathy Corder, Mark Shapiro, Anna Jordan, Tameka King, Althoria Taylor, Martha Story, Liza Bryant, Cheryl Kopec Nahmias, Susan N. Wood, Hannah Gerber, Tresha Layne, Rosemary Bunn, Debi Rice, Jennifer Dail, Karen Shipley, and Patricia Buckley. I give special thanks to Jan Graham and Mark Shapiro, teachers at Elizabeth Cobb Middle School in Tallahassee, Florida, for allowing me to photograph their students in action and to include samples of their students' work in the book. I extend special thanks, too, to Kathy Corder and Mary Carpenter, teachers at Augusta Raa Middle School, Tallahassee, Florida, for allowing me to include samples of their students' work in the book.

    This book would not have been possible without the indulgence of my Florida State University colleagues and students in English Education. They covered other bases for me, which gave me time to work on the manuscript. Thank you, Susan Wood and Mike Rychlik and our English Education undergraduate and graduate students. Thank you, also, to John S. Simmons, my now-retired colleague who never stops helping with solid suggestions, careful reading, and moral support.

The following reviewers gave me great advice, especially in helping me bring cohesion to this ambitious book project: Ellyn Arwood, University of Portland; Alexandra G. Leavell, University of North Texas. I am very grateful to them. Thank you.

Aurora Martínez Ramos, Allyn and Bacon editor, has been an extraordinary help and source of enthusiastic encouragement since we first spoke about this project. Thank you, Aurora.

Finally, I thank Joe Donoghue, my husband, a scientist with a fine eye for editing; you know that I always depend on your patience, kindness, and sense of humor.

ABOUT THE AUTHOR

Pamela Sissi Carroll is professor and coordinator of English Education at Florida State University, Tallahassee, Florida. A former teacher of middle and high school English, she now spends significant amounts of time in secondary classrooms, working with prospective and practicing teachers of English /language arts and their adolescent students on research and teaching projects.

Reflecting her long-lasting interest in young adult literature, she served as editor of The ALAN Review from 1998 to 2003. She has written and edited books, chapters, articles, and research reports about the genre of young adult literature, its authors, and its place in the secondary classroom. She has also written about the characteristics of today's young adolescents, and the ways that teachers of English can use those characteristics to inform student-sensitive instruction.

She says she often does her best thinking away from a desk, while running, swimming, biking, or playing in her garden.

Integrated Literacy Instruction in the Middle Grades

1

Spontaneous Overflow of Young Adolescents' Literacy in Language Arts Classrooms

"Poetry is the spontaneous overflow of powerful feelings; it takes its origin from emotion recollected in tranquility."
—William Wordsworth, from the Preface of the 1800 edition of *Lyrical Ballads*

Young adolescents' spontaneous overflow of energy for language.

Adolescents are, for me, what poetry was for Wordsworth: the source of delight, intrigue, surprise, and sometimes dismay with their "spontaneous overflow of powerful feelings." As teachers of literacy in language arts classes, we can help young adolescents channel their energy and enthusiasm for full participation as learners and thinkers in their families, schools, communities, and the world. We can have a profound effect on the ways they see themselves and the ways they become involved in their world—not only in the real world of the future, but now, at this moment in time. Young adolescents already are active in the real world. Our challenge is to help them understand how to use their energy, insights, and knowledge to participate more fully, confidently, and effectively even while they are 10, 11, 12, 13, and 14 years old.

I am convinced that we can meet that formidable challenge through integrated literacy instruction. Integrated literacy pedagogy encourages students to take advantage of their instincts as language users, their interests as young adolescents, and their perspectives as thinkers in the twenty-first century to make sense of and know the world.

What Do We Mean by *Integrated*?

I believe that literacy instruction is most effective when it is integrated across the language arts. We misrepresent the process of learning when we base our teaching on the belief that every bit of knowledge is attained—and every skill is developed—in isolation. A better representation of learning accounts for the importance of learners' interest in finding answers to problems, and for the cognitive and social overlaps that occur as they seek answers both inside and outside school. Examples of the learning overlap, the integration of cognitive and social skills, include these: We improve as writers when we learn to review our work with the eye of a reader. Conversely, we read more critically if we approach a text with the question, "What kinds of clues has the writer left for me here?" By referring to an *integrated literacy pedagogy* throughout this book, I am suggesting that we envision a pedagogy in which the ways that students use language—as speakers, writers, listeners, readers—are viewed, taught, and practiced as unalterably connected elements.

We will, by necessity, need to highlight different aspects of literacy as we consider the contributions of individual components of the language arts curriculum to the overall goal of literacy development. Nevertheless, in this book I promote an approach in which we will draw on all of the language arts to support the development of each of the individual components that will result in literacy. These individual components include the following: reading (Chapter 3); literature (Chapter 4); writing (Chapter 5); listening, speaking, and language (Chapter 6); and visual and nonprint media (Chapter 7). By giving critical attention to each component, we will be able to see its unique properties, as well as those that it shares with the other literacy components.

The element that each of these components shares is language: Language is the vehicle that we can teach students to rely on for meaning making, for knowing one's world. Skill as a user of language—in its spoken, written, and other symbolic forms—is an essential characteristic of literacy.

What Does Integration Have to Do with Literacy?

Literacy is the ability to make sense of, to know, one's world. According to this definition, literacy demands are present within classrooms and beyond the boundaries of educational institutions. We develop literacy so we can participate actively in our lives. A young adolescent will demonstrate some of the kinds of literacy that are usually associated with language arts classrooms when she does the following: reads a poem, writes a journal entry about how it makes her feel, discusses the poet's use of figurative language within the poem, and offers ideas about what the poem means for her. This demonstration usually occurs on the request of a language arts teacher, and the student may even receive an evaluation and a grade as a measure of the success of her literacy performance. But this same young adolescent will also demonstrate some of the kind of literacy associated with participation in life when she does the following: reads and evaluates magazine advertisements for two different brands of shampoo, weighs the claims of the advertisements against her friends' opinions about the two brands, and then decides on the better choice in terms of her own purposes and priorities. This demonstration is unlikely to happen within a classroom, and its success is measured by the adolescent's satisfaction with her choice. It gives us one picture of how adolescents draw on literacy in the world beyond schools and classrooms.

The deceptive simplicity of my definition of *literacy*, "the ability to make sense of, to know, one's world," hides enormously complex questions about what it means to "know." What, for example, do we mean when we suggest that students know a work of literature, or a song, or one author's narrative style? What do we mean when we say that adolescents should know how to write an essay or that they should know how to behave when buying movie tickets at the mall? For teachers, the epistemological question of *knowing* and the pedagogical question of *teaching* are connected: How can we teach so that others can know?

Are these questions new to our Information Age? Not at all. Roman orator Quintilian addressed them when, in the first century A.D., he asked, "For what object do we have in teaching, but that the student might not always have to be taught?" Comenius, in the seventeenth century, explained that the purpose of teaching was "not so much to make men learned as to make them wise, to give them understanding of their own ends and the end of all things" (Rusk & Scotland, 1979, p. 65). Rousseau, in the eighteenth century, spoke through his student Emile to explain that children learn best through firsthand experience. While he believed that the aim of education is "the liberty and happiness of the child," he recognized that "liberty and constraint are compatible" (Rusk & Scotland, 1975, p. 107). Froebel, through the mid-nineteenth century, pushed for a doctrine of education that encouraged children to explore their worlds with an ultimate aim that, through exploration and play, a young person's spiritual nature would be awakened. He suggested that good education leads one to be in conformity with his or her highest nature (Rusk & Scotland, 1979, p. 178). From the first year of the twentieth century, John Dewey insisted that attention be given to students' experiences, interests, and interpretations. In *Democracy and Education* (1916), he declared, "The pupil must learn what has meaning, what enlarges his horizon, instead of mere trivialities" (p. 186).

Through my experiences as a teacher of young adolescents in middle grades language arts classes, and as an observer of hundreds of middle school teachers, preservice teachers, and young adolescent students, I have learned that the primary dilemma of our profession is difficult to reconcile: We are experts who are paid to share our knowledge. However, it is only when we teach our students how to make sense of and know their worlds for themselves and not to rely just on our interpretations, information, and formulas, that we have succeeded. The best teachers are wise and experienced enough to know when the information that they hold in their minds and the attitudes that they have developed through their own learning may interfere with their students' growth. They know the moment when information should be withheld or deferred so that their students will have an opportunity to engage in making sense of and knowing the world for themselves.

In the twenty-first century, integrated literacy education for young adolescents can incorporate the best of pedagogies from former centuries, including attention to a broadly defined knowledge base, intellectual and spiritual exploration, and personal connections with what has meaning for the learner. This book explores ways to integrate literacy instruction in language arts classes. For example, we focus on writing instruction, and within that focus, we explore ways to use writing to support young adolescents' literature learning. We focus on instruction in listening and speaking, and within that focus, we consider how listening skills can support young adolescents' critical viewing of nonprint media advertisements. Our goal throughout is to teach young adolescents to develop their own abilities to make sense of, and know, their world.

A Bit of Personal History

I recommend this integrated literacy pedagogy because I would have found it helpful when I was a new middle school teacher. After completing a university degree and a stringent teacher certification program, I was hired to teach English at the high school level. My responsibilities included ninth grade basic and advanced and eleventh grade general and honors courses. It was exactly the kind of position I had imagined for myself. My students and I read *The Red Pony*, *I Know Why the Caged Bird Sings*, *The Great Gatsby*, and *The Catcher in the Rye*. They performed crucial scenes from *A Raisin in the Sun*. They wrote books of poetry and recorded their favorites as songs. Despite the fact that I thought I had to wear my hair in a tight bun to appear teacherly, and despite the fact that one student challenged me to an arm-wrestling match over a grade that he received and did not like, it was a great year. I was where I was meant to be and planned to stay there.

To my surprise, I was fired on the last day of school that first year. Well, I wasn't really fired, but I was released. The county in which I worked announced that all new teachers had to be released from duty, due to a funding crisis. What I got, along with a few sweet end-of-the-year notes from students, was a pink slip.

Fortunately, the principal at the high school where I had worked put in a good word for me at the county office. In late August, I got a call from another principal, asking me to interview for a teaching job. When I arrived for the interview, the reality of the situation struck me: This job was located in a *middle school*. The subject I would be asked to teach is called "language arts," not the comfortable, dependable, always-capitalized "English." More important, at a middle school, I would be expected to teach *young adolescents*. They are not almost college-aged, like many of the high school students with whom I had bonded the previous year. I had seen middle school students seated in large packs at the food court in the local mall, and what I saw made me nervous: young teens and preteens, 10- to 14-year-olds. Prepubescents and pubescents. 'Tweenagers. These and other ugly labels rushed into my thoughts. Yes, I had learned during my teacher preparation program about the differences between middle schools, junior highs, and high schools. I could design a thematic unit, complete with evaluative matrix, that would be appropriate for teaching to a group of sixth graders. I was familiar with authors who were featured in the literature anthologies that seventh graders were assigned. I knew that some clever teachers were capable of helping eighth graders produce entertaining essays as well as identify the parts of speech correctly. I even understood the cognitive developmental stages for 11- to 14-year-olds as described by Jean Piaget. But I saw myself as a teacher of *high school students*. Young adults. People with whom I could have real conversations about issues that mattered. What in the world would I do with middle school kids?

When I accepted the position (I have to confess that I needed the money and the respect that came with saying that I had a full-time job), it was with a sense of having been demoted. I felt as though I had failed high school and had been sent to middle school as some sort of delayed punishment from the principal's office. But my attitude changed in less time than it took me to welcome the first group of students I met that August to their eighth grade language arts class. Those students, their classmates, and those who followed during the next several years proved to me that having the opportunity to teach young adolescents is a gift. Shortly after I started teaching eighth graders that second year of my teaching life, I realized that I had not been demoted but promoted to what I believe is the most challenging, interesting, frustrating, and wonderful teaching position that exists today: teaching language arts in the middle school. Middle school students taught me that they use language in a combination of ways as they work to make sense of and know their world, to articulate their place within it. They showed me that their writing improved when their interest and skill as readers increased. They showed me that they wanted to know how to be informed viewers of television and magazine advertisements so that they would not fall victim to advertisers' manipulations. They taught me that language arts instruction requires the ability to keep one eye focused on a primary curricular concern, while also accounting for other concerns—personal, social, and academic.

Developing the flexibility to consider more than one focal point at a time did not come easily for me. For example, during that first year, I asked my eighth grade students to prepare and deliver persuasive speeches for their classmates. My curricular focus was on the product: the speech itself. The students taught me that I had failed to consider all of the literacy skills they would need to draw on to develop and present a successful speech. They had to use their skills as researchers and as readers who could separate significant information from less important ideas. They had to rely on their knowledge of rhetoric and their skills as writers to craft persuasive arguments. These were curricular connections that had not occurred to me when I first designed and gave the "Create and present a persuasive speech" assignment. There were personal and social aspects of the lesson that I had failed to account for as well. Students needed to feel comfortable in the role of speaker so they could present their speeches with convincing authority and oratorical success. Yet some were so nervous that, when it was their time to give their speeches, their words were inaudible. Some were unable to control the shaking of their hands. Some were embarrassed to the point of tears when they stood alone as the center of the class's attention.

I was mortified that I had failed to account for complex ways in which the literacy tasks associated with giving a persuasive speech were integrated. The integrated literacy pedagogy that I present in this book, in a sense, came directly from middle school students who taught me their way. If I could apologize to those eighth graders for my lack of understanding of the ways they use language to make sense of and know their world, I would. Instead, I have written this book to help you understand what eluded me when I started teaching: the power of an integrated literacy pedagogy for teachers of young adolescents.

Language and Literacy Demands of a Middle School Student

Let's take a moment to consider a scenario that demonstrates a tiny fraction of the kinds of literacy demands that a middle school student must face in order to make sense of her world:

In a half-hour, Krista will leave the house for a before-school workout: Krista is a swimmer who is interested in good nutrition, since she knows that her speed in the water depends in part on the strength and condition of her muscles. When she groggily stumbles into the kitchen, she must decide which of three cereals in the pantry is the best breakfast choice. She reads the competing claims of Kellogg's advertisers, who insist that the snap, crackle, and pop of Rice Krispies provide 10 essential vitamins and minerals and 110 calories, with only 2 grams of fat. She weighs that information against the message of the Post advertisers, who point out that the wholesome, sweetened rice cereal Cocoa Pebbles has 10 vitamins and minerals, plus real cocoa, and is low fat, too. Then she turns to the box of Heartland Granola Cereal, where she reads that the ingredients include whole grain rolled oats, whole grain rolled wheat, brown sugar, and raisins (none of which she saw on the other two boxes). She sees that this cereal has more grams of fat and more calories and uses a smaller serving size.

How does Krista make an informed decision? Does she want taste, fat content, or number of calories to have the strongest influence in her choice? How much does she know about how many calories she will need to fuel her swimming workout and stave off hunger until lunchtime? Does she know the difference between calories gained from carbohydrates and those that come through protein? Perhaps her decision will come down to the appeal of a cereal box: Rice Krispies has an Ernie and Bert Global Adventure game on the back— it almost looks like the page of a geography book, with photographs of animals found in Kenya; Cocoa Pebbles has a cartoon-enhanced Cocoa-Stone National Park game, including riddles, on its back panel; Heartland Granola has an old-fashioned oval picture of a farmer cutting wheat stalks above several paragraphs of narrative text. Wanting to swim well, she selects the granola, convinced that she'll need the extra fat calories to fuel her workout.

The print and nonprint information that Krista must process to make the best decision regarding a breakfast cereal is only a preview of the kinds of literacy skills she will use during her school day. At school, she will use literacy skills to make sense of her social and academic settings. Before the opening bell, she will begin to sort out the difference between fact and opinion in the information and gossip that she and her friends exchange. She will determine how much of what she hears is reliable and legitimate and then decide whether or not she will write a note to her best friend about it during math class. She will use literacy skills in a more formal way in each of her classes. During her first period language arts class, she will read a short story and write an essay about the effectiveness of one author's use of figurative language. During science class, she will collaborate with a partner to prepare a diagram that depicts the results of their recent photosynthesis experiment. In mathematics, she will interpret instructions for a set of bonus questions (and the substitute teacher, who is filling in while her regular teacher is out sick, does not know how to assist her at all). Krista will go with her social studies class to the media center, where she will use the Web to locate information for her project on the Holocaust, yet she will run into difficulty when she finds some visually appealing but troubling sites that claim that the Holocaust never happened. And when she gets to physical education, the teacher will ask Krista to help the new student from Bolivia, since he cannot understand the teacher's directions about how to serve the ball.

This hypothetical outline of Krista's school day provides a glimpse into the kinds of challenges that young adolescents face when trying to make sense of their world. The following list delineates the kinds of literacies that Krista had to deal with in one day:

- Engaged in use of prior knowledge of nutrition and exercise connections;
- Read three cereal boxes with a critical eye toward her specific needs;
- Thought critically about how to separate facts from opinions when she heard and participated in school gossip;
- Read a story to enjoy it and also to take information from it;
- Wrote an essay about the nature of the author's use of language within the story;
- Collaborated orally with classmates to produce a graphic (symbolic) explanation of a science experiment;
- Interpreted print text;
- Used Web-based technology to conduct research;
- Thought critically to evaluate the contents of Web site information;
- Listened and spoke carefully to a classmate who was an English language learner.

Today's literacy requires being able to read and write; to view television, movies, videos, and advertising critically; and to distinguish between helpful and accurate information and misleading or even dangerous information, especially when it is presented in flashy ways on the Internet. Literacy means being able to calculate or compute numbers and use formulas from sources as different as national nutritional guidelines and the kinds of coins needed for parking meters and subway tickets. Literacy also requires being aware of different racial, regional, social, even generational dialects within the context of the social and academic power and prestige that we associate with language. The definition of literacy is thus situational, dependent on what a person needs to be able to do at a given time to make sense of the world, to know it.

Teaching Literacy and Encouraging Languaging

Those who teach today's middle school students must acknowledge that the job extends beyond preparing students for the demands they will face as readers and writers. Today, our job requires that we help them recognize and deal with the demands they will face as they strive to make sense of the practices, values, and beliefs of people from a variety of ethnic and cultural backgrounds. In the twenty-first century, personal literacy must include elements of cultural and social literacy along with academic knowledge.

Today, we must move away from the former definitions of *literacy* that were based on the belief that the discipline of English includes three discrete subjects and treats them in isolation: literature, written composition, and spoken language. Instead, we must strive to incorporate attention to our students' world into our literacy curricula. The curricula that we develop should allow students to explore their world with the one vehicle that all of the broad-based elements of literacy have in common: using language to think, to make sense of the world. This vehicle for thinking is what I refer to as the act of using literacy, or "languaging." I use the gerund form because it suggests a sense of the dynamic nature of interplay of words, phrases, sentences, and other language structures in spoken and written forms. In the section that follows, I explain how the notion of languaging functions as the foundation for the integrated literacy pedagogy. Languaging has a lot in common with *metacognition*; both are concerned with our ability to think about our thinking. Languaging goes a step further, because it implies that we not only think about our thinking but we also act on what we find in our thoughts: We synthesize and evaluate our ideas as we work toward the process of making sense of—and knowing—the world.

The Integrated Literacy Pedagogy: A Focus on Languaging

In this book, the term *integrated literacy* denotes a pedagogy, or approach toward teaching and learning, in which four core beliefs are interrelated and inseparable, and in which the goal is to help young adolescent students master languaging: (1) a recognition that students come to us both as individuals and as members of many groups, including at least one group in which we, as teachers, have a significant presence: our classrooms; (2) a willingness to put our students' immediate and future needs as learners and as humans in front of other classroom or personal goals; (3) a definition of *literacy* that is as broad as possible, with constant attention to students' use and interpretation of language, to inform all of our decisions about curricula and learning activities; (4) a habit of consulting professional standards as guidelines that complement our own intuition, observations, and knowledge about what needs to occur in our classrooms. Each of the core beliefs is described in the paragraphs that follow.

Belief One	Belief Two	Belief Three	Belief Four
Young adolescents are individuals; young adolescents are members of many groups.	Our students' needs and interests must take precedence over all other classroom goals.	We must draw on a broad definition of literacy to prepare today's young adolescents to participate in the twenty-first century.	We must balance our own intuitions and observations with professional standards when making teaching and learning decisions.

FIGURE 1.1   Four Core Beliefs of an Integrated Literacy Pedagogy

Belief One: A recognition that students come to us both as individuals and as members of many groups, including at least one group in which we, as teachers, have a significant presence: our class.

This belief requires that we, as teachers, rely on a current and dynamic base of knowledge about the world that our students inhabit and about what young adolescents experience in general. We need to incorporate information about the immediate realities that affect our students with a broad understanding of the physical, psychosocial, and intellectual characteristics of young adolescents in general. We need to know the linguistic backgrounds that our students bring as part of their family identities, and to learn about the cultural affiliations that influence them, so that we will treat them with the genuine respect that will allow us to build relationships with them. We cannot merely make assumptions about the prevalent attitudes and values of today's middle school students based on what the general public believes, since their perceptions are often colored by negative reports about adolescents and tarnished memories of adolescence. Instead, we must build a base of knowledge that is informed by our adolescent students' actual perceptions of their world and their place in it, including the world we share with them: our classrooms and schools. Too, we must learn what we can about what sets young adolescents apart from the children they once were, and the older adolescents whom they will become. (See Chapter 2, "Today's Young Adolescents," for specific information that can provide a starting place for this knowledge base).

In practice, this belief means that we view a student like Krista, in the previous vignette, as much more than a female student in our language arts class. She is also a daughter, a friend, an athlete. As her teachers, we must remember that she brings each of those roles and group memberships with her when she enters our classroom. We must be willing to study Krista, to know her as a thinker and as a person, as an individual and a member of the class group, if we want to help her learn to use literacy to make sense of her world.

As teachers who espouse an integrated literacy, we must even be willing to talk with other school professionals, including media specialists, counselors, and administrators, to help our students become more skilled languagers, better meaning makers. We must be willing to find ways to get the parents of each of our students involved in the activities and goals of our classes. We must be committed to talking frequently with our students to uncover their insights as experts on the literacy demands on youth when we need to add new dimensions to our perceptions. In short, the integrated literacy pedagogy assumes that we, as teachers, are obligated to use our experience and expertise to help students grow. Further, it assumes that teachers are prepared and eager to provide not only carefully structured academic guidance for our students but also personal and social support for the young adolescent students in our classrooms.

Belief Two: A willingness to put our students' immediate and future needs as learners and as humans in front of other classroom or personal goals.

This belief, which is closely connected to the first, must be evident in all facets of our classroom lives: when we are involved in planning instruction, assessing students' current situation, choosing texts, evaluating students' growth, reflecting on the effectiveness of lessons, and communicating with other school professionals, our students' parents, and the students themselves. The belief requires that we intentionally create and implement instructional goals, assessments, lessons, extensions, and evaluations that reflect not only our subject expertise but also what we know about our particular students in our specific school settings. This is the part that every teacher has to learn for him- or herself; no one has the opportunities to observe, talk with, and ponder your students the way you do when you are in your classroom with them.

This belief indicates that the integrated literacy pedagogy values student-sensitive approaches over the student-centered ones in which teachers repudiate their classroom authority in the name of allowing students full academic freedom. As teachers in student-sensitive classrooms, we are obligated to improve our ability to understand our students and to find ways to help them develop as languagers. We show our concern for students not only through the ways that we interact directly with them but also by continually developing our professional knowledge bases (your reading of this book is one example of your professional development). We then are able to combine our professional knowledge, our observations of the realities of our students' lives, and our instincts and intuitions about the needs of our students. We learn to rely on what Catherine Snow, a Harvard researcher and former president of the American Educational Research Association (AERA), refers to as "personal knowledge" (Snow, 2001, p. 3).

We must pay careful attention to our students' physical, psychosocial, and intellectual characteristics and listen with respect to what Richard Beach and Jamie Myers refer to as our students' "concerns, issues, and dilemmas" (Beach & Myers, 2001, p. 17). We must pay particular attention to those students who, by virtue of linguistic barriers, poverty, special physical or emotional needs, are less empowered, and whose voices are weaker than their classmates' voices. Then we must rise to the (gigantic) challenge of creating and implementing lessons that account for this mix of student characteristics and concerns and our professional and personal knowledge. To do anything less is to abrogate our responsibility as a teacher of the young adolescents who are members of that group to which we also belong: our class.

Teachers who approach teaching and learning with a student-sensitive stance recognize that students need to be active participants in their literacy development. These teachers make students' interests, concerns, and issues apparent in the curriculum. For example, these teachers may choose to include the adolescent novel *Hatchet* (Paulsen, 1987) as a part of a unit on survival, because they know that many middle school readers have responded positively to the book for many reasons, including the length of the book (it is short and the reading difficulty level is low); the age of the protagonist (Brian is a young teen); the narrative voice (Brian's); the intriguing setting (a desolate location in the Canadian wilderness); the plot situation (young Brian is the sole survivor of a small plane crash; his parents' impending divorce is on his mind as he tries to stay alive); and the themes (self-sufficiency and dependence, family relationships, what really matters).

Yet advocates of the student-sensitive integrated literacy stance also insist that teachers assume a strong directive and supportive presence in the classroom. For example, instead of merely handing students a copy of *Hatchet* and telling them that they might want to read it, a teacher who practices a student-sensitive integrated literacy pedagogy will actively lead the class in the study of the novel. He may introduce a prereading activity such as having small groups list the things that they believe they would need to survive if left alone in the wilderness. The teacher might conduct short during-reading lessons that focus on Paulsen's development of characters in *Hatchet* by having students track the decisions that Brian has had to make for himself up to the page they are on. From the tracks that Brian leaves, they can draw conclusions about whether or not Brian is becoming more self-sufficient, more mature, or more unsure of himself. The teacher might ask students from different ethnic backgrounds to describe how an adolescent from their home culture would react—what he would do first, what would he tell himself, and so on—if he became stranded in a frozen wilderness like the protagonist in this story. The teacher could conduct a wrap-up activity in which students go to the Web to collect information and photographs on Canadian wilderness areas, including the habits of the animals and typical weather patterns in those areas and then use that information to create Brian's survival journal.

The point is that when we incorporate a student-sensitive integrated literacy pedagogy, we work not only as time and activity managers, as we might do in a student-centered classroom, but also as experienced readers, writers, thinkers, and meaning makers who recognize that our adolescent students benefit from our guidance, encouragement, and expertise, as well as from the freedom that we give them as they seek answers for themselves. The difference between this student-sensitive perspective and some more traditional teaching stances, however, lies in this fact: Instead of being controlled solely by a set of pre-established lesson plans, the flow of our lessons must also be determined by the directions that our students' responses to the novel, the writing assignment, or the viewing of a film take the class.

In practice, this belief means that we would acknowledge a student like Krista not only when she writes a compelling essay but also for her contributions to the swim team. We could encourage her to engage in activities that draw on her interest in athletics as a vehicle for developing her abilities to think critically and express her ideas appropriately and powerfully—student-sensitive languaging activities.

Belief Three: A definition of literacy that is as broad as possible, with constant attention to students' use and interpretation of language.

This belief implies that we are willing to redefine and reconceptualize *literacy* by thinking of it in its plural form, *literacies*. Our lessons need to reflect the variety of understandings that today's young adolescents must be able to negotiate in order to read a wide range of messages, while focusing on the central place that language has as a medium for communication and expression. The development of literacies will require that our students learn to give critical attention not only to linguistic and numeric symbols but also to graphic, musical, dance, and multimedia representations of ideas as they work to make sense of the world they inhabit. We must help them learn, for example, to think critically about the messages regarding appropriate behavior that they watch on television, the promises they hear in politicians' speeches, the claims of fulfillment that they see offered by advertisers.

This belief leads us to look for ways to acknowledge the impact of popular culture on our young adolescent students. It also prompts us to bring samples of popular media into our classrooms, where we can help students find ways to critically read them, and to discover ways that they can create media as well as the ways that media creates them. It encourages us to allow discussion of the cultural, racial, and linguistic stereotypes from the perspectives of members of dominant and minority groups, so that students and teachers will learn to look beyond their perspectives when considering the impact of media on adolescents. (See Chapter 7, "Overflowing with Competing Messages: Critiquing Popular Media" for more on media literacy.)

This belief also carries with it an obligation that those of us who practice a student-sensitive integrated literacy pedagogy consider multicultural differences among our students, especially as they relate to learning and performance in our classrooms. When we define literacies, we need to consider what they look like, and how they are used, in terms of students of various genders, races, and ethnicities and for those who live in poverty or with special physical, emotional, or learning needs. All of today's young adolescents need our help in learning how to draw on multiple literacies as languagers.

In practice, this belief means that we help Krista recognize the multiple sources of information that she must navigate through, from the competing claims of breakfast cereal makers to the pleas of her friends. It means, too, that we help her learn to think about and respond effectively to the sometimes competing sources of information so she can make well-informed choices.

Belief Four: A habit of consulting professional standards as guidelines that complement our own intuition, observations, and knowledge about what needs to occur in our classrooms.

This belief posits that we, as teachers, are willing to refer to reliable standards and use them as resources when we assess students' knowledge and skills, establish instructional goals, implement instruction, and evaluate learning and growth. We need to be willing to recognize the curriculum and performance standards most closely associated with our state and local school systems, and use them as guidelines or resources when planning and implementing instruction and evaluation of our students. We also benefit from familiarity with the standards established by leaders in the national and international organizations that we respect, such as the National Council of Teachers of English, the International Reading Association, and the National Middle School Association (an outline of the professional standards of these three groups is included in the appendix).

However, this component also requires that we realize that even the most desirable standards statements should not, and cannot, take the place of our own careful observations, analyses, and evaluations of our students' particular learning strengths and needs. As classroom teachers, we are in the position to learn about the various personal, social, intellectual, and environmental factors that influence our students' attitudes toward learning and their growth as thinkers. We are obliged to consider the skills and interests that students arrive with, not just the skills or products that they are able to demonstrate or present following time spent in our classes. For example, it would be wrong to use the same criteria when evaluating the linguistic dexterity and mechanical correctness of an essay written by an English language learner and an essay written by a native speaker of English.

An Aerobics Class Example

This situation, in which one set of standards is applied across the board indiscriminately, reminds me of a realization that I had during one of my previous jobs as an aerobics instructor. I taught an advanced aerobics class at 5:30 in the afternoon. The participants in that class were veterans of aerobics instruction. They were eager to attend the advanced class and arrived three days a week with energy and enthusiasm for the session. All of the participants had established clear, reasonable individual goals for increases in their fitness and flexibility. They were using the class to help them attain those goals. They checked their progress regularly and were happy when they could report solid evidence of gains in fitness and flexibility.

In contrast, I taught an advanced aerobics class at 6:00 in the morning, three days per week. The participants in that class were employees of a nearby manufacturing firm. They were required by their company to attend the class, just as they had been required to attend the three-month beginners' class earlier in the year. No one (not even their instructor!) wanted to be on the aerobics floor at 6:00 A.M. during the first few weeks of that course. I found quickly that the dance routines that members of the 5:30 P.M. class learned with ease were almost impossible for the members of the 6 A.M. class to learn. Therefore, I had to change the dance routines that I taught (fewer steps with less movement). I also had to change my tone of voice (make it a little less demanding) and my attitude (make it much less perky) in order to be sensitive to the participants in the early morning class.

Regardless of my Herculean efforts to make accommodations, I could not force those early morning aerobics class participants to enjoy the class or to try hard enough to realize any positive results from it. To further complicate my problem, I learned that although the company required that its employees attend the class, it had no plans to measure their accomplishments. Therefore, the employees saw no incentive related to improving their fitness. As a result of all of those factors, some of the participants were no more fit or flexible after three months in the 6 A.M. class than they had been when they started it.

How does this scenario relate to the issue of measuring individual students' progress against externally imposed standards? I believe that it demonstrates the following: (1) It is a mistake to assume that everyone who enters a class has the same amount of background preparation for success in the class. (2) It is a mistake to assume that what motivates one learner will motivate all learners. (3) It is evident that instruction must be tailored to the ability and interest levels of the participants in the class. (4) It is inappropriate to begin instruction before assessing the abilities and interests of the students. The afternoon exercisers were like students who had done well in language arts classes for years. They were eager to participate, to set goals for their success, and to celebrate their accomplishments. The early morning exercisers, on the other hand, were like many of our students who have had little, if any, success as students in language arts classes. We cannot expect them to rise to the level of those who begin the year with a head start. We must meet them where they are and then gently lead them further. We must be sensitive to the circumstances that have contributed to their lack of success. We must treat them as individuals, not merely measure them against the standards and find them lacking. We must not, even unintentionally, hold the students responsible for the circumstances that have kept them at arm's length from success in the past.

In practice, this means that we plan activities that will interest, appeal to, and intellectually challenge all of our students. For students like Krista, who have been successful in school, we can pair our own intuitions with the standards of our profession to guide us in making decisions about academic curricula and appropriate learning activities. For those who have been less successful, we must rely heavily on our knowledge about how to assist learners who bring various barriers to our class with them. We must balance the standards with our own knowledge of who they are as learners and as humans.

This fourth belief, then, points us back to the first one, that students come to us both as individuals and as members of many groups, including at least one group in which we, as teachers, have a significant presence: our class. It acknowledges that we need to place our own instructional priorities, and those of our specific students, within the broader context of what young adolescents can be expected to do, according to the standards of the professional organizations that we trust. At the same time, it requires that we also place our instruc-

Young adolescents enjoy developing multiple literacies.

tional priorities within the narrower confines of the kinds of educational experiences that each student brings with him or her to our class.

Goals of an Integrated Literacy Pedagogy

As teachers and prospective teachers of English language arts who incorporate integrated literacy approaches, we are dedicated to providing middle school students with a low-risk environment in which they can experiment with their newly emerging adolescent personalities, value systems, and understandings. Academic activities like the following encourage students to explore questions about their own identities and nudge them beyond egocentrism to broader, more socially aware perspectives. They encourage students to engage in languaging to make sense of and know their world:

- Preparing a written, illustrated report after conducting research and taking photographs of places in the community that are significant for the student;
- Planning and recording interviews with older people in a community-based oral history project;
- Reading and responding to stories by and about people from cultures similar to and different from those of the students;
- Seeking and synthesizing information about the habits and attitudes of teens from around the world, using the Internet;
- Writing and illustrating fables and other stories to present to elementary school students during story time;
- Watching television advertisements and critically evaluating them in terms of the messages they intend to send viewers;
- Evaluating movies critically, in terms of the hidden messages they send to adolescents about violence or love or family loyalty, for example.

These are activities through which young adolescents begin to make sense of their own communities and the people of other communities. Through engaging in these kinds of activities, young adolescents can learn to think critically about what is happening in their own homes, schools, and communities. With technologies, they can also think critically about what is happening in various communities around the world.

In an integrated literacy classroom, students are challenged to learn to *think*, not merely to learn to *remember* information. For example, a teacher who is a proponent of integrated language practices does not insist that students memorize what she believes to be the meaning of the title of Robert Frost's poem, "Nothing Gold Can Stay." Instead, the teacher encourages students to use reading response journals and class discussion to construct their own meanings for the title, requiring only that students consider the title within the context of the poem itself. Discussion of the poem then involves an exploration of different students' readings and interpretations; the teacher is involved in meaning making with students and is not just transmitting information to them.

In classrooms in which teachers practice an integrated literacy pedagogy, students are also treated as writers who have real purposes for writing. Instead of composing an essay whose only audience is the teacher, for example, an eighth grader might write a letter to a group of fifth graders about what they can expect in middle school. A seventh grader might write to the city's park association and request information about the recreational soccer program for adolescent females. A sixth grader might write a narrative about his fishing trip with his grandfather, with the intention of giving the story to his grandfather at his sixtieth birthday party. Each of these writing activities is based on the student-writer's desire to communicate an idea that is important to him or her to a real audience. An important point is that none of these writing activities serves merely to produce a sample of composition that a teacher can read and evaluate. Rather than writing solely for a grade, the effectiveness of the compositions is determined by readers' responses and reactions.

Teachers who encourage students to engage in languaging activities help them connect new learning with their previous experiences and knowledge. They help students learn to make sense of their world. Teachers who employ an integrated literacy pedagogy know that it is at the intersection of new and past understandings that learning occurs. They understand, too, that learning occurs in a social context and that intellectual development happens as a consequence of minds being engaged in the kinds of languaging activities that lead to authentic meaning making that is characteristic of the integrated literacy pedagogy.

Integrated Literacy Instruction in the Middle School Classroom: The Our Generation's Heroes Project

The Our Generation's Heroes project provides a clear and detailed portrait of what a student-sensitive integrated literacy pedagogy can look like. The project demonstrates how teachers can design engaging integrated languaging activities that lead to cognitive and social growth. Each of the four beliefs that underlie the pedagogy is apparent in the design and implementation of the project: Students are treated as individuals and as members of the class group; students' needs and interests are a primary focus; *literacy* is broadly defined; professional standards provide a guideline for the teachers' decisions about the project.

In regard to belief four, the Our Generation's Heroes project is an example of how student-sensitive integrated literacy pedagogy can be guided by and address the National Council of Teachers of English/International Reading Association (NCTE/IRA) and National Middle School Association (NMSA) standards for the instruction of middle school students. A few examples include the following: during the project, students read a wide range of print texts and engage in interviews while gathering research for the project (NCTE/IRA standard 1); they build an understanding of human experience by speaking directly to those who were involved in World War II about personal recollections of that time in history (NCTE/IRA standard 2); and they use a variety of technological and information resources to extend what they learn during reading of print texts and interviews (NCTE/IRA standard 8). Further, they are engaged in learning experiences that help them make sense of themselves and the world about them (NMSA position one) and in learning environments that expand beyond the school (NMSA position three). (See Appendix: Professional Standards and Positions for a list of the NCTE/IRA Standards for English Language Arts and an NMSA Position Statement on Middle Level Curriculum.)

The Our Generation's Heroes project began almost by accident. Eighth graders at the Augusta Raa Middle School were studying World War II. Language arts teacher Mary Carpenter, social studies teacher Kathy Corder, and media aide Gena Varn suspected that students could benefit from a more personal connection to the people directly involved in the war, so they invited three World War II veterans to speak to their students. Following the session with the guest speakers, the initial idea grew into a major project.

Every student's first task was to conduct an in-depth interview with an adult partner, someone who had participated in or had been directly affected by World War II. The media specialist was able to gather a group of adult volunteers for those students who had no personal contacts on which to rely. Surprisingly, several of the adults noted that the school-based conversation was one of the first times that they had talked about the war and its personal costs for over fifty years. Though many had grandchildren the age of their interview partners, they had not discussed their war experiences with them. The students' invitation for the adults to share their stories opened doors for further communication. The student/adult conversations and interviews were recorded, with participants' permission, on videotape.

The students' next task was to study their interviews and probe them for topics on which they could conduct detailed research. One student decided to focus, for example, on how racial segregation affected the African American officer whom he interviewed. Another chose to describe how rationing coupon books affected the lives of those at home. Others discussed the specific jobs (clerks, truck drivers, signal men) or battle sites (Pearl Harbor, the Pacific theater, the European fields) that their senior partners recalled.

While writing their histories, the students studied Tom Brokaw's *The Greatest Generation* (1998), mining it for ideas about how to combine interview and research notes into prose narrative. From the interviews and their research, the students composed individual histories, rich accounts of one slice of life during World War II. They drafted and redrafted copies of their histories and had to earn final approval of final drafts from two tough groups of readers: their teachers and their senior partners. Once their drafts were perfected, they were collected. With a local printing company donating its services, *Our Generation's Heroes* (Carpenter & Corder, 2002) was professionally printed and bound.

The student-authored book was unveiled at a ceremony attended by the students and their parents, school administrators and teachers, and the World War II seniors with whom the adolescents had collaborated. In a moving sequence, students stood and, one at a time, read their histories aloud, and then presented copies of their book to their senior partners. At the request of a member of the Florida House of Representatives, copies of the book and a videotape of the interviews and the ceremony have been donated to the Museum of Florida History.

While engaged in the project, students assumed roles as purposeful languagers. They learned about the power of language to reach across generations, across historical events, across realities. They were involved not only in authentic, primary source research but also in the exchange of meaningful conversations with another segment that, like adolescents, often feels misunderstood and alienated: senior citizens. Student Daniel McRae summed up the experience when he commented, "As a student, I saw it as just another project, but I soon saw it differently as a person."

Instead of a traditional test that would measure their understanding of the impact of World War II on American citizens, the eighth graders were able to demonstrate their understanding in a much more meaningful and poignant way. Here are a few brief excerpts from student-written bio-histories:

> Stanley told me there was no way around making friends. However, it was extremely sad when you saw them killed, especially when they had family. He had one good friend, named Roger Martin, who also survived the war. He saved Stanley's life quite a few times, and Stanley saved his. (Evan Goldstein, p. 38)

> Saima Matt was born in Estonia, one of the three small Baltic countries next to the Soviet Union. . . . She helped around the garden and lived a life just like any other kid would in those days. . . . When Saima was five years old, her father was captured and taken for questioning. The Russians told her mother that he was safe and to send warm clothes and food for him, which she did. They later learned that their father had been killed a long time before, and the Russians used the clothes and food they sent. (Jessica Binnun, p. 34)

> Wil Varn was working his shift at one of two theaters in Panama City. He was projecting a movie onto the big screen. . . . A breaking news flash reported that the Japanese had bombed Pearl Harbor, and that America would have to enter World War II. He was not as shocked as some because he knew the war was coming, but nobody suspected this. The date was December 7, 1941. (Andy Bates, p. 131)

> I can only imagine how hard it was for [Mr. George], having an all Black training camp with all White officers. Blacks were confined largely to service rather than combat units and were excluded entirely from the Army Air Corps, Marines, and from the Navy, except as waiters. However, in 1940, President Roosevelt forced the Army to say that it would become 10 percent Black. In 1942, President Roosevelt ordered the Navy, much against its will, to enlist Blacks for general service. Keep in mind that Mr. George had enlisted in 1941, so he had to deal with racism and segregation in the military. (Tim Lewis, p. 86)

Teacher Kathy Corder (2002) described the project and its impact during the book unveiling and presentation ceremony:

> The writing of *Our Generation's Heroes* was an extensive project which entailed three months of work for our students. The book, which features the stories of over 50 people who exhibited valor, courage, honor, and a sense of duty during a difficult time in our nation's history, is more than just a class project or book. It is a tribute to greatness. . . . When the stories in students' interviews started coming to us and we began reading them, we suddenly realized we had more than just a successful class project. The stories were full of courage, duty, and honor. I'd like to share with you our observations about the outcomes, the tremendous learning and literacy benefits for the students, that grew out of this project.
>
>   First of all, our students learned about World War II from people who were there. What an amazing opportunity for them. If you pick up the history book which they had issued to them this year, you will find a dry report of this period in our history, a book in which D-Day is captured in two paragraphs and a whopping two pages is devoted to the Holocaust (and the Holocaust is a required subject of study for eighth graders in Florida). This project has taught our students and it has reminded us that history is in the people and the places around us. It's in our parents, our grandparents, and in us. It's not just about our individual

stories, but it is about our role in history, the ways in which we impact history's outcome, and the events that shape the lives of others.

Another lesson our students learned is that storytelling is an important vehicle and art form, not just for the sake of academic gains—but to our families and our sense of self and belonging. How often do we sit down with our parents and grandparents and ask them to tell us about the War, about the sixties, about the assassination of John F. Kennedy, about the day the bomb was dropped on Hiroshima?

. . . And finally, our students have truly learned what the writing process entails. In our state, high-stakes testing has threatened to reduce the teaching and practice of writing to lessons and assignments that prepare students to compose an expository or descriptive essay on a topic that has no personal significance to them, and to do the writing, start to finish, in a 45-minute time period. . . . Our students understand what real writing involves.

Today, as we unveil the students' work and their tribute to the wonderful individuals whom Tom Brokaw has coined "The Greatest Generation," we wish to thank especially the men and women who so graciously offered their time so that our students could learn from them. We realized after we read many of the stories that the act of telling them wasn't always that easy. Some stories were sad, tragic, or almost too horrible to discuss. But you did anyway. And for that we thank you. Our kids need to know the truth, and we're glad you were willing to share your truths so that they might go out and exemplify what you have demonstrated in your stories. We want them to develop that same sense of duty and desire to serve the community, country, and world that you have shown them. Thank you so much.

We also want to say to our students, "We are so proud of you." People are so quick to point out the things that young people do that aren't honorable: the drinking, smoking, and other activities which we choose not to mention and often try not to think about. But when we look at you and we see what you are made of, we are optimistic about the future of our country. I feel good knowing that you young people will be looking after us in the years ahead. You show great promise for a life committed to service. Thank you for teaching your teachers such invaluable lessons.

The Our Generation's Heroes project resonates with the notion that literacy instruction can treat language as a social construct. In the words of Gere et al., in *Language and Reflection* (1992), for teachers like Kathy Corder and Mary Carpenter, and others who treat language as a social construct:

[T]eaching English means teaching reading and writing as an active, dynamic process where meaning is generated through the interaction of students, their teachers, and various texts, both spoken and written. In other words, teaching English is teaching literacy. The challenge is not to cover a specific set of texts or objectives in a specific period of time, but to engage students in activities that ask them to discover and make sense of whatever they have chosen to study. These themes have as a common denominator a concern for collective community life. . . . Reading and writing play critical roles in . . . students' ability to understand, respond to, and participate in community life.

The concern for community—the classroom community and the communities in which the students live—stems from another important element of the language-as-social-construct perspective, which recognizes that schooling takes place in particular social and cultural contexts. (p. 187)

When language is perceived to be a social construct, it must be treated as a power tool, not as a lifeless artifact. Students who participate in classrooms where teachers have adopted an integrated literacy pedagogy read, study, interpret, and create literature, movies, television shows, magazines, electronic sites, multimedia productions, popular music, dance, advertisements, and other artistic and informative expressions. Students in these classes study the ways that they shape—and are shaped by—popular culture and popular media. They learn to become active critics who are able to use the power of language and literacy as an ally to guard against the possibility that they will be vulnerable to those who use symbols to persuade, confuse, tempt, or deceive young adolescents.

In classrooms that are informed by an integrated literacy pedagogy, students become engaged as informed, thoughtful participants in society. The students who participated in the Our Generation's Heroes project proved that they are capable of full participation as thinkers in our society. They learned that their words and actions can and do matter—not just to themselves and their families but also to the others with whom they share the world in which they live.

Channeling the Spontaneous Overflow of Young Adolescents

A student-sensitive integrated literacy pedagogy can accommodate the spontaneous overflow of young adolescents' emotions, ideas, and actions. It allows us, as teachers, to view the young adolescents with whom we work first as humans and then as students. It allows us to tap into virtually every aspect of life experience as our subject matter, since so much of experience is mediated through language. In the chapters that follow, first we spend time learning about and confirming what we know about young adolescents (Chapter 2). Then we consider ideas for giving specific attention to the individual components of the integrated literacy curriculum: reading (Chapter 3), literature (Chapter 4), writing (Chapter 5), oral language (Chapter 6), and nonprint media (Chapter 7). We close with ideas about how you can encourage your colleagues to create interdisciplinary units that employ integrated literacy (Chapter 8). Doing so allows us to consider the student-sensitive integrated literacy pedagogy in light of the students who fill our classrooms.

The ultimate goal of a student-sensitive integrated literacy pedagogy is to equip adolescents with the ability to generate and regularly use specific critical criteria to make sense of their world. While working toward that goal, we want our adolescent students to be able to separate the good from the bad, the sublime from the pedestrian, the moving from the boring. We want them to understand the difference between what is real and what is illusion each time they are called on to participate as readers of the print and nonprint texts that they encounter and of those that they create. We want them to become effective and intelligent languagers.

Works Cited

Beach, R., and Myers, J. (2001). *Inquiry-based English instruction: Engaging students in life and literature.* New York: Teachers College Press.

Brokaw, T. (1998). *The greatest generation.* New York: Random House.

Carpenter, M., and Corder, K. (Eds.). (2002). *Our generation's heroes.* Tallahassee: Target Printing.

Corder, K. (May 15, 2002). Unpublished speech, Our Generation's Heroes ceremony. Museum of Florida History, Tallahassee, Florida.

Gere, A. R., Fairbanks, C., Howes, A., Roop, L., and Schaafsma, D. (1992). *Language and reflection: An integrated approach to teaching English.* Upper Saddle River, NJ: Prentice Hall.

Paulsen, G. (1987). *Hatchet.* New York: Laurel Leaf.

Rusk, R. R., and Scotland, J. (1979). *The great educators*, 5th edition. Houndmills, England: Macmillan.

Snow, C. E. (October, 2001). Knowing what we know: Children, teachers, researchers. *Educational Researcher 30*(7): 3–7.

2 Today's Young Adolescents: Spontaneously Overflowing with Powerful Feelings

Each young adolescent is an individual and member of many groups.

We've all had it happen to us. We tell our friends that we are interested in teaching young adolescents in the middle grades or that we are employed as a teacher of language arts at a middle school. Our friends respond by asking, bluntly, "Are you crazy?" and continue with some version of the following: "Those kids don't care about anything but themselves. They are either giggly, wiggly, and silly, or they are sad, sullen, and angry. Nothing pleases them, and they think they already know everything. Why would you choose to have to deal with them on a daily basis?"

What we often don't tell our friends is that we ask ourselves those questions, too, and that on some days, we would describe young adolescents just like our nonteacher friends do. And yet we are drawn to teach this age group. We see possibility, hope, and the future in the students. And as teachers of literacy in language arts classes, we have a great opportunity: We can use language, potentially the most democratic of all school subjects, as a vehicle through which we can connect with our young adolescent students and help them grow to be positive, productive, effective, happy humans.

A Middle School Scene

Mark Shapiro, middle school counselor and teacher of language arts and social studies, is frequently asked to give university students a tour of the middle school where he works and where they will spend a semester as tutors for sixth, seventh, or eighth graders. I was there recently with a group of English education students, many of whom had not been in a middle school since they were 13-year-olds themselves. The first thing that Mark showed us was the ceiling beams in the hallway outside his office. The beams, set about twenty feet apart, protrude down from the eight-foot ceiling about one foot. When one of my group asked about the significance of the beams, Mark explained this way:

> On those beams are the handprints of many of our students from the past and present years. As sixth graders, many of them stop and look up at the beam, take a few jumps toward it, and realize that they are not going to be able to leap high enough to put their handprints there yet. By the time they reach eighth grade, though, they are able to skip down the same hallway, lift like hurdlers, and tag one beam after the other. I guess the best way to describe middle school students is that they strive to achieve their goals by hitting specific points—the beams in their lives—and that they keep trying until they can reach them, and go even further. They are always reaching, stretching, and searching. (October, 2002)

Just as he finished talking, the tone that signaled the end of the school day sounded. As students poured into the hallways, we all watched the young adolescents' spontaneous overflow of energy and enthusiasm and saw at least four of them jump up toward the beams.

In this chapter, we take a general look at many of the issues that have an impact on the ways that our students experience life. We try on the lenses through which they begin to form a picture of the world and their place in that world. We look at the characteristics that are common to adolescence and a few of the pronounced social problems that plague some of the students with whom we work. We will be able to connect with the young adolescents whom we teach only when we know them as humans as well as students.

After we learn some of the facts about the world as it appears to young adolescents today, we can begin to understand why they behave as they do. Knowledge of some facts about characteristics of young adolescents will help us recognize a few of the barriers that students construct to keep others, especially adults, at a distance. Some of these barriers are *physical:* For example, a student might become uncomfortable sitting still on a hard desk chair during a 50-minute class period, since his bones have grown faster than the supporting tissues that would add padding to his seat. The result is that he moves around too much, and we accuse him of being a distraction for his classmates, when the real problem is that we need to add more opportunities for movement and action in the class period. Some of those barriers are *personal:* A student is shy about participating in class because she doesn't want to draw attention to her "funny accent," for example. Our reaction might be to give her a low grade for class participation, when the real problem is that we have misinterpreted her reluctance as refusal to participate. Some are *intellectual:* A student who has not learned to read fluently insists that she has forgotten her literature book day after day when the class is reading a story aloud. The result might be that we assume she is lazy or insolent, when the real problem is that she wants to hide her inability to read well. Some barriers exist because a student brings differences into the classroom: A student who has immigrated to the United States with his non-English-speaking parents, who are working in the nearby strawberry fields, scowls and puts his head down on his desk when we call on him in class. We might be irritated with what we assume is his bad attitude and lack of participation, when the real problem is that he is eager to learn English and is frustrated because he doesn't yet know enough to have casual conversations with his classmates. He will require us to stretch our understanding and our willingness to make accommodations, to adjust expectations, and to promote progress. He will require us to find ways to allow him to protect and maintain the integrity of his cultural and linguistic heritage even while he learns English and learns how to be a student in our school and young teen in our community.

Once we learn enough about young adolescents to recognize them as humans who are eager to put their trust in us, we will be more likely to empathize with them as they deal with life issues—even on those days that we ask them to sit in our third period class and listen to us discuss the proper use of the exclamation point. Once we know more about young adolescents, we are better equipped to create lessons that invite their thoughtful participation and develop their skills as critical thinkers and language users. Once we know them, we will be prepared for and welcome their spontaneous overflow of powerful feelings in our classrooms.

In this chapter, we consider some basic information about the physical, psychosocial, and intellectual traits that are characteristic of today's middle school students. This information is a brief overview only. It is meant not to replace focused study of the characteristics of young adolescents but to suggest how middle school students' physical and emotional characteristics color the educational environment of the classroom. We also focus on a sample of the kinds of serious issues that today's young adolescents are likely to bring into the classroom—extreme poverty and violence among them. This information, again merely an overview, is designed to remind us that we are working with humans who have complex lives outside of our classrooms. With this information, we begin to understand why it is as important to promote a student-sensitive pedagogy that, in the words of Henry Giroux, reflects an "ethic of concern, self-responsibility, and compassion" (1997, p. 60) as it is to create a classroom in which students' standardized test scores soar.

After we begin to understand and appreciate who young adolescents are, we move to our other subject: encouraging languaging among young adolescents, with an integrated literacy pedagogy. In considering our first subject, the young adolescents themselves, and our second subject, literacy instruction in the middle grades, we are continually guided by the four core beliefs of an integrated literacy pedagogy, as described in Chapter 1 and restated here in a slightly different form: (1) We must treat middle school students as individuals and as members of many groups. (2) We must design instruction with a primary focus on meeting our specific students' needs and interests. (3) We must operationalize a broad definition of literacy that incorporates forms that have not typically been valued or promoted in traditional language arts classroom settings, such as oral, visual, multilingual, and technological literacies. (4) We must be willing to use professional standards to guide our choices and to help us hold reasonable expectations, without limiting ourselves to someone else's description of what our students are capable of accomplishing.

Biopsychosocial Characteristics

Bodily changes create changes not only in appearance but also in self-esteem, values, goals, and directions. The intersection of the physical, psychological, and social changes is sometimes referred to by the umbrella term, *biopsychosocial characteristics*. I like using this term and concept when thinking about who our young adolescent students are, because it reflects the fact that no category of change exists separate from or independent of the others. All weave together in the fabric of adolescence.

Physical Changes

Females enter puberty earlier than do their male counterparts (a fact that, in itself, generates plenty of commotion in many middle school classrooms). For females, the physical changes of puberty usually begin between the ages of 10 and 14; in other words, their puberty corresponds with grades six, seven, and eight almost perfectly. In general, we can expect our middle school females to experience their major growth spurt around age 12. This spurt will be manifested in increases in height and breast size and in rounding of the hips, creating a change from an androgynous look to a more womanly figure. During this time, females begin menstruation, and some experience problems including cramping, headaches, and mood swings that accompany the hormonal changes that lead to menses. Hormonal changes also account for activation of sweat glands that produce body odor and secretion of oils that may lead to pimples or acne. Further, hormonal changes create variations in metabolism. Young females are likely to have alternating bouts of sluggishness and high energy.

For young adolescent males, the physical changes of puberty usually become apparent between ages 12 and 16. While some young males reach puberty during middle school, others retain a childlike physical appearance until they are in high school. Any postponement of physical maturation is personally troubling and socially trying for many young males.

The physical changes that accompany a male's puberty include increases in height and body hair, the definition of muscle mass, enlarging of the penis and testicles, and, for some, deposits of adipose tissue on the chest. In addition, males' voices change, sometimes squeaking and scratching before ultimately deepening during puberty. Like females, males experience changes in hormones that lead to the activation of sweat glands, secretion of oils, and energy swings. For both, too, bones grow faster than some tissues, often creating discomfort, for example, for someone who has to sit still on bony protrusions for an extended period.

Psychosocial Impacts

There are many other physical changes associated with puberty for males and females. These introductory-level lists are important for us, as teachers of middle grades literacy, because they note changes that are observable from the outside, and thus they mark changes that potentially have huge impacts on how our students feel about themselves and about their classmates. In normal classroom interactions, physical changes can exacerbate self-consciousness and can fuel distractions as well.

Here are a few realistic examples: The female who grows four inches in six months is likely to feel a shift in her center of gravity that results in awkwardness. If she is asked to distribute papers to her classmates, she may refuse, fearing that she will trip when walking across the floor. A male who has not experienced puberty may be reluctant to stand in front of the class as a member of a panel, since he is shorter than everyone, including the females in the class, and since his voice is high-pitched. A female who has acne may be too self-conscious to participate in a small group discussion, preferring instead to sit at her desk where she can hide behind a book. A male who has become physically stimulated by the sight of a female classmate's midriff may not be able to stand and walk to the teacher's desk if asked to do so. The dramatic activity that appeals to some students will seem to require too much of an effort for others. A female is so distressed by the biologically appointed rounding of her hips that she is determined to lose weight; she skips breakfast and lunch every day. Her friend, whose culture shows greater appreciation for rounded female figures, is thrilled when she gains weight and dimensions. A male is preoccupied with building his muscles and skips doing homework to spend extra time at the gym each afternoon. His friend is too self-conscious about his lack of physical maturation to participate in physical education class, since doing so would require that he shower among his classmates. He chooses to fail the course instead. And the group of males and females that began the year as best friends may be experiencing broken ties as the females seek males who are more physically mature than their age-mates.

In addition to physical development and the psychosocial changes that can be related to them, young adolescents are in a period during which they are trying to develop their own sense of self, their own value system. This endeavor means that young adolescents, in addition to being quite sensitive to others' perceptions, exhibit conflicting behaviors. They may be brave and nervous, gregarious and shy, confident and insecure, idealistic and pessimistic, passionate and noncommittal. These contradictions confuse their families and friends, and sometimes create communication barriers just at the time that young males and females need to make connections.

Intellectual Characteristics

Middle school students, despite the challenges of adolescence, are inquisitive and intensely curious. Whether eager to learn what it is like to be a teenager who has a driver's license or to understand how weather satellites assist meteorologists, they want answers—and they are not particularly patient as they wait for them. They seek out information from resources that range from adolescent novels and magazines to older friends, from church groups to the Internet. Unfortunately, they often fail to discriminate between reliable information and misrepresentations.

We, as adults whom they learn to trust, can help. Most young adolescents enjoy being active in their learning more than being passive recipients of others' information. Middle school students are beginning to use abstract reasoning, and thus they enjoy activities that allow them to generate more than one solution for a problem, to engage in hypothetical-deductive (if . . . then) reasoning and contrary-to-fact reasoning. They also enjoy playing with meanings; word games, riddles, puns, and axioms interest them. They are willing to explore symbol systems that transcend our alphabet and language, such as algebra and music.

We can use these intellectual characteristics to the advantage of our students and our lessons in literacy classes and across the curriculum in middle school settings. Middle school students, because of their intellectual characteristics, are primed for language study. The study of similes and metaphors, for example, expands their skills in using various symbol systems, including figurative language, visual art, and numeric equations. When we ask them to consider how a character *could have* responded to a situation and contrast those answers with how he *did* respond to a situation, we help them to develop their contrary-to-fact reasoning skills. If we ask students to suggest the potential results of a hypothetical situation such as, "The principal gives you authority to make decisions about the school for an entire week," we help them develop their hypothetical-deductive reasoning skills.

Their intellectual growth also demands that we provide as much guidance and support as we can. We can teach study skills to help young adolescents learn how to organize their thoughts and activities. We can teach mental habits that will help our students learn to use metacognition (the ability to think about their own thinking). We can teach habits of mind that will encourage students to develop their skills, interests, and talents. It is important for us to remember that students do not develop intellectually in all areas at the same pace. Some may manifest strides in linguistic abilities that are not matched, for example, by increases in logical thinking. Further, and perhaps more vital, we must remember that physical maturity and social maturity are not indicators of intellectual maturity. Often, we see young teens who look grown up and then expect that they will be able to think like adults. I have made that mistake many times. I recall being exasperated with the rowdy behavior of my eighth grade class one day. After trying unsuccessfully to channel their energy in positive directions, I put my hands on my hips and snapped, "Why are you all acting like kids?" No one responded, but I am sure that several thought to themselves, "We're acting like kids because we *are* kids!" An important lesson for us to remember is that physical maturity is not an accurate predictor of social maturity. Young adolescents, by definition, are still growing, experimenting, learning, or, as Mark Shapiro says, "always reaching, stretching, searching." (See Chris Stevenson's *Teaching Ten to Fourteen Year Olds*, 2nd edition [1998], and Callahan, Clark, and Kellough's *Teaching in the Middle and Secondary Schools* [1995] for more information on the biopsychosocial and intellectual characteristics of young adolescents and the ways that those characteristics interact. I have merely scratched the surface here.)

What Today's Young Adolescents Bring to the Classroom

Unfortunately, the changes that adolescents go through often contribute to teacherly assessments that our students "don't want to participate in our classes," that "they just don't want to learn," that "they are lazy," that "they are contentious and snotty," or that "they are wishy-washy." What we need to consider, perhaps, is that often they are actually unsure, confused, embarrassed, shy, frustrated, and eager to move beyond the in-between world in which they are no longer children and not yet young adults. We need not only to accept their occasional reluctance to stand alone in front of an entire class or group but also to provide opportunities for them to perform in front of their classmates as the center of attention on occasion, too. We need to be aware that for some, being singled out, even with praise, is terrifying, while for others, it is essential. We need to understand that our students define themselves based on their interpretation of how others see them, rather than by how others actually do see them or by who they really are. We need to be aware of the dual tendencies of adolescents to exhibit what child development expert David Elkind (1998) calls the "imaginary audience" (p. 40) and the "personal fable" (p. 44). The "imaginary audience" is a teen's belief that everyone notices every one of her shortcomings. The "personal fable" is a teen's feeling that the kinds of problems he is experiencing are unique to him and that no one else can understand.

We need to recognize the changes that are typical of people their ages, so that we will be compassionate instead of impatient with them. We need to be prepared to teach sixth grade boys who build forts to play in on the weekend and those who arm themselves with real weapons; seventh grade girls who play with Barbie dolls, and those who look like Barbie; eighth grade couples who blush when a pair kisses on movie screens and those who give birth to their own babies.

As their literacy teachers, we are obliged to help young adolescents find ways, through our class activities and curricula, to use languaging to arrive at and articulate answers to the most important questions of young adolescence: "Who AM I?" and "Where do I fit?" We have myriad opportunities to help them grow and to help them express what they are learning about themselves and their world as they seek answers. We have opportunities to watch our students become more accomplished and artistic users of language, to nudge them toward developing habits of critical thinking, to acknowledge them as they celebrate achieving new levels of knowledge and understanding. Finally, when working with today's teens, we need to acknowledge that there are other pressures, in addition to the ones they have in common, with which many are dealing. In the following section, consider some questions regarding three of these pressure points. These pressure points will help us understand and be sensitive to the realities that many of our students must navigate today.

Ambiguity and Absence of Adults in Parenting Roles

How many of our students have parents who are inconsistent or absent in their parenting roles as a result of having to deal with too much difficulty in their own adult lives? In *All Grown Up and No Place to Go: Teenagers in Crisis* (1998), child and adolescent development expert David Elkind contends that today's adolescents are struggling as the result of a shift in society to a postmodern period in which "the needs of children and youth are often weighted less heavily than are the needs of parents and the rest of adult society" (p. xiii). Elkind continues by saying that the contemporary world has become a time and place in which "we as a society have abrogated our responsibility to young people" (p. xiv). Are our students among those whose parents, like two-thirds of those studied by David Hamburg (1994), admit that they are "less willing to make sacrifices for their children than their own parents would have been" (p. 34)? Do our students seek acceptance through social groups when they can't find it at home (Brown, Lohr, & Truhillo, 1990)? As teachers, we need to consider how we would answer the following: What kind of impact might a young adolescent's feeling of alienation or outright neglect at home have on his or her performance in our middle school language arts classes?

Poverty

How many of our students live in extreme poverty, particularly those in the minority student population? Do their school experiences include bad schools? Do our students walk down wide bright hallways, past student-tended flower gardens and sunny courtyard gazebos, and into well-stocked media centers and buzzing technology hubs? Or do they wander down dark and uninviting hallways, through fenced yards, and into stale air that hangs heavy in thick pockets of humidity and poverty? Have we learned firsthand that school failure rates are highest in the middle grades among minority youth, especially those who do not speak English at home and that high school dropout rates are also highest among minority youth (Carnegie Council, 1989, p. 27)? Would we agree with David Hamburg's assessment that "No problem in contemporary America is more serious than the plight of children and youth in our decaying cities. Almost a quarter of the nation's children grow up in poverty—and all too many of them are in smashed families and rotting communities" (Hamburg, 1994, p. xvi)? Do we recognize the children who are labeled as slow learners because they start school with underdeveloped attention spans, verbal fluency, academic skills, social skills, and energy levels? We need to formulate an answer to this question: What can we do in our classrooms, as teachers, that will provide an emotional, social, and intellectual balance for what students living in poverty experience outside of our classes?

High-Risk Behaviors and Violence

How many of our students are involved in high-risk behavior, for example, sexual experimentation, and in the violence of gangs, hate groups, or rebels? Will we teach a student like the teen mother whom child psychiatrist Robert Coles interviewed and photographed for *The Youngest Parents: Teenage Pregnancy as It Shapes Lives* (1997), who told Coles that she did not know that her baby cried when he was hungry, so that she often just leaves the room to avoid his wails, and that she keeps him in dirty diapers because she hates to clean them? She tries to explain:

> I feel fine, I'm doing fine; and then, all of a sudden, I'm not doing fine anymore! I'm bad, real bad—I'm in trouble. A big cloud from the sky has come down through the window and surrounded me. I'm in the middle of it. I'm trying to find the sun. Where are you, sun? (I'm asking.) Then, no telling when and why, that cloud decides to move on (to someone else, I guess) and there I am, in broad daylight again, the warm sun making me feel good again. (Coles, 1997, p. 107)

And will our class rolls include young students who are among the approximately 5 percent of 12- to 15-year olds who are victims of robbery, rape, or assault each year (Hamburg, 1994, p. 191)? Will some of our African American males be victims of homicide, which is the leading cause of death for African American males between the ages of 14 and 44? Will one of our students commit suicide, the third leading cause of death among adolescents, after accidents and illness (Hamburg, 1994, p. 193)?

Will these victims and other students sit in small group discussions with classmates who have perpetrated the kinds of delinquent behaviors that David Huizinga found common among the 1,500 11- to 19-year-olds whom he studied over a period of ten years, including aggravated assault, robbery, gang fights, rape, hitting to injure, throwing objects to injure, snatching purses, carrying hidden weapons, burglary, theft, joyriding, fencing, using credit cards illegally and committing other fraud, avoiding payment (sneaking in a theater, for example), arson, running away, skipping school, vandalism, public disorder, prostitution, and selling drugs (Huizinga, 1995, p. 22)? Again, we need to begin to try to answer a huge question: What impact will these realities have on what I teach, which activities I choose, which works of literature I assign, and how I assess and evaluate student progress in my language arts classroom?

Valuing the Lives of Young Adolescents

I worry about how well prepared we are to teach young adolescents who live without consistent adult guidance, who live in poverty, who speak other languages at home, who take risks, and who are victims or perpetrators of violence. Too often, don't we see students who come with these kinds of problems as "deficient"? After all, when they enter our classrooms, they come without having had adequate food, without having had a positive conversation with a caring adult, without skills to communicate in English, without relief from violence, without having had a chance to set realistic learning goals for the day. We need to find what it is that they come *with* when they enter our classrooms.

There is evidence, for example, that there are family and social benefits for adolescents even when they live in dire poverty. In *Children of Immigration* (2001), an account of one portion of the largest longitudinal study of immigrants and their families, Harvard University researchers Carola and Marcelo M. Suarez-Orozco point out that the kinds of neighborhoods that immigrant families settle in shape the lives of immigrant children in many ways.

They concede that concentrated poverty breeds diminished opportunities for meaningful and legal work, especially for adolescents, who often either leave the home neighborhood or become involved in the underground economy of illegal substances that is supported by gangs and that produces neighborhood violence. Further, they note that "the outcomes can be devastating" when poverty and racial segregation are paired. They cite a "large-scale sociological study" that concluded, "people who grow up and live in environments of concentrated poverty and racial isolation are more likely to become teenage mothers, drop out of school, achieve only low levels of education, and earn lower adult incomes" (Suarez-Orozco & Suarez-Orozco, 2001, pp. 130–131).

Nevertheless, the researchers refer to sociological studies that suggest that even poor communities can have a positive impact on the lives of children and teens within them. One of the studies indicates that "culturally constituted patterns of community cohesion and supervision can 'immunize' immigrant youth from the more toxic elements in their new settings"; another demonstrates that "when communities are cohesive and when adults within the community can monitor youngsters' activities, the children tend to do better. Children who live in such communities are less likely to be involved with gangs and delinquency and are more focused on their academic pursuits" (Suarez-Orozco & Suarez-Orozco, 2001, p. 131).

College-educated and therefore privileged teachers must learn a great deal about the students who have little adult guidance, who are living in poverty, and who are involved in high-risk behaviors or violence. Since our goal is to help all students develop critical and multiple literacies, we cannot pretend that all parents are involved in their children's education, that poverty stays politely at the door when young adolescents walk into our classrooms, that our students will treat each other kindly. We are obligated to find ways to help our young adolescent students tap into their own family and community situations to help them make sense of their worlds there.

Those of us who choose to practice an integrated literacy pedagogy will find that natural opportunities to interact with our adolescent students, as humans, regularly emerge in our classrooms. The positive learning environment that is associated with this pedagogical base allows us to establish and enjoy the kind of relationship with students that is most appropriate: Instead of trying to entice young adolescents into cooperating with us by assuming the role of friend, we can elicit their participation by demonstrating that we are adults whom they can trust. Again, we can be guided in part by the four beliefs that serve as the foundation of the integrated literacy pedagogy—attention to students as individuals and as group members; an instructional focus that considers our students' interests and needs; the use of broad definitions of literacy; and reliance on professional standards as guides to support and sustain this kind of positive learning environment. (See Chapter 1 for a more detailed explanation of these four beliefs.)

In classrooms that feature an environment of mutual trust, we will be able to recognize the remarkable characteristics of young adolescents and celebrate their spontaneous overflow of enthusiasm for learning, of inquisitiveness, of wonderment. Through instruction in reading, literature, writing, listening/speaking, and nonprint media, we can tap into the power of their enthusiasm. One of the best places to feel that enthusiasm is through young adolescents' growth as readers, the topic of the chapter that follows.

Works Cited

Brown, B., Lohr, M. J., and Truhillo, C. (1990). Multiple crowds and multiple life styles: Adolescents' perceptions of peer group stereotypes. In R. E. Muuss (Ed.). *Adolescent behavior and society: A book of readings*, 4th ed. New York: McGraw-Hill, 30–36.

Callahan, J. F., Clark, L. H., and Kellough, R. D. (1995). *Teaching in the middle and secondary schools*, 5th edition. Boston: Allyn & Bacon.

Carnegie Council on Adolescent Development, Task Force on Education of Young Adolescents. (1989). *Turning points: Preparing American youth for the 21st century*. Washington, D.C.: Carnegie Council on Adolescent Development.

Coles, R. E. (1997). *The youngest parents: Teenage pregnancy as it shapes lives*. Durham, NC: Center for Documentary Studies, in association with New York: W. W. Norton.

Elkind, D. (1998). *All grown up and no place to go: Teenagers in crisis,* revised edition. Reading, MA: Addison-Wesley.

Giroux, H. (1997). *Channel surfing: Race talk and the destruction of today's youth*. New York: St. Martin's Press.

Hamburg, D. (1994). *Today's children: Creating a future for a generation in crisis*. New York: Times Books of Random House.

Huizinga, D. (1995). Developmental sequences in delinquency: Dynamic typologies. In Crockett, L. J., and Crouter, A. C. (Eds.). *Pathways through adolescence: Individual development in relation to social contexts*. Mahwah, NJ: Lawrence Erlbaum Associates, pp. 15–34.

Stevenson, C. (1998). *Teaching ten to fourteen year olds*, 2nd edition. New York: Longman.

Suarez-Orozco C., and Suarez-Orozco, M. M. (2001). *Children of immigration*. Cambridge, MA: Harvard University Press.

3 Reading Goals for Middle School Students: Learning to Use Reading Skills Spontaneously

Teacher Jan Graham gets a class excited about literacy learning.

Reading Instruction Today: Controversies and Confusion, Possibilities and Promise

Several years ago, the principal of a nearby middle school telephoned to ask if I would conduct a reading workshop with the language arts faculty at her school. After I told her that I would be happy to lead the workshop, she mentioned the catch: The school's faculty was firmly and, it seemed, inexorably divided in their views regarding what constitutes effective reading instruction for the middle school grades. One part of the faculty believed that reading instruction should be modeled after what happens at the local elementary school: Students are given opportunities to build phonemic awareness and practice phonics, lists of high-frequency sight words are constantly displayed on the wall, and tests frequently include an evaluation of how well students can produce the sounds of nonsense words. Students in these teachers' classes learn to read word parts, then words, then short sentences before working their way through complete paragraphs and stories. The teachers of this faction explained that their middle school students needed and benefited from this phonics-based approach, noting for justification that many of them performed below the state average on the standardized tests that they took. The teachers argued that, since their students were poor readers, they had to start from the beginning and that it was their job to focus exclusively on teaching the reading skills that their students were missing. They were confident that the most effective away to concentrate on those skills was to teach them as discrete elements, in isolation. They believed that attempts to combine reading skills instruction with other aspects of the language arts curriculum would lead to confusion for the students who, these teachers argued, could not be expected to deal with literature or composition since they could not read.

The other faculty group held that reading instruction at the middle school level should be centered on the interests of the young adolescents and grounded in literature. The teachers in this group shared a large collection of texts from which their students selected materials for their daily sessions of sustained silent reading. The collection included novels for adolescents and adults, as well as picture books for young children; teen, sports, fashion, and music magazines; local, regional, and national newspapers; nonfiction including biographies, autobiographies, history, and self-help books; poetry collections; and miscellaneous print texts such as restaurant menus and album covers. Instead of directly teaching reading skills, the teachers in this group determined that their role meant they should provide three things: choices (from the collection), time (one day per week during the language arts period for reading), and evaluation (students had to demonstrate to the teacher, and often to their peers, that the time spent reading contributed to their growth as readers and thinkers). Students could demonstrate their growth in a variety of ways, each taken from a list that the teachers developed together. The list included the following kinds of items:

- Give whole-class story shares about the books they read;
- Create an illustrated time line for historical texts;
- Collaborate to create and present advertisements for real or imaginary products that they linked to the print texts, such as a motorcycle that was prominent in one story, a beauty parlor from another, and the daily lunch specials from the restaurant menu.

The teachers assigned a grade to each reading demonstration; the grade was weighted with several other reading grades earned during each nine-week period.

The division at that rural school exemplifies a debate that has occurred in schools across the United States and has fueled the current situation, one that leaves teachers wondering which stance to take on reading instruction. Some have become convinced that reading instruction is about using carefully sequenced and organized lessons to teach sound, letter, and word skills and strategies. These teachers have aligned themselves with the "phonics" movement. Others have countered that reading instruction should be about creating lifelong readers, and thus it involves finding ways to get middle school students interested in books, regardless of the genre or subject. These teachers are still sometimes called by the now derisive term *whole language proponents*. I suggest, in this chapter, that the two factions can find an area of common ground. My contention—that there is an area of common ground where phonics-based and whole language arguments dissolve and an integrated literacy pedagogy—is based not on blind optimism as much as on the fact that proponents of both factions share the same ultimate goals: to help middle school students become more proficient as people who read and to help them find that reading is a pleasure that they can enjoy throughout life. We need to be flexible and informed enough to know when and how to use ideas from both schools of thought. Before we turn our attention to instructional ideas that will address our students' specific needs, let's take a moment to participate in the current national conversation about reading instruction. It is a conversation in which we, as practicing and prospective teachers of language arts, have a voice, and one in which we have a stake.

The National Reading Panel

Today, questions about reading instruction arise in political arenas, as well as in educational circles. In preparing its influential report, *Teaching Children to Read: An Evidence-Based Assessment of the Scientific Research Literature on Reading and Its Implications for Reading Instruction* (2000), the National Reading Panel (NRP) conducted a meta-analysis of 115,000 experimental or quasiexperimental studies of reading from the mid–twentieth century to the present. The NRP claims that it has been able to identify the most effective ways to teach children to read, based on its analysis of the thousands of individual studies of reading. Its findings related to reading instruction prompted the NRP to publish instructional recommendations that include the following:

1. Explicit, systematic instruction in phonemic awareness to improve children's reading and spelling;
2. Phonics instruction for young readers and especially those with reading difficulties, including children with learning disabilities, those who are low achievers, and children from low socioeconomic levels;
3. Use of a variety of approaches for specific students;
4. Use of guided oral reading by children to their teachers, parents, or others capable of giving them feedback for developing reading fluency;
5. Teaching of systematic comprehension strategies such as recall of information, question generation, and summarizing of information. (NRP, 2000)

It is important to note that there have been many loud objections to the work of the National Reading Panel. (See the Open Letter in the June/July 2001 *Educational Researcher* by neurophysiologist Steven Strauss, who argues that the National Reading Panel and its leader have neglected "both the social underpinnings of illiteracy" and "certain psychological components of reading" [p. 26], and Elaine M. Garan's *Resisting Reading Mandates* [2002] for more on this situation.) Naturalistic studies were excluded because they typically cannot be replicated; therefore, in building its database, the National Reading Panel excluded studies of individual readers and ethnographies of particular classrooms, both of which produce qualitative instead of quantitative data. Many argue that this omission renders the information that informs the report limited and thus flawed. Another concern that more directly affects teachers of middle school students is that the report addresses instruction for beginning readers, but does not offer much direction for teachers of students who are experienced but unskilled readers, and those who are competent readers who choose not to read.

Despite these and other criticisms, federal and state funding for reading programs clearly reflects a preference for an alignment with the "scientific and research-based" instructional approaches identified by the National Reading Panel. In other words, state textbook adoptions and the programs promoted through county in-service providers are likely to reflect the experimental research-based preference of the National Reading Panel. These sources are likely to exclude programs that are supported by qualitative, classroom-based research (programs that in the past would have been closely associated with whole language approaches). Therefore, teachers and administrators in schools and offices at all levels, and those who will soon be entering the profession, need to be familiar with the basic findings and recommendations as they relate to reading instruction. I mention the long-term schism in reading instruction and the impact of the NRP for two reasons: One, they suggest a place to begin to examine what we know and what middle school students need to develop as readers. Two, I believe that beginning and experienced teachers need to recognize the history and the political aspects of the profession to make decisions that are informed by their knowledge of, and experience with, what is educationally sound, regardless of what is politically popular.

The Integrated Literacy Pedagogy Framework

It is possible that the school where you will work, or the one in which you work now, has teachers who stand at both extremes of the professional conversation about reading instruction. Some teachers believe that reading instruction is best treated as teaching a set of skills that students can learn to apply to all assignments; for them, teaching students to use their reading skills means teaching them problem-solving skills. Other teachers in this school see reading instruction as a means toward the goal of creating within students a desire to seek out books, to shape meaning and personal significance during reading experiences, to enjoy spending time with texts. Neither approach is wrong, but each is incomplete when used to the exclusion of the other. We can turn to the four core beliefs of the integrated literacy pedagogy as we set our course for reading instruction in the middle grades (see Figure 1.1):

Belief One: Because we believe that students come to us as individuals as well as group members, we recognize that our middle school students will demonstrate a range of abilities as readers. Some will be unskilled readers, others will be struggling (and often therefore uninterested or reluctant) readers, and some will be both skilled and eager readers.

Belief Two: Because we believe that our role requires that we attend to the needs and interests of our particular students, we realize that we will have to draw on the best examples for all of the strategies for teaching reading that we can find. For students who are unskilled readers and who have little understanding of the letter–sound correspondence that is a necessary prelude to reading print texts, we might provide direct instruction in phonemic awareness. For struggling or uninterested readers, our focus will be on identifying and addressing their particular reading problems and on finding ways to make reading attractive to them. For skilled and eager readers, we will seek ways to spark the intellectual charge that occurs when readers bring their own ideas to the transaction and, together with the author's words, create meaning. For all students, we will seek ways to connect reading to their lives, to introduce possibilities for exploring the impact of texts from internal and external perspectives, from self-conscious to socially-conscious elaborations.

Belief Three: Because we believe that today's language arts classes require the use of a broad definition of literacy, we will push all students, unskilled and skilled languagers alike, toward developing critical skills for reading words to reading the world.

Belief Four: Because we believe that professional standards should guide our decisions, we will consider those as we address the needs of our students.

The NCTE/IRA standards provide the following guidance to beginning teachers about expectations for readers:

> Standard 3: Students apply a wide range of strategies to comprehend, interpret, evaluate, and appreciate texts. They draw on their prior experience, their interactions with other readers and writers, their knowledge of word meaning and of other texts, their word identification strategies, and their understanding of textual features (e.g., sound–letter correspondence, sentence structure, context, graphics). (Farstrup & Myers, NCTE/IRA, 1996, p. 3)

Teaching Reading Is Not Synonymous with Teaching Literature

As language arts teachers, few of us are also reading specialists, yet we will be expected to teach reading skills that middle school students can apply across the curriculum. Therefore, we need to acquire a starter set of reliable assessment and instructional strategies that we can take into our classrooms and use with our students. But where do we begin when it comes to reading instruction for middle grades students?

First, many of us need to remind ourselves that teaching reading is not synonymous with teaching literature. While the desire to share our love of literature with adolescents is responsible for bringing many of us into the teaching profession in the first place, we have to recognize that we will not succeed in teaching literature if our students cannot read and make sense of print texts. Reading instruction, then, is the part of our role that involves teaching the skills that readers need to make sense of any print text (and, as we will see in Chapter 8, reading can also involve nonprint texts, such as the pictures in magazine advertisements).

A few examples of the skills that are frequently the focus in middle grades reading instruction include the ability to:

- Decode words (recognize the words that are encountered as words they have heard or seen before or words that sound like English words);
- Construct an organizational framework from which to make the parts of a text, such as subheadings and cross-references, fit together (consider how the parts fit into the whole of print text);
- Recognize cause-and-effect relationships (follow the structure of the text to make predictions about relationships);
- Differentiate between fact and opinion (use knowledge of word cues and other context clues that denote fact and opinion);
- Distinguish between explicit and implied or inferred meanings (notice when writers are directly stating information and are more subtly leading readers, and use that information appropriately);
- Determine the meaning of unfamiliar vocabulary words (take advantage of available context clues to generate plausible definitions for unfamiliar words).

Reading occurs in each school subject; good readers learn to transfer reading skills to fit the various reading tasks and challenges that they face. Teachers of all disciplines need to consider ways to help students make sense of the print text that is common in their subjects so they can assist the students as they read for information. Look at NCTE/IRA standard 3 on page 37 again, with an eye toward the interdisciplinary nature of reading skills. But notice, too, that as literacy teachers in language arts classes, we have the best opportunity among our colleagues to teach reading as part of our subject content because our medium is primarily spoken and written words. Our goals in reading instruction include a tall order: They range from ensuring that students develop the skills to decode and define unfamiliar words, to ensuring that they can comprehend, analyze, and evaluate unfamiliar texts. In reading instruction, our focus must encompass small units of analysis, such as word sounds (phonemes) and word parts (morphemes), and it must consider the relationship of sounds and meaning (phonemic awareness). In addition, it must expand to encompass large units of analysis, such as the comprehension of a novel or the evaluation of a short story.

I wonder if you are like I was as a beginning teacher of middle school students: I simply assumed that students would know how to read by the time they arrived in my middle grades classes. During my first two years of teaching eighth graders, I assigned a lot of pages of reading; I regularly checked students' comprehension with essays and multiple choice tests, games, and dramatizations; I gave vocabulary lists and Friday quizzes; I expected students to focus on main ideas and required that they monitor their progress in reading response logs as they moved through texts. But it took me a couple of years to discover the difference between *telling* them *to* read and *teaching* them *how to* read.

A Plan for Reading Instruction

We can now explore issues related to reading instruction and consider several ideas for identifying and meeting the needs of a variety of readers. First, we consider ways to assess the phonemic awareness and phonic knowledge of students who seem to be unskilled readers and explore possibilities for bringing those students into reading activities that not only address their interests but also improve their skills. Next, we consider ways to identify the kinds of reading problems that our struggling readers manifest. We examine the possibility that those struggling readers frequently hide their lack of skill and confidence behind curtains of reluctance, resistance, or lack of interest and explore possibilities for bringing those readers on board in classroom reading activities. Third, we consider ways to increase the interest and enthusiasm of those students who come to us as skilled and eager readers. The chapter concludes with a sample lesson plan that could be used in the many classrooms in which all three types of readers—unskilled, struggling and uninterested, and skilled and eager—sit side by side. This sample is followed by a list of the ways that the ideas of the chapter support an integrated literacy curriculum and a list of the NCTE/IRA standards that are addressed in the activities recommended in the chapter. The chapter closes with a list of strategies that are particularly helpful for promoting the reading development of English language learners.

Unskilled Readers

Identifying Problems

I recommend that teachers of language arts ask the following questions when they find a student who is having an especially tough time reading. The questions, based on a list of indicators of special needs for readers by Reutzel and Cooter (1999), are designed to help the language arts teacher in a middle school classroom identify students who have severe reading difficulties and who need special instruction:

Can the student tell you what the alphabet is and what it is used for?

Can the student name the letters of the alphabet when shown them?

Can the student produce letters in writing?

Can the student identify rhyming sounds?

Can the student recognize or identify the specific letter sounds in different words?

Can the student put spoken sounds into written letters? (p. 109)

I recommend, too, that we pay attention to the indicators that Kylene Beers, in *When Kids Can't Read, What Teachers Can Do* (2003), points to when describing a student who is an unskilled reader:

Has no strategies for recognizing unknown words;

Has limited sight word vocabulary;

Does not know how to use the context as a clue to help with word recognition or word meaning;

Does not have or use knowledge of word parts to help with word recognition or word meaning;

Reads haltingly, one word at a time;

Reads aloud or whisper reads when silent reading would be more appropriate;

Reads very slowly, with no attention to punctuation;

Reads aloud with little or no expression;

Reads too fast, blurring words, rushing through punctuation;

Does not visualize the text;

Does not "hear" the text when reading silently;

Does not reread to clarify meaning;

Reads to finish rather than to understand. (p. 24–25)

When we answer "no" or "in a limited way" to the questions on the Reutzel and Cooter (1999) list, or when we notice a student having difficulty with the indicators that Beers (2003) cites, we know that a student needs special focused reading instruction. In ideal school settings, we will be able to call on the services of a reading specialist to assist with those students. If we do not have the option of a reading specialist, we will need to develop some simple yet effective strategies to address the needs of readers who are struggling.

Most of our middle school students will demonstrate understanding of the alphabet and will be able to hear sounds and write words using their knowledge of the relationship between sounds and letters. Yet many will still demonstrate the kinds of problems that Beers lists. So we, as teachers of language arts, find ourselves back to the Big Question for this chapter: What is a teacher of middle school students to do about reading instruction? The next question is equally challenging: What shall we do when we have unskilled readers in our classrooms, sitting among more skilled, confident, and enthusiastic readers? Do we treat unskilled readers as beginners and prepare lessons that reflect the research-based practices that are promoted for early elementary school classrooms, with phonemic awareness or phonics instruction? For most of us, the answer will be "No."

Unskilled Readers Are Not Beginning Readers

Here is why we will want to look beyond the first pair of findings and associated recommendations of the National Reading Panel when we begin our reading instruction: Most of our 10- to 14-year-old students, even those who are unskilled as readers and those who are English language learners (non-native speakers of English), have had experiences with print texts. They are not beginners. Most know what it means to read, to interpret print symbols as letters and words. Most have developed some level of phonemic awareness. With their ten years or more of experience as languagers (listening to, generating, and making sense of words), our middle school students have come to understand that spoken words are composed of sounds that can be separated from each other. They know, intuitively, that phonemes, or sounds that are considered the smallest signals in a language, account for the different meanings associated with words. They have used language enough to understand that individual sounds (phonemes) are strung together to produce words and that individual sounds also create meaningful contrasts between sounds, so that we can distinguish, for example, between *kick* and *cook*.

Further, most young adolescent languagers understand that the sounds are only roughly connected to the letters of the alphabet. For example, a sixth grader is likely to know that the sound of "a" in *math* is different from the sound of "a" in *social*. He could conclude from that example that one letter of the alphabet can have more than one sound, and perhaps, too, that the sound of the specific letter is determined by the letters that surround it. The flip side is also true. He is likely to know that the initial sound in the word *fish* is the same as the last sound in the word *tough* despite their different spellings. He might be able to articulate the phonemic rule that explains what he knows, as a languager, to be true: The same sound can be represented by different letters, depending on the word and place within the word in which the sound occurs. It is true that phonemic awareness is deemed "highly predictive of success in beginning reading" (Graves, Juel, & Graves, 2001, p. 102), and therefore teaching phonemic awareness necessarily takes a central place in the elementary school literacy curriculum, where students might first learn to connect the sounds they hear with the print they see. However, at the middle school level, our students are more likely to be unskilled or unmotivated readers (or both) than they are to be beginning readers. I suspect that few have had no experience using the sound–word–meaning relationship. Few cannot understand that sounds and letters of the alphabet have a relationship that extends into the sound and meanings of words.

Assessing and Assisting Unskilled Readers

Assessing Phonemic Awareness

If we suspect that a student has not acquired phonemic awareness (the understanding that the sounds we use when we speak are represented symbolically by letters of the alphabet), we can use the rhyming words assessment. We would use this assessment if, for example, a student is performing well below her classmates on reading and comprehension tasks. For this task, we should provide the student with a two-column word list that has twenty words in each column (Figure 3.1). The words should be no more than two syllables in length. On the list, fifteen of the word pairs rhyme, and five of the pairs do not rhyme. The student's task is to listen as the teacher reads the word pairs aloud and then to tell the teacher whether or not the two words in each pair rhyme. Students who are unable to achieve a score of at least 75 percent on this assessment, because they either fail to recognize rhyming pairs or claim that a pair rhymes when it does not, demonstrate a lack of phonemic awareness. These students will need extra help in learning to hear the individual sounds in words.

Teaching Phonics

Teaching phonics in isolation to middle school students may not be a good solution, because phonics instruction may divert attention from more meaningful reading instruction, where our goals are to increase students' ability to make sense of print texts and increase the likelihood that they will develop good reading habits. If this seems farfetched, see the study of students' writing by Finlay McQuade (1980), in which students who received strict grammar instruction performed more poorly on writing tasks after several months than did their classmates who had no formal instruction. McQuade's conclusion was that the time spent on grammar was detrimental because it displaced time that could have been spent on writing. Unlike first graders, our young adolescent students are likely to have had experiences with the letter–sound correspondence on which the English alphabet is based.

FIGURE 3.1   Rhyming Word Pairs for Assessment of Phonemic Awareness

swim	Jim
like	Mike
snake	lake
bar	far
task	mask
lamp	camp
nowhere	there
brick	tick
picture	mixture
tree	tall
phone	loan
show	snow
screen	mean
mane	plain
box	rock
man	fan
boy	big
girl	swirl
cat	car
phone	few

Modified from Ruetzel and Cooter, 1999, pp. 104–105.

Rimes.   Teachers who do choose to teach phonics in isolation at the middle school level emphasize the correspondence of letters and sounds by having students pronounce lists of word parts. Typically, rimes, which are composed of a vowel and the letter(s) that follow it, are the word parts that are featured in direct phonics instruction. In this type of phonics instruction, the rimes *ock*, *ick*, *ink* might occur on the same list. Students demonstrate their grasp of phonics when they are able to say the different sounds correctly, despite the fact that the sounds themselves carry no meaning. Eventually, students learn that these sounds are word parts and that they can be attached to beginning syllable sounds ("onsets") to become words, such as *clock*, *brick*, and *think*. One benefit of emphasizing rimes as a vehicle for teaching beginning readers to predict the sound of words is that the vowel sound remains constant when onsets are added to the rimes. For instance, the rime *ide* sounds the same when it is heard as a part of each these words: *hide, chide, slide, tide, side*. Once students learn the consonant sounds associated with the letter(s) of the alphabet (or the onset sound that precedes a rime) and a collection of rimes, they can determine the sounds of many words in print texts. The use of rimes is an important concept in phonics instruction; because it is virtually impossible to pronounce a consonant in isolation, unskilled readers need to learn to pronounce consonants in combinations. (Take a moment to experiment with this concept: Try to pronounce the consonant *B*. Do you hear only an unvoiced bilabial flap [imagine the sound that one drop of water would make if it leaked from a faucet], or do you hear *B* followed by a vowel sound, probably something like *eee*, after your lips touch and separate to form the *B*?)

In *Language Arts: Content and Teaching Strategies* (2002), Gail Tompkins lists the following essential rimes and gives some examples of the words in which the rimes occur:

> ack (black), ail (snail), ain (brain), ake (wake), ame (game), an (can), ank (bank), ap (cap), ash (trash), at (cat), ate (gate), aw (claw), ay (play), eat (heat), ell (shell), est (chest), ice (mice), ick (brick), ide (hide), ight (bright), ill (kill), in (grin), ine (fine), ing (king), ink (pink), ip (ship), ir (fir), ock (block), oke (joke), op (chop), or (for), ore (shore), uck (truck), ug (drug), ump (lump), unk (junk) (p. 156)

Tompkins's list might be useful for those of us who have middle school students who seem to have no knowledge of rimes or of the ways that sounds combine to create words.

Phonic Generalizations. Another common approach for phonics instruction that may be more useful for middle school students who are unskilled readers, because it deals with complete words instead of the letter–sound correspondence only, involves practice with single-syllable and short multisyllable words that are almost identical. Using this approach, *cat*, *cut*, *crate*, and *car* might appear together on a list. When studying the list, students learn about the property of the letter *c*: It can be pronounced with the hard sound of /*k*/. When they learn another list of words that begin with *c*, such as *cease*, *city*, and *cycle*, they learn that *c* can also have the soft sound of /*s*/. The lesson will continue to demonstrate how *c* has a hard sound when it starts a word and is followed by *a*, *o*, or *u*; it has a soft sound when followed by *e*, *i*, or *y*. When the student can say these and other words that include *c*, he demonstrates his understanding of one part of the English letter–sound correspondence, which is the heart of phonics instruction.

In the middle school classrooms in which I have observed phonics instruction, a lesson that demonstrates a generalization for single-syllable and short multisyllable words usually progresses toward having students add more generalizations. For example, students may first focus on the consonant–vowel (CV) generalization, which says that when one vowel follows one consonant in a single-syllable word, the vowel sound is usually long, as in *go*. (*To* and *do* are exceptions that these students will have to memorize as rule breakers.) They may then add other generalizations about consonant–vowel combinations, such as the consonant–vowel–consonant (CVC) generalization. This rule describes how, in one-syllable words that have one vowel that is between two consonants, the vowel sound is usually short, as in *can* and *ton*. A third consonant vowel generalization is the final *e*, or CVC*e* generalization, which says that when there are two vowels in a single-syllable word, and the second one is a final *e*, then the first vowel is long and the final *e* is silent, as in *home* and *care*. (Again, there are exceptions, like *love* and *move*, that students simply have to memorize.)

Perhaps it will be useful for language arts teachers to keep a chart of phonic generalizations handy. Even proficient readers forget what the rules state regarding pronunciation. For some of our students, learning to apply these rules will open up the possibility of decoding words, an essential step toward learning to make sense of a print text, or languaging as a reader. See Figure 3.2 for a list of some of the most common phonic rules.

FIGURE 3.2   Common Phonics Generalizations

1. CVC pattern	When a one-syllable word has only one vowel, and that vowel comes between two consonants, it is usually short.
	Examples are **cat, bet, wit,** and **tub.**
	(Exceptions include **night, cold, tow, mow.)**
2. Final *e* or CVC*e*	When there are two vowels in a one-syllable word, and one of them is an **e** at the end of the word, the first vowel is long and the **final e** is silent.
	Examples are **cape, safe,** and **flute.**
	(Exceptions include **have** and **love.)**
3. CV pattern	When a vowel follows a consonant in a one-syllable word, the vowel is long.
	Examples are **be** and **go.**
	(Exceptions include **the, to,** and **do.)**
4. Two sounds of *c*	The letter c can be pronounced as /k/ or as /s/.
	When *c* is followed by *a, o* or *u,* it is pronounced /k/ (the **hard c** sound).
	Examples are **cat, cold, cup.**
	When *c* is followed by *e, i,* or *y,* it is pronounced /s/ (the **soft c** sound).
	Examples are **cease, city, cycle.**
5. Two sounds of *g*	The sound associated with the letter *g* depends on the letter following it.
	When *g* is followed by *a, o,* or *u,* it is pronounced as /g/ (the **hard g** sound).
	Examples are **gas, gone, gulp.**
	When *g* is followed by *e, i,* or *y,* it is usually pronounced /i/ (the **soft g** sound).
	Examples are **gentle, ginger, gypsy.**
	(Exceptions include **get** and **give.)**
6. -i*gh*	When *gh* follows *i,* the *i* is long and the *gh* is silent.
	Examples are **night** and **slight.**
	(Exceptions include **neighbor.)**
7. *Kn-* and *wr-*	In words beginning with *kn-* and *wr-,* the first letter is not pronounced.
	Examples are **know, knit, wrong, write.**
8. *R*-controlled	Vowels that are followed by the letter *r* are overpowered, and are neither short nor long.
	Examples are **bird** and **car.**
	(Exceptions include **fire** and **tired.)**

Source: Clymer, T. (1963). The utility of phonic generalizations in the primary grades. *The Reading Teacher, 16,* 252–258.

These strategies, assessing phonemic awareness and teaching phonic generalizations, focus unskilled readers on word parts. A productive set of strategies for middle school students who are unskilled readers, but who understand that words are composed of letters that represent different sounds, give attention not to word parts but to words the strategy then move into recognizing words in appropriate contexts. Some ideas related to teaching words that will help unskilled readers navigate through print texts are described in the paragraphs that follow.

Teaching High-Frequency Sight Words

Some middle school students who are unskilled readers may not have learned basic high-frequency sight words (sometimes called *function words*). As Vacca, Vacca, Gove, Burkey, Lenhart, and McKeon suggest in *Reading and Learning to Read* (2003), a total of 300 sight words comprise 65 percent of all written texts. (See Figure 3.3.) High-frequency words include so-called function words that connect ideas within a phrase, clause, or sentence, such as the following: *of*, *at*, *is*, *was*, *the*, *and*, *on*. They also include short words that are used to describe information-bearing words such as these: *good*, *sentence*, *city*, *earth*, *life*, *feet*, *side*, *white*, *four*, *list*, *song*, *color*, *music*. If our students learn to recognize those 300 words, they can "more readily read across *any line of print*" (Vacca et al., 2003, p. 205). Therefore, for unskilled readers, direct instruction in high-frequency word recognition, complemented by instruction and reinforcement of a set of self-monitoring word recognition strategies, is appropriate. One approach that Vacca et al. recommend is the "language experience strategy," in which a single function word is the focus of a mini-lesson. I recently tried the language experience strategy with a small group of unskilled seventh grade readers. The words I wanted to focus on were *and* and *like*. First I asked the readers to name their male and female role models, or "a man and a woman they like a lot." I wrote their choices on the board, creating simple sentences that I read aloud as I wrote. I also underlined the two focal words as I wrote the sentences:

We *like* Michael Jordan *and* Britney Spears.
Mohammed Ali *and* Mia Hamm are people I *like*.
They *like* George Bush *and* Julia Roberts.

Next, I asked the students to pick out the two words that were in all three sentences. They quickly recognized the underlined *like* and *and*. We read the sentences aloud, in unison. At this point, they had been introduced to the two focal words and had seen them used in an appropriate context. Like most high-frequency words, these are not words that they have trouble using when they speak; they are merely words that they have trouble recognizing when they read.

To continue the language experience lesson on *like* and *and*, I asked them to tell me two things that they really like about school. As they spoke, I wrote the words, but omitted the function word; the list that I wrote, based on their word pairs, looked like this:

recess   lunch
friends   talking
playing   learning

FIGURE 3.3 **High-Frequency Sight Words**

1–25	26–50	51–75	76–100	101–125	126–150
the	or	will	number	new	great
of	one	up	no	sound	where
and	had	other	way	take	help
a	by	about	could	only	through
to	word	out	people	little	much
in	but	many	my	work	before
is	not	then	than	know	line
you	what	them	first	place	right
that	all	these	water	year	too
it	were	so	been	live	mean
he	we	some	call	me	old
was	when	her	who	back	any
for	your	would	oil	give	same
on	can	make	now	most	tell
are	said	like	find	very	boy
as	there	him	long	after	follow
with	use	into	down	thing	came
his	an	time	day	our	want
they	each	has	did	just	show
I	which	look	get	name	also
at	she	two	come	good	around
be	do	more	made	sentence	form
this	how	write	may	man	three
have	their	go	part	think	small
from	if	see	over	say	set

151–175	176–200	201–225	226–250	251–275	276–300
put	kind	every	left	until	idea
end	hand	near	don't	children	enough
does	picture	add	few	side	eat
another	again	between	while	feet	face
well	change	own	along	car	watch
large	off	below	might	mile	far
must	play	country	close	night	Indian
big	spell	plant	something	walk	real
even	air	last	seem	white	almost
such	away	school	next	sea	let
because	animal	father	hard	began	above
turn	house	keep	open	grow	girl
here	point	tree	example	took	sometimes
why	page	never	begin	river	mountain
ask	letter	start	life	four	cut
went	mother	city	always	carry	young
men	answer	earth	those	state	talk
read	found	eye	both	once	soon
need	study	light	paper	book	list
land	still	thought	together	hear	song
different	learn	head	got	stop	leave
home	should	under	group	without	family
us	America	story	often	second	body
move	world	saw	run	late	music
try	high	food	important	miss	color

From Edward Fry, *Elementary Reading Instruction*, 1977, as presented by Vacca, Vacca, Gove, Burkey, Lenhart, and McKeon, in *Reading and Learning to Read*, 5th edition, Allyn and Bacon 2003, pp. 203–204.

I then asked students to come to the board to put the words into sentences like they did with the list of people they like. Copying the structure of the previous sentences that they had read aloud in unison, they wrote:

> We like recess and lunch.
> Friends and talking are what I like.
> They like playing and learning.

One volunteer came forward to underline the words that show up in all three sentences, *like* and *and*. Then again we read the sentences aloud, in unison. I noticed that the students seemed more confident, even with the other words in the sentences, during the second oral reading. I think that the practice of reading aloud encourages that kind of confidence, when the entire group is comprised of readers who are having similar problems with reading.

To finish the language experience lesson, I asked them to do one more activity: They turned in their literature books to Toni Cade Bambara's "Raymond's Run" (1997), a story that I had previously read aloud to them as they followed in their books. They enjoyed the story and were eager to return to it. I explained that one thing good readers do is that they "recognize most words automatically" (Beers, 2003, p. 35). Then I asked the unskilled readers to count how many times the two words we had just focused on, *like* and *and*, appeared in the first column of the story, while I read the column aloud to them. They were surprised to find *and* repeated twelve times in that first column, and to discover that *like* was used once, in the opening sentence, "I don't have much work to do around the house like some girls" (p. 53). One student commented, "It doesn't mean *like* the same way we meant it when we said I *like* talking, but it is still *like*." (This comment reminded me that we should not expect unskilled readers to be uninterested in language itself; many middle school students who are unskilled readers have learned to depend on listening carefully and using oral language skillfully. Although they may not be readers, they are thinkers.) The lesson ended with their request that they be given a chance to read the paragraphs in column one for themselves, following my lead.

This direct instruction model incorporates modeling, group practice, and then individual practice. The lessons learned through direct instruction can be reinforced by teaching students metacognitive strategies by which they monitor their own recognition of new words. Vacca et al. (2003) recommend the use of high-frequency word walls, in which newly learned words are written on a semipermanent list that is kept on display in the classroom, to be used as a quick-reference list by student readers (p. 206). I saw this idea extended in a middle school that I visited recently: The mathematics, social studies, and science teachers on a grade-level team agreed that they would all copy "word wall words" from the language arts teacher's wall every Friday afternoon. On the next Monday, when students arrived, they found the words that they had learned in language arts posted in the mathematics, social studies, and science classrooms. This interdisciplinary reinforcement helped students see and think about those words throughout the day. I have no solid evidence that the teachers' cooperative effort contributed to students' ability to read those words, but I would be willing to bet that it did.

Teaching Environmental Print

The use of environmental print (Reutzel & Cooter, 1999, p. 111) is a starting place for many young adolescents who cannot read. It involves at least two stages. In one, the teacher labels the items in the classroom and points to the labels when the words are spoken. For example, *table* and *mesa*, if your class includes speakers of Spanish, or the word for *table* in whichever home language your students use, are written on a note card in large print and taped to the table. In the other stage, the student records printed words that he observes in the environment and uses contextual understanding to learn to say and reproduce the words. For example, the student who passes by a Men Working sign on the way to school each day would bring in the words that he copied from the sign and then learn, with the help of the teacher, a classmate, or an aide, what the words say. He would then practice saying and spelling them orally and on paper. This strategy is only a starting point that may help unskilled readers understand that sound/symbol/word meaning connection that is necessary for them to progress as readers.

Other Instructional Strategies

Other possibilities for self-paced and self-monitored instruction in sight words include these: (1) Have students create illustrated glossaries, in which they write the word in as many different ways as they can (fancy script, block letters, across the corners of their pages, top-to-bottom of a page, and so on) to practice its letter combinations; (2) have students group similar sight words according to categories that they create (such as a "people" category for *mother*, *father*, *he*, *she*, *they*, *them*); (3) and have them create magazine advertisements for their favorite products (cars, sneakers, shampoos, etc.), incorporating a specified number of their sight words in the slogan that they create.

Struggling and Uninterested Readers

A word of relief here: Approximately twenty years of experience working with young adolescents has convinced me that most middle schoolers have at least some rudimentary knowledge of reading, and therefore the number of students for whom you, as a middle school language arts teacher, will have to implement lessons on phonemic awareness and phonics is probably going to be few. Instead, the biggest reading barriers that we are likely to confront are related to fluency and comprehension. When we focus instruction on these two interrelated and virtually inseparable aspects of reading, we promote development of discrete reading skills and also build students' interest in the content of reading.

We can comfortably lean on the remaining recommendations of the National Reading Panel (2000) when we look toward instruction in fluency and comprehension, since the recommendations call for the use of a variety of approaches for specific students. The recommendations also call for the use of guided oral reading by children to their teachers, parents, or others capable of giving them feedback for developing reading fluency, as well as the teaching of systematic comprehension strategies such as recall of information, question generation, and summarizing of information.

Using drawing to express comprehension of The Cay.

The following scenario illustrates what happened when one teacher of struggling readers taught a teacher-directed phonics-based lesson and followed it with a student-sensitive oral story sharing lesson during one class period. I suggest that the students' responses to the two distinctly different lessons speak to the importance of integrated literacy instruction for middle school languagers.

A student teacher was working with a mentor teacher in a sixth grade language arts class. The class was in a school that was populated primarily by students who lived in poverty. For several years, the school had performed badly on state tests, and as a result of the test scores and the neighborhood in which it was located, the school has a bad reputation in the town. In the past two years, due to tireless work by the administration and teachers, partnerships with parents, local businesses, and collaboration with some of the local university's teacher education programs, the school had experienced success: Students' state test scores were climbing, and there was a sense of possibility that previously had been missing. In an effort to prepare students in this school for the year's next high-stakes standardized test, and to try to maintain the school's recent increase in self-respect, the principal announced that the entire school would go into intervention mode for four weeks. For the teacher, this meant abandoning plans for integrated literacy lessons to implement the phonics-based reading program that the principal asked all teachers of language arts to use for the coming month.

In previous visits to this classroom, I had seen the teacher working elbow-to-elbow with her students. She helped as they illustrated a poem and when they charted temporal connections in two different stories. She encouraged them to use explicit details in their writing by having them send "silly request notes" to three of their classmates (she made the pairing to be sure all were included). Everyone tested the effectiveness of the silly request notes by watching as the recipient tried to fulfill the silly request. One student delighted his classmates, for example, when he stood up and sang "Mary Had a Little Lamb" while substituting a "w" each time an "l" appeared in the original lyrics.

When I observed her this time, the teacher was leading the class in a phonics lesson. She was reading directly from a teacher's edition of the phonics workbook, an edition that instructed her about when to pause for emphasis, when to point to letters on the publisher-provided overhead of partial words, how many times and how loudly to pronounce word parts, and so on. Initially, students were timid participants in the lesson, but then they began responding more eagerly. Finally, they sounded like a chorus when the teacher asked them to chant lists of rimes from their workbooks. They sang out "*ock oak op or.*" Some added a rhythmic beat. The lesson was energized; the students were jazzed; they enjoyed the sounds they were generating. They were having fun with the phonics lesson. I wondered, though, if the fun would carry over into an increased understanding of the relationships of the sounds that they were repeating to the word parts they would continue to study the next day.

This group had been working through the workbook for five class sessions prior to my observation. (Each workbook lesson was designed to fill approximately forty minutes; at this school, each class session lasted a total of fifty minutes.) Despite the pleasure of seeing students enjoying the lesson, I was troubled: These students would not be reading a paragraph, or indeed any text longer than a sentence, until lesson day thirteen of the phonics program. They would spend forty minutes of class for twelve days of calling out word parts, saying sounds. Was this reading instruction? Would it even help prepare these sixth graders for the standardized test?

The workbook portion of the class period contrasted dramatically with what happened during the closing few minutes. After students finished the day's phonics lesson and neatly stacked their workbooks on a shelf, the student teacher took a seat in the middle of the class. From there, she continued reading from a story she had begun with them five days earlier—a story about a boy whose father was killed by a shark. The students, who had literally been singing sounds a few minutes earlier, were quiet and intensely focused on the story.

When the bell rang, the spell of the story sharing session was over, but the impact of the story did not evaporate. The students enthusiastically discussed the story as they left the room, and they were still talking about it an hour later, when they returned to line up for an assembly. The story. The shark. Huge teeth. The water. The fear. None of the sixth graders mentioned pronouncing *dock, dock, dock, dope, dope, dope, door, door, door,* despite the fact that they had seemed to enjoy participating orally in the phonics lesson that day. Instead, they were talking about the languaging event that was *meaningful* for them: the story. I overheard one mention that he'd seen on television a news report of a recent shark attack in nearby Destin Beach; another announced that her friends had claimed to see sharks when they were fishing off the Panama City Beach pier. Unlike the collection of word parts that they sounded out, the story held the potential for real meaning for these students. Through the story sharing time, they were invited to use their own background and experiences as adolescents who had grown up near the ocean to make sense of the story. The boy, his father, the shark, were more than fiction in their minds.

For those of us who advocate an integrated literacy stance, a primary goal in reading instruction is to teach students to use reading as a means of making sense of their world. A related and significant goal is to help our students develop habits of people who read. Notice that in the scenario described above, the five minutes of story time accomplished more toward reaching these goals than did the forty minutes of phonics instruction.

Sparking Fluency, Comprehension, and Motivation in Struggling and Uninterested Readers

Third-year teacher Tameka King comments on the connection between fluency and comprehension when she explains her concern:

> My main concerns regarding my students' reading comprehension skills are that students who are able to read aren't necessarily able to comprehend what they have read and that those who are not fluent readers aren't able to comprehend because they can't get through the text. Some of my students just don't seem to be concerned with the fact that "calling out words" does not equal "reading." They just like to "get finished with" reading assignments. (June 6, 2002)

Tameka's comments give rise to more specific questions: What do we need to know about fluency and comprehension so we can design reading instruction that develops these crucial and interrelated skills? What kinds of goals should we establish for working with students whom we identify through listening to their oral reading and observing their habits during their silent reading? What should we do when we identify some as struggling readers? What kinds of goals should we establish for assisting students who are well on their way to performing as competent, critical readers? In order to work toward practical, student-sensitive answers for these questions, within the framework of an integrated literacy classroom, let's look at fluency and comprehension as two interrelated, inseparable, key components in the reading focus in a middle grades language arts class.

Building Fluency and Comprehension among Struggling and Uninterested Readers

Fluency, in regard to reading, is the ability to read words quickly and accurately. Comprehension is the ability to make sense of those words, and it may occur at literal and figurative levels. A problem that many of us find at the center of middle school language arts classes is this: Some of our students are fluent; they can decode words quickly and accurately, so we assume that they are able to comprehend texts. Yet fluency, while required for comprehension to take place, is not sufficient to allow comprehension to take place. Skilled readers do more than decode words quickly and accurately. One job that we must accept, as teachers of reading within the framework of an integrated literacy pedagogy, is to help students use fluency as they build comprehension. The distinction between students who can decode words, and thus read them—sometimes quickly and with ease—and the students who can both decode words and make sense of them within a given context, or comprehend them, is frequently difficult for teachers to see. We must carefully attend to students' meaning making while they read; this process is time intensive because it demands that we spend time individually with all of our students, listening to them summarize the main points of an article or retell a story, for example. Unless we listen to them individually and probe their comprehension of print texts, we may be misled to equate fluency with comprehension.

Unlike those who read quickly (and who may or may not be able to make sense of the words they decode), many young adolescent students lack fluency; they have trouble maintaining the momentum necessary to allow for comprehension because they are not fluent readers. Richard Allington, in his NRP-defiant research-based text, *What Really Matters for Struggling Readers* (2001), insists that we should spend class time concentrating on building fluency to develop comprehension, and he promotes the use of free reading periods and student choice of materials as part of his method. His student-sensitive approach stands in stark and welcome contrast to more traditional teacher-dominated fluency and comprehension instruction that includes a stop watch, word count charts, and publisher-produced multiple choice comprehension quizzes.

As Allington points out, the simple equation that the more time readers read, the more fluent they become, is often ignored in classroom instruction. When adults choose to spend time reading, we are almost always free to vary the kind and difficulty of text that we select, depending on our purposes, time, mood. Yet in classrooms, we sometimes forget that students need to learn to be people who read, not merely students who have to read. Consequently, we emphasize the reader-as-student definition at the sacrifice of the reader-as-person goal. We ask students to deal with texts that will challenge them to higher levels of comprehension and sophistication. But how often do we invite them to get lost in a book, to crawl or to fly through it if they wish, to experience it the way that they most enjoy?

Why do we avoid issuing these invitations? One answer lies in what we believe about our role in our students' literacy development and lives. I could argue that, given the limited time available for reading in our classrooms, I have to make every minute count by including in it educational reading material (in other words, literature that introduces new vocabulary, complex themes and imagery, complicated or archaic syntax, and so on). Yet you can counter that argument by suggesting that since reading fluency is one of my primary goals for young adolescent students, then I need to allow time for easy, fast reading in my classroom, too. And you would be right on target: I must provide students with time to read the books that they can read without assistance or frustration. Like young children who beg to pore over the same picture book again and again and again, unaware that their familiarity with the text is contributing to the development of their emerging reading skills, young adolescents benefit from reading texts that they can move through unimpeded.

If I want to improve fluency, I need to provide students with time to practice with texts that they can move through fluidly. The simple truth is that we impede our students' reading performance when we refuse to allow them access to texts that they can read fluently, because the more words per minute they read, the more likely they are to improve their reading.

Does this mean that I am suggesting that teachers should avoid using books that challenge students toward development of higher, more sophisticated reading skills? Not at all. Yet it does mean that I advocate treating young adolescents in my classroom as people who read, not merely as students who are required to read. There is a difference. Think again about the reading experiences that adults who are teachers enjoy: Sometimes we choose to read challenging material slowly and with great care toward our comprehension of it; at other times, we choose to spend time with texts that entertain us and that we can finish without much effort. We read differently when we are perusing changes in our retirement plans, the latest short story in *The Sun*, or a poem in *The New Yorker*. Yet when we go to the dentist and sit in the waiting room, or when we sit on a jet, aren't we as likely to read a *People* magazine or a John Grisham novel as we are to delve into a tome by Thomas Hardy? Why do we choose to take advantage of these different kinds of reading experiences? Because sometimes we want to read purely for pleasure. And because we are reading with pleasure as our purpose, we continue reading only if we are able to do it with fluency and comprehension.

Assessing Fluency and Comprehension

Establishing a Baseline   In *Reading and the High School Student*, Judith L. Irvin, Douglas R. Buehl, and Ronald M. Klemp (2003) note that struggling adolescent readers are often experts at "mock participation" in reading instruction. Students who demonstrate the following may be giving us signals that they are struggling as readers: "avoid eye contact with the teacher, engage in disruptive behavior, become a good listener, rely on a 'with it' classmate or a good reader, seek help from friends, forget to bring to class books and other materials that may be needed for reading, use manipulative techniques in and out of class to gain teachers' positive perceptions" (p. 80). We must take specific actions to determine whether or not a middle school student can read with fluency and comprehension and to discover which kinds of texts he or she can read easily, as well as which kinds of texts he or she will read. Further, we must try to discern whether or not uninterested readers in our classes are truly bored and apathetic, as they often claim to be, or if their resistance is actually an attempt to hide the fact that they are struggling as readers, as we often discover.

The first and most direct assessment that can provide us with insights into the practices and habits of middle school readers involves having students read aloud while their language arts teachers keep records. The second assessment involves having students read silently and think aloud about their reading process, using a method known widely as a "think-aloud." The assessment activities are described in the sections that follow.

Informal Individual Reading Skills Inventory   The initial assessment should involve each student in the class individually. By conducting this seven-step assessment, you will be able to gather baseline information about students' oral reading proficiency and habits, as well as their ability to comprehend fiction and nonfiction texts. The information will contribute to a data source that you can use to inform later decisions about appropriate reading instruction for individual students.

First, to prepare for the informal individual reading skills inventory, identify and photocopy three short works of narrative fiction and three works of expository nonfiction that are no more than 300 words in length. I recommend these kinds of texts because middle school students spend more time reading narrative and expository texts than any other kind of text. The text samples in each category (fiction/nonfiction) should reflect variation in readability (below, at, and above grade level). Second, write two or three literal-level comprehension questions, and one personal-connection comprehension question for each of the six texts. (Please see the sixth step for sample questions.) Third, distribute a copy of all six written texts to each student. Do not distribute the questions; you will use them during the student-teacher conference (see the sixth step). Fourth, instruct your students to select the one fiction and one nonfiction piece from the sets that they feel most comfortable reading aloud to you for the oral reading assessment. They can make this selection by reading the first paragraph of each passage or by reading to a certain point that you have marked with a check on the copies of the passages. (For this assessment, it is important to alert your students to the fact that they will be sitting with you in the reading corner and that they will be reading loudly enough for only you to hear them. This announcement will relieve some anxiety, particularly for the poor readers in the class.)

Fifth, when you are ready to begin individual assessments, call a volunteer to the reading corner, and begin the assessment by recording the student's answer to an important question: "Which two passages did you choose to read to me?" The student's answer to this question gives you an unscientific yet extremely helpful clue to the student's perception of her reading level. Sixth, ask the student to read the two student-selected passages aloud. After the student completes the first passage, ask her to answer two or three literal-level comprehension questions and one personal-connection comprehension question, each of which is designed to gauge her ability to make sense of the text. Repeat the process with the second passage.

For example, after reading Ray Bradbury's "All Summer in a Day" (1996) you might ask literal comprehension questions like these: "What are the children waiting for at the start of the story?" "How do you know?" and "What makes Margot different from her classmates?" You should also ask personal-connection comprehension questions such as "How did you feel about Margot being locked in the closet?" "How would you feel if you were Margot or one of the students in her class?"

For David Owen's nonfiction "Lego" (1997), an essay about a woman who landed her dream job as head of the Lego company's model-design staff, you might ask these literal and personal-connection comprehension questions: "What one thing does Francie like to do more than any other activity?" "How do you know?" "What is her job today?" "Which of your hobbies could become a paying job when you are older?" The answers to these questions will reveal whether or not each student has been able to make sense of the text. It is important that you question all students as they finish each passage, even those who appear to have no trouble completing a passage; the questioning will help you ascertain whether or not the readers who appear to be fluent are comprehending the text or are merely decoding it well.

Seventh, create a running record on a sheet of paper that has only this student's name, the date, and the titles of the passages he has chosen to read on the top. Note carefully how the student answers the comprehension questions. Record the student's exact words, where possible. Before you call on the next student to come to the reading corner, take time to jot a note about any behaviors that the student demonstrated while reading aloud. Look for body language that denotes ease or discomfort. These questions may help you notice signs of discomfort:

- Is the student sitting up straight or slouching?
- Is he or she mumbling or whispering or speaking with a confident tone and an appropriate volume?

- Does he or she ask you to tell what the words are when he or she comes to ones unfamiliar ones, or does he or she try to work them out by sound or another method?

Some behaviors that warrant particular attention, because they strongly indicate that the reader is struggling with the task, include these:

- Pointing to words with a finger while reading;
- Moving the lips before vocalizing words;
- Skipping unfamiliar words;
- Not trying to pronounce unfamiliar words;
- Replacing unfamiliar words with familiar words that make no sense in that context.

These running record notes comprise an initial reading skills inventory for the student. They provide a wealth of information for you as you gather information on the reading strengths of the individuals in your classroom, as well as on the range of readers with whom you are working. You will want to make a special note of any student who, during the reading skills inventory, demonstrates great difficulty reading the below-grade-level passages. The recommendations for assessment of phonemic awareness at the beginning of the chapter might be helpful for working with these students.

Silent Reading/Think Aloud   The silent reading/think aloud assessment requires that the student read silently and then talk aloud about his reading process—the connections he is making, the glitches he struggles through, the roadblocks he can't crawl over. It is important to assess the silent reading of all students, since some of the cognitive moves of silent reading are different from the ones we use in reading aloud. (For example, one strategy that skilled readers use when reading silently is called *metacognitive comprehension monitoring*. As skilled readers, when we realize that what we are reading does not make sense, in terms of what we have just read, we are likely to reread—to retrace our steps to try to determine where we went wrong and then correct ourselves. This kind of internal activity, which is an important part of self-monitoring, rarely occurs when we read aloud.) If conducted early in the school year, results of a silent reading/think aloud assessment, when paired with the results of the reading skills inventory, can further assist us in making an informed decision about an individual's reading strengths and experience level. By the end of the second assessment, we will have enough baseline information to determine which students need extra help in reading skills instruction and to confirm or refute preliminary analyses regarding those who appear to be ready to use their skills in grade-level and more advanced reading tasks.

The silent reading with think aloud, when used as an assessment tool, has three main components: preparation, teacher modeling, and student reading/thinking aloud.

1. Preparation: To prepare for the silent reading/think aloud, select a passage from one of the books that your students will be using in your class. Make a copy of the passage for each student in the class, and distribute the copies to the students, so that they can follow the text when you model the think aloud protocol.

2. Teacher modeling: The think aloud is a cognitively challenging activity that few middle school students have had experience with. For that reason, you need to take time to model the think aloud process and to provide examples of the metacognitive conversation that the reader has with himself or herself before asking students to engage in silent reading/thinking aloud. We will follow an example of Dirk, a teacher of eighth graders, as he models silent reading and thinking aloud in a scenario below.

3. Student reading/thinking aloud assessment: During the actual silent reading/think aloud assessment, you will sit with an individual student in the reading corner; both of you will have a copy of the text that the student will read silently. The other students should be reading silently at their desks. You will remind the student of your demonstration of how to read silently and think aloud and then ask him or her to try to do the same. As the student vocalizes his or her thoughts, you will note what he or she says and record any reading behaviors, such as slouching, pointing to words, subvocalizing, repeating or skipping lines or words, and so on. Your notes will be written directly onto your copy of the text that the student is reading to pinpoint areas of strength and weakness.

An important component of this assessment involves the way you use the notes. You will want to pair them with notes from the initial assessment of oral reading to develop a clearer picture of each reader in terms of oral and silent reading and in terms of the way each reader approaches an in-school reading task. The paired comments will allow you to draw some preliminary conclusions about which students are ready to advance as readers and which need extra help in order to participate fully in the language arts class and in their other classes as well.

Modeling a Think Aloud   Try to envision the silent reading/think aloud modeling that follows. While following Dirk's actions, beginning with his preview of the story and his prediction making, we can consider whether or not the silent reading/think aloud model could work for us and our students.

Step One: Preparation   Dirk has prepared for the silent reading/think aloud modeling session by selecting a text from one of the class anthologies. He has made twenty-eight copies of a short story, "The White Umbrella," for his students. When class starts, he distributes copies to them. Although he knows that some will have difficulty with the text, he asks them all to read the story silently, and to write a brief "gut reaction" to it in their literature logs. He then asks them to discuss their reactions to the story itself, reinforcing the idea that one purpose for reading a story is to enjoy the experience of reading. He also asks them to describe any parts of the story that they didn't understand or didn't believe as readers.

This discussion is important because it gives the students an understanding of the story, so that they can focus their attention on Dirk as he demonstrates for his students the silent reading/think aloud strategy in the next few minutes.

After the short discussion, he asks his students to put their copies on the desk and then tells them, "During this part of the lesson, your job is not to read but to watch how I act as a reader and to jot down notes about anything you notice. My job is to show you how I make sense of a story as I read. I suggest that you pay particular attention to the way I ask myself questions as I go and visualize what is happening and who is involved. That way, you will notice what an experienced, good reader does before, during, and after reading." He notes that he is modeling what he will ask them to do as readers during individual conferences with him. The conferences will occur when they have their next reading assignment. He ends his instructions by telling them that they are watching him read a text that he has read earlier and is familiar with due to class discussion but that the read silently/think aloud strategy is usually used by readers when they first encounter a new text. He is merely using a familiar text so that they can focus on him and not on trying to make sense of the story itself.

Step Two: Teacher Modeling of Silent Reading/Think Aloud In the prelude to the silent reading/think aloud, Dirk reminds his class that he wants them to pay attention to the mental moves that he makes while he reads the story. To help them follow his moves, he is going to try to do two things at once: say his thoughts aloud and read the story silently. His first step, he announces, is to make predictions regarding the contents of the story, based on the title alone. He reads the title aloud. Then he says aloud, "Hmmm . . . 'The White Umbrella' [by Gish Jen, 1997]. I'd guess that the story deals with an umbrella as an important possession—something that someone in the story treasures. And since the umbrella is white, not the more usual black or dark color, it must be special, somehow. Maybe it is more like a parasol, to shield someone from sun, rather than to keep rain off. I need to look for some clues to see if it is raining in the story and to see where it takes place and who its characters are. I can do that before I really start reading it."

Then Dirk spends several moments quietly flipping through the story. Students are watching him intently. After a minute, he looks up and announces a couple of predictions about the story's contents: "I saw a photograph of a girl playing the piano; she looks like she might be Chinese—and there is mention of 'the other Chinese family' in the first paragraph, so this story must involve a Chinese family. And I notice, now, that the author has an unusual name, Gish Jen. I wonder if she is Chinese American. From the illustration, and some of the lines I glanced at, I could tell that a piano lesson was going on. The person telling the story arrived all wet at the piano teacher's place. There is an umbrella on the floor. It must someone else's."

Next, in an essential step, Dirk talks about how he came up with his predictions. He says, "I looked at the title, scanned the story (generally looking for guiding features such as subheadings, graphics, and other organizing features) and skimmed it (seeking answers to specific questions about the story, such as which names are repeated and who seems to be involved with whom). Then, he admits, "I spent a few extra seconds looking at the pictures of the girl playing the piano and the picture of someone under a white umbrella on the first page of the story," and that he "read the first and last few lines of the story."

Dirk announces that he now has several ideas, or predictions, about how the story pieces will fit together. So that he and the students can check his predictions later, he jots them on the board: white umbrella is a valued object; Chinese piano student needs an umbrella, and an earlier student left an umbrella; the wet Chinese student will take the white umbrella when she leaves the piano lesson. He then says that it is time to read the story so he can check his predictions.

Dirk explains to his class that while he reads silently, he will not be completely quiet because he will be talking as he goes along. In this step, Dirk verbalizes the mental moves that he makes as he reads the text. This talk brings his comprehension monitoring strategies to the surface, where students hear them. As Beers (2003) notes when recommending the use of the think aloud strategy, "This is the time when your thinking (which is normally invisible) becomes visible" for students (p. 43).

In talking metacognitively, Dirk explicitly highlights these mental moves to help his students follow them: (1) visualizing the characters ("I see the narrator's mother as a clean, pretty, small Chinese woman who carries herself with dignity even though she is wearing old clothes" and "I see the sisters as petite and shy, quiet and polite, but not smiling"); (2) confirming initial predictions ("The narrator sees the umbrella on the floor during her sister's piano lesson, and wants it badly; the umbrella really is used for the rain); (3) raising a question about what will happen next ("I bet the teacher will let the narrator take the umbrella, but the narrator will refuse, pretending like she doesn't want it, because she is ashamed of not having one"); (4) checking understanding by rereading a short portion of the story to himself ("Who is the older sister? Ah, there it is.").

When he finishes reading the story, Dirk closes it on his desk and says, "Well, I never saw that car wreck coming! The fact that the girl is reluctant to let her mother see the umbrella proves—at least to me—that she knows her mother wouldn't approve of the gift. I feel sorry for the girl, since she so wants the kinds of things that other American girls have. But I am glad that she sees how much her mother cares about her."

Dirk follows the modeling episode by leading a discussion about what the class saw and heard him doing as a reader. They generate a list of his mental moves and put it on the overhead. The list includes these items: making predictions, checking predictions, and (sometimes) changing them; visualizing; prereading. Then Dirk asks his students which of the moves they usually make as readers. Their additional strategies are listed beside Dirk's strategies on the overheard. He asks them to create a third list, one that cites the kinds of mental moves that they make when they read their science, mathematics, and social studies books. This list includes items such as these: figure out the charts; practice the sample problems; check the glossary; list the dates; draw the people involved. This third list leads to a lot of conversation about the ways readers approach texts, and the impact of readers' purposes for reading on the ways that we engage in making sense of texts. The students finish the session with an understanding that different kinds of texts demand the use of different reading strategies but that with all texts, the reader has to be active as a meaning maker.

In the class periods that follow, all of Dirk's students have an opportunity to approach new texts in reading silently/thinking aloud. Their engagement in silent reading gives Dirk the chance to meet individually with each reader for about five minutes. During that meeting, the individuals read silently and think aloud. Dirk records each student's think aloud comments, aware that the comments tell him what each reader is doing in order to make sense of the story. The recorded comments help him identify students' reading strengths as well as their problem spots. When he combines each student's think aloud comments with notes from the initial assessment, he has solid data to inform his decisions about which reading skills to teach to the whole class, which ones to emphasize for individual students and which ones have already been championed by his students. (See Figure 4.4, Directed Individualized Reading, for a practical solution to the problem of finding time to sit with each student for five minutes as he or she reads silently and thinks aloud.)

For more information on the use of the silent reading/think aloud strategy, and for slight variations, please see these books that focus on reading instruction: *When Kids Can't Read, What Teachers Can Do*, by Kylene Beers (2003), whose recommendations for using think alouds as part of a plan for helping dependent readers become independent readers, pages 41–44, are practical and sound; *Strategic Reading*, by Jeffrey D. Wilhelm, Tanya N. Baker, and Julie Dube (2001), whose variation for reading poetry, pages 192–194, is especially useful, and *Teaching Reading in Middle School*, by Laura Robb (2000), whose section on "In-the-Head" reading strategies, pages 135–137, is particularly helpful for language arts teachers.

Modified Reading Miscue Analysis for Struggling and Uninterested Readers   During these two one-on-one reading sessions with your students, you will probably identify some who have difficulty reading with enough momentum to sustain comprehension and students who read without expression and proper phrasing. You will need to further assess the strengths and weaknesses of these students as readers. A modification of reading miscue analysis can provide the kind of diagnostic information that will help you make informed choices about how to treat individual students who are not performing well as readers in your language arts classes. The process that I describe in Figure 3.4 is a modification of what Kenneth and Yetta Goodman describe and use in much greater detail for the diagnosis of specific reading skills problems and strengths (see Goodman, Goodman, & Hood, 1989). The modifications are not intended for reading specialists in pull-out programs; instead, they are intended to be used in the regular language arts classroom by a student-sensitive classroom teacher. This classroom-based reality dictates, for example, that the time spent with each

---

This assessment method requires that the teacher reproduce two copies of an approximately 100-word, on-grade-level print text. Ideally, both copies will be reproduced with extra margin space and with at least three spaces between each line, to allow room for notes that the teacher will write as the student reads aloud.

In addition, the teacher makes a grid of the kinds of miscues and errors that are common among struggling middle school readers (a list of six follows) and copies the reading passage into the left-hand column of the grid, so that as the student reads each phrase, clause, or sentence, the teacher can note any deviations from the print text at the point at which they occur.

The teacher asks the student to read the 100-word passage aloud and marks a check on the line and in the column of each miscue as it occurs. After the reading is completed, the teacher tallies the number of miscues and errors and then analyzes them in terms of whether or not they are the kinds of deviations from the text that are likely to impede comprehension. Patterns in students' reading behaviors become apparent during the modified reading miscue analysis so that the teacher can design instruction that addresses specific reading needs based on the information garnered from the assessment.

FIGURE 3.4   Modified Reading Miscue Analysis for the Language Arts Teacher

(continues)

The word *miscue* is used to refer to deviations from the print text that readers make as they read that do not count as errors, because they do not interfere with the reader's ability to make sense of the text. For example, if the text states, "He came home from the grocery and ate a piece of apple pie" but the student reads, "He came home from the grocery store and ate a piece of apple pie," (adding "store" after "grocery"), the miscue has no impact on the reader's comprehension of the sentence or of the story in which the sentence occurs. Frequently, readers try one word, and by the time they read beyond it, realize that it was incorrect and go back to correct themselves. An example of this kind of miscue occurs when the reader says, "He came home from the grocery and ate a pie of apply pie" then corrects himself by returning to the last clause to read, "a pie of apple pie." Of course in some cases, the addition of "store" could create an interpretation problem; in that case, it would be an error, not a mere miscue. Similarly, if a reader self-corrects so often that he loses his ability to comprehend the passage, then self-correction of initial misreadings becomes an error instead of a miscue.

Six common miscues and errors that language arts teachers can easily detect and note during reading miscue analysis include the following:

Word call miscues or errors: This occurs when the reader sees one word and says another that looks similar, like saying "awesome" for "awful," thus demonstrating the use of graphemic cues. When the reader sees one word and says a synonymous one, like saying "cool" for "cold," he demonstrates use of context clues. These errors are noted on a miscue grid by writing the word that the reader used directly over the word that actually appears in the text.

Attempts to decode: This occurs when the reader starts to pronounce a word and stops before she finishes, then tries again, often starting over with the initial sound, such as reading "rendezvous" as "re . . . renda . . . rende . . . rende-z . . . rende-z-voues . . . rendezvous." These errors are noted on a miscue grid by writing the sequence of attempts, as accurately as possible, over the word that causes the reader to stumble.

Self-correction: This occurs when the reader realizes, sometime after calling a word, that he has used an incorrect one, based on the context surrounding that word, and returns to the spot of the mistaken word and corrects himself. For example, when the reader initially reads, "There were forty soldiers on the file when the first gunshot sounded," and then recognizes that "file" should be "field," he corrects his mistake by returning to a portion of the sentence and rereading, "forty soldiers on the field when the first gunshot sounded." These errors are coded on the miscue grid by writing the initial attempt(s) and the actual word that the reader finally arrived at immediately above the word that caused the reader to stall.

Insertions: This occurs when the reader adds words that are not in the original text. These insertions are miscues if they do not contaminate the reader's ability to make sense of the text as it is, but they are errors if they do get in the way of using the cues embedded in the text to make sense of it. For example, if a reader adds the word in brackets in the following, she is likely to have to reread the entire sentence to make sense of it because the insertion contaminates the text: "When will you clean [under] out the bird cage?" This error is coded on a miscue grid by drawing a caret and then writing the inserted word above the print text in the place where the reader inserted it.

FIGURE 3.4   Continued

Omissions: This occurs when the reader skips a word. Without self-correction, this may cause an interpretation problem similar to the one caused by uncorrected insertions. For example, in the sentence, "Nobody could remember what happened early in the year," if the word *early* is omitted, the sense of the sentence is altered and the reader's ability to make sense of it is impeded. This error is coded on a miscue grid by circling, on the print copy of the text, the word that was not read aloud.

Repetition: This occurs when the reader repeats a word that is not repeated in the print text. Often, inexperienced readers sometimes seem to need to approach a sentence or clause with a head start and solve that need by repeating a few words. Only when this becomes a habit or interferes with comprehension is it a problem, yet in round-robin reading, as most of us remember, teachers traditionally corrected students immediately if they repeated words. This error is noted on a miscue grid by underlining any repeated words one time for each repetition.

Gail Tompkins (2003) provides guidance with the recommendation that we consider these three text issues when trying to determine whether or not a miscue is an error that is likely to impede comprehension. To each of Tompkins' three categories, I have added questions that you might ask yourself as you review the kinds of miscues and errors that you record for each student reader:

> **Semantics** Does the student's rendering have a meaning that is similar to the text or that is different?
>
> **Phonology** Does the student's rendering sound similar to what is written in the text, or is it obviously different?
>
> **Syntax** Does the student's rendering work, in terms of normal English syntax, or does it create a structure that does not resemble English or that does not fit the context?

The teacher's copy of the story and the accompanying miscue grid for a 104-word excerpt of the O. Henry short story "After Twenty Years" are provided below. As the teacher and assessor, you would add marks to this type of copy of the text to indicate the reader's miscues and then go back to the grid and indicate whether or not the miscues seem to impede comprehension of terms by virtue of their alignment with the semantics, phonology, and syntax in the print text. Students should read the passage from a copy of the text that appears in its normal format.

See if you can follow the marks to determine how the student read the first sentence and whether I interpreted the miscues being related to the reader's use of semantic, phonological, or syntactic clues. The student's initial miscues are given in parentheses.

	word call	decode	self-correct	insert	omit	repeat	*semantics/phonology/syntax*
(bear . . bea . . t)							
The *policeman* on							
the beat		x			x		/
(Av . . avon . . aveno)							
Moved up the avenue							
impressively.	x					/	

FIGURE 3.4   Continued

(continues)

The impressiveness was habitual

And not for show,

for spectators were few.

The time was barely 10 o'clock at night,

but chilly gusts of wind with a taste of rain

in them had well nigh depeopled the streets.

Trying doors as he went, twirling his club

with many intricate and artful movements,

turning now and then to cast his watchful eye

down the pacific thoroughfare, the officer, with

this stalwart form and light swagger, made a fine

picture of a guardian of the peace. The vicinity was

one that kept early hours.

Note: The student read the first sentence this way: "The policeman policeman on the bear . . . bea . . . t . . . beat moved up the av . . . avon . . . aveno impressively." I interpreted the repetition of policeman as a noninterfering feature and thus did not code it under the three categories of semantics, phonology, or syntax. However, I thought the student's inability to come up with the word *avenue* would interfere with her ability to interpret the text, so I coded it as a semantic miscue. I would have to look further to see if this kind of miscue was habitual for this student before deciding if it needs direct attention and instruction.

Because you are using an approximately 100-word passage, the modified reading miscue analysis is fairly easy to score. Every word that is read without deviation from the print text receives one point, so the total score is 100. Every miscue that does not impede comprehension is counted as if it were not a deviation, just like a correct word. You will have to use professional judgment to determine whether or not a deviation is a miscue or an error, using your markings on the part of the grid that notes the reader's use of semantic, phonologic, and syntactic clues for reading and interpreting the text.

In general, the decision about whether or not the student's rendering of the print text impedes comprehension requires that you look at how the student constructed the passage, using context clues, and that you look for patterns in the reader's habits. Once you consider these issues carefully, you will be ready to decide whether or not an isolated word call miscue, omission, insertion, or so on is a problem for that reader. The following chart shows student scores and the corresponding reading achievement level. Remember that the passage is taken from a textbook that is intended for use in your classroom. Individuals who score at the frustration level will confirm your prediction that they need special attention when you make in-common reading assignments. If several students in any one class read a grade-level text with accuracy that denotes the frustration level, you will probably need to make adjustments in your choice of book.

FIGURE 3.4   Continued

95–100% accuracy   independent level

90–94% accuracy   instructional level

89%–below accuracy   frustration level

Please note that these scores should not be the only source you use when you are trying to gauge the reading achievement level of an English language learner in your language arts class. These students should be given extra time to preread the assessment passage. Extra time allows them to draw on a limited amount of familiarity with the printed words during the assessment. It also gives them an opportunity to make sense of whatever cultural or regional words, structures, or ideas are included in the text before they are asked to decode and interpret the words orally and for an audience, even when the audience is limited to one—you, the teacher.

This modification is based on the theoretical work regarding miscues of Goodman, Goodman, and Hood (1989), the running record method of Marie Clay (1972), and the Flynt/Cooter Reading Inventory for the Classroom (1998).

FIGURE 3.4   Continued

student is limited, since we cannot pretend that twenty-nine students will sit quietly and work while we spend several minutes with the thirtieth student.

Eager Readers

I remember taking piano lessons as a child. Mrs. Dykes, the veteran teacher, insisted that I pay close attention to the sheet music that she laid out in front of me. I became fairly competent at reading and interpreting music from those printed pages. But it took me years to realize that I had within me the power to change what was on the printed sheets; I could embellish the passages that I loved in my favorite pieces, and I could ignore a note or two— even skip an entire refrain—if I chose. I was astounded with these simple revelations, because I had grown tied to—and restricted by—the printed sheets of music. I had assumed that the music itself resided there, in the print texts, and that if I were true to the printed notes, exactly as they were, I could play the piano piece correctly. In other words, I saw my contribution as a player as being responsible for rendering someone else's musical intentions into sound. But I finally came to realize that my assumption was flawed. I had given myself too little a role in creating the music. I did not understand that as the player, I was involved in the creative process and could make choices about my participation.

The Gift of Choice: Efferent and Aesthetic Reading

It seems to me that middle school students often make this same erroneous assumption when it comes to reading of print texts, particularly in school settings. They simply may not know that they can approach print texts with different stances, read with different purposes, and contribute to the creation of meaning by transacting with the text. When we teach our skilled and eager readers about the kinds of decisions they are free to make as readers, we give them a gift of intellectual freedom. Sometimes, it may make the difference between choosing to be a reader and choosing not to be one.

Literature theorist Lousie Rosenblatt, whose *Literature as Exploration* (originally published in 1938 and still influential today, in its 5th edition, 1995) presents an argument for teaching students that they can adopt both efferent and aesthetic stances when they read texts, depending on their purpose for reading. We approach a print text with an efferent stance when we want to finish the reading event with a collection of facts or information. It is the kind of reading we do when we pore over a local newspaper article because we need to know where a crime took place. We take an efferent stance when we read the instructions on a bottle of cough syrup because we want to relieve our symptoms without taking too much medicine. We read with an efferent stance when we read a historical account of the movements of the Mohawk tribe when our goal is to collect a list of dates and name places. Too often, we ask students to approach short stories and novels from an efferent stance, as if the goal is to take away facts and information about the plot, setting, and characters, instead of to enjoy the time spent in a fictitious world. Think of the assignment that asks students to read the often-anthologized story, "Flowers for Algernon," and then write an answer to the questions: "How many times did Algernon win the maze race against Charlie?" "What is the name of the female technician?" In order to answer these literal-level questions, students must read with an efferent stance. Ideally, when we design assignments that require students to take away information from literature, we will also ask them to tell us their personal responses and connections to the text, so that they will be encouraged to balance the efferent stance with an aesthetic one.

The aesthetic stance is one in which we read for the pleasure of the experience. When we have no obligations associated with a text, but read it purely for our own pleasure, we are likely to approach it from an aesthetic stance. When we dive into our favorite author's newest book because we love the way she uses language, we are reading with an aesthetic stance.

As skilled readers, we use neither stance exclusively. Even within the same reading event, we may alternate between them. For example, when I reread William Faulkner's *The Sound and the Fury* recently, I marveled over the author's word choices, his syntax, his miraculous language. Yet I did perform efferent tasks, even when reading the novel for no purpose but pleasure: I drew on my knowledge of geography to visualize the setting of the novel; I wanted to be able to keep the characters' names and roles separate in my mind, so I wrote down each new name that I came to while reading, and plotted a rough-hewn character chart. My ability to visualize the events of the novel, and my pleasure as a reader, were enhanced by my acts of taking away specific information from the text.

On the other hand, when I recently read an advertisement for a brand of running shoes, my purpose was primarily to take away information about the shoes. I approached the advertisement with an efferent stance, with the goal of gathering information about the weight of the shoe, its durability, its shape, and so on. I read quickly, with a strong singular purpose. My only criteria to determine the value of the advertisement were its clarity, conciseness, and completeness. However, I shifted into the aesthetic stance when I noticed that the advertiser used intriguing figurative language beneath the photograph in the ad, "Run like a kite, suspended with legs of the wind gods," to convince me that the shoes are worth their price. I forced myself to return to my efferent stance because I did not want to be swayed by figurative language; my goal, as a reader, was to make a decision based on information that I took away from the advertisement.

We give middle school readers a gift of choice when we explain these two stances to them. Many are delighted—liberated—to learn that they don't have to read their favorite magazines with the same kind of intensity with which they read their social studies homework assignments. When we introduce the concepts of efferent and aesthetic stances to them and help them explore ways to focus their reading according to their purpose, we are teaching them an essential comprehension strategy. Students need to be able to decide, at least on occasion, their reasons for approaching a text, choose the more appropriate stance, and then read from that stance. Further, as teachers we must recognize that when we evaluate our students' growth as readers, we cannot assume that their in-school reading demands the efferent stance exclusively, that they are reading only to take away information. We must find ways to account for their growth as readers when they are reading to experience the pleasure of the encounter with and co-creation with the author of art as well.

Encouraging Skilled Readers to Make Appropriate Choices

In teaching reading, then, we must attend first to the reader—who she is, what she brings to the reading event in terms of background knowledge; experiences; attitudes toward the topic and toward reading; and skills for generating, monitoring, and guiding her own comprehension. Next, we must attend to the reader's stance, with attention to her goals and reasons for reading this text at this time. Third, we must reinforce students' ability to attend to clues provided by the text and author, so that they will participate with the author and text in making sense of the text.

There are many activities that we can use to encourage good and eager readers to fine-tune their skills by attending to the stance they choose when they approach a text and the choices they make as they move through a text. Following are a few that I recommend:

In *Dancing with Words*, Judith Rowe Michaels (2001) describes a close reading activity in which students examine the impact of a single important word in a work of literature (pp. 49–56). They choose one word from a text that encapsulates the gist of the text or labels a significant theme within the text. Then they write about it or write using it. To write about a word, they might consult a dictionary and a thesaurus; record definitions, synonyms, and antonyms; and write questions for their classmates to try to answer. To write using the word, they might use the voice of the protagonist in the story, and write a letter or essay from the character's perspective, explaining why that word is significant to him or her within the story. For example, after reading "Thank You, Ma'am," students might decide that *hungry* is a significant word, both in its literal and its figurative senses. They could then write definitions, synonyms, and antonyms for *hungry* to explore the literal meaning, and then write about the word from the main character's perspective to explore possible figurative meanings, as well. This kind of word-focused activity encourages good readers to pay attention to authors' subtle uses of language and to consider the impact of the words that authors choose to present to readers.

In "*Reading Don't Fix No Chevys*," Michael W. Smith and Jeffrey D. Wilhelm (2002) describe how students become eager readers when they are able to add action to reading assignments (pp. 102–103). For example, Smith and Wilhelm watched as a group of formerly resistant readers produced documentaries about the families and historical situations that are presented in *Romeo and Juliet*. The students researched text-related topics, such as the role of dueling, and even created their own histories of the family feud between the Montagues and Capulets. They followed this active engagement with the text by creating a video documentary about the play. According to Smith and Wilhelm, "the boys indicated that when teachers created contexts that allowed them to pursue active responses and projects, they felt better able to meet the challenge provided by their reading" (p. 103). In addition, these students learned how to make a literary text, even one written in the 1600s, their own.

In *Teaching Reading in Middle School*, Laura Robb (2000) recommends having students write readers' theater scripts for favorite texts and then read them for the class (p. 308). Alternatives might include asking students to write and perform dramatizations of scenes or to prepare radio scripts and perform them, with sound effects added. These activities, although simple in design, require that students identify which parts of the text are meaningful, powerful, or otherwise significant for them and then bring those passages to life.

In *Teaching Ten to Fourteen Year Olds*, Chris Stevenson (1998) points to the benefits of arranging for students to meet in reading interest groups, according to their interest in common topics, genres, authors, or titles, and then using that point of interest as the springboard for discussion when group members meet. (This idea is similar to the literature circles and book clubs that are introduced in Chapter 4.)

One final recommendation that may work with eager and skilled readers is to simply provide them with adequate time to read. In commenting on her readers' habits, veteran teacher Cheryl Kopec Nahmias points to the importance of providing some reading-only time, not reading-and-doing-an-activity time, for middle school students:

> My biggest concern is that students don't read extensively because they don't see reading as an enjoyable activity. My students' ability to develop vocabulary and critique ideas is often severely limited by their refusal to read outside of the minimum required for their classes.

Have you ever felt like Cheryl feels? Perhaps the problem is that students are always asked to do something to prove that they have done the reading, and that they have understood the text. Sometimes, perhaps the best strategy we can use to motivate our skilled and eager readers is to let them read. Read. Read. Period.

Teaching Reading to the Whole Class

One method of planning instruction that can benefit an entire class of young adolescent readers incorporates what Frank Smith refers to as the "focal and global predictions" that skilled readers make as they read (1986, p. 168). Smith uses the analogy of a trip in an automobile to explain the difference in these two aspects of prediction: When we begin a trip in a car, we have an expectation about when we will arrive at the destination and make predictions about when we will pass various landmarks along the way and how many times we will probably need to stop en route. If we want to visit a sight that is not on our route, we plan extra time for the trip. The tentative decisions that we make, as we plan the trip, are analogous to "global predictions," in that they "tend to influence large parts of the journey" (p. 167). On the other hand, we make instant decisions while we are on the road. We might have to swerve to miss a truck that strays into our lane, or we may need to stop to check under the hood if our car starts smoking. These instant decisions are analogous to "focal predictions," the kind that "concern us for short periods of time only and have no lasting consequence for the journey as a whole" (p. 167). Smith explains how the two aspects of prediction interact during reading:

> Your focal predictions about my next sentence will depend to some extent on your comprehension of the present sentence but also on your expectations about this paragraph, this chapter, and the book as a whole. Conversely, the global predictions that we make at the book and chapter level must be constantly tested and if necessary modified by the outcomes of our predictions at more focal levels. Your comprehension of one sentence could change your view of a whole book The entire process is at once extremely complex and highly dynamic. (p. 169)

The earlier think aloud demonstration with Dirk provides evidence that skilled readers make predictions while they work to make sense of texts. Even when reading for pleasure, skilled readers generate guesses about what comes next and how that relates to what has come before. As I read Virginia Euwer Wolff's *Make Lemonade* (1993), for example, I make a focal prediction about why Wolff writes a particular sentence, "All the time Jolly kept insisting she was nobody's kid, ever" (p. 151). I tell myself, "I know that everyone has had a biological mother, at least. But Jolly is not much more than a child herself; she must feel like she was abandoned from birth, and expected to become a mother before she was finished being a child. Maybe she is using her lack of a mother model as an excuse for her ignorance about how to treat her own two babies." As I continue, I make global predictions about how Jolly's lack of a mother role model will affect the rest of the story, telling myself, "Ever since the first few pages about Jolly, I knew she was in over her head. I bet that Jolly will unintentionally harm her children. She might even get so frustrated that she can't deal with them and just leave." In the act of generating these global predictions, I have created a focus for my reading: I will look for clues that support or refute my predictions. When we teach students to make predictions while they read and to test their predictions against what they find as they read, we give them a useful tool for making sense of texts. A sample whole-class lesson set that incorporates the notion of making focal and global predictions to encourage growth in unskilled, struggling, and skilled readers, follows.

A Sample Lesson Set

In the short story "Thank You, Ma'am," by Langston Hughes (1997, originally published in 1958 and often anthologized), a 14- or 15-year-old boy named Roger tries to steal the purse of Mrs. Luella Bates Washington Jones. He falls when he grabs the purse; the large woman traps him and then drags him to her apartment. Twice she asks if he has anyone at home to "tell you to wash your face" (p. 255) or to fix him a bite to eat for supper, and twice he tells her that he has no one at home who takes care of him. Once they arrive at her humble apartment, Mrs. Jones invites Roger to wash his face and to have dinner with her. She shares all of the food that she has, down to her $.10 cake. Instead of running away when he has the opportunity, Roger realizes that he wants to gain her trust. He confesses that he was trying to rob her so that he could buy some suede shoes. Mrs. Jones sends him away, but not before she gives him money for the shoes and a stern but loving warning that he should not try to grab her purse, or anyone's, for shoe money, since "shoes got by devilish ways will burn your feet" (p. 257).

This short story reads as if it were a quick scene in a television show; the characters and their actions are strong and vivid. However, since Mrs. Jones's actions are unexpected and even unpredictable, it is an ideal story to use when our goal is teaching students how to make and check focal and global predictions to make sense of what they are reading.

First, ask your students to describe how they would photograph a person if they wanted the photograph to show every single wrinkle or pimple. Someone in the class is likely to suggest that he would use a close-up lens or that he would zoom in on the person. Then ask what kind of lens they would choose if they wanted to photograph an entire street scene. Someone is likely to say that she would use a wide-angle or broad-view lens. If possible, show them photographs that use zoom and wide-angle lenses, so that they can see the difference in perspective produced by each.

Second, write the words *focal* and *global* on the board/overhead/LCD panel, and ask students to decide which lens, zoom or wide angle, would be more closely associated with creating a focal or global perspective. Help them understand that the zoom lens notion can be closely related to the term *focal*, since it deals with what can be seen up close. Likewise, help them see that the wide-angle lens notion can be closely associated with the term *global*, since it deals with the big picture that includes smaller items. Then have them brainstorm other words that they associate with the two key terms, and list those.

Third, end this part of the conversation by asking someone to provide definitions for *focal* and *global*, and add them to the board. Explain that the students are going to use the ideas of focal and global perspectives when they read—that they will learn to read with a zoom lens to pick up on the tiniest details and a wide-angle lens to get the big picture. Explain, too, that the photographs that they create in their minds will help them see what they read more clearly.

Fourth, ask them to guess who the speaker in a title like "Thank You, Ma'am" might be. (It might promote discussion to ask questions such as "Who would be likely to say this, and to whom? What kind of people are involved? Who do you see in your mind when you read the title and say it aloud?") This simple step prepares students to think about both the specific character (focal features) and the type of character (global features) represented in the title and thus introduces an example of the way readers can attend to focal and global issues simultaneously.

Fifth, read the first paragraph aloud, as students follow, and then ask them to stop and write (or verbalize) a general prediction about what will happen. (See the box for the first paragraph of the story.) Answers such as "The big woman is going to call the police," or "She might try to take his money," or "The boy is going to get up and hit the woman and run"

Opening Paragraph of "Thank You, Ma'am," by Langston Hughes

She was a large woman with a large purse that had everything in it but a hammer and nails. It had a long strap, and she carried it slung across her shoulder. It was about eleven o'clock at night, and she was walking alone, when a boy ran up behind her and tried to snatch her purse. The strap broke with the tug the boy gave it from behind. But the boy's weight and the weight of the purse caused him to lose balance. Instead of taking off full blast, the boy fell on his back on the sidewalk, and his legs flew up. The large woman simply turned around and kicked him square in his blue-jeaned sitter. She shook him until his teeth rattled. Then she reached down and picked the boy up by his shirt.

Source: Hughes, Langston. (1997). Thank you, Ma'am. In *Literature and Integrated Studies*, Grade Eight. Glenview, IL: Scott, Foresman and Co., pp. 254–257.

are all text-supported response possibilities that students might give. After several volunteers read or state their predictions, ask them to discuss what it was in the paragraph that *led them to* these predictions. Point out that the clues they are using to make their predictions show readers what kind of person Mrs. Jones is because they show what she does when the boy tries to steal her purse. We know how she acts in this one scene (focal information gathered), and therefore we can guess how she might act in general (and we will look for further evidence to check our global predictions about Mrs. Jones and whether or not we have read her correctly as we continue the story). The specific information about Mrs. Jones allows us to make focal predictions—we can guess her very next moves. The insights about who she is as a person allow us to make global predictions—to look beyond this particular scene and guess what kind of person she is and thus prepare us for her actions in the future. Some students might want to bring their visualizations of Mrs. Jones to the surface by drawing her.

Sixth, ask your students to make two columns on their notebook paper; one should be labeled Mrs. Jones and the other Roger. In the appropriate column, have students record any clues—words or phrases—from the first paragraph of the story that help them visualize the character and make predictions about how they will act. Explain that they will continue to build these character charts as they read the rest of the three-page story to collect information and record ideas that will allow them to make and check predictions about Mrs. Jones and Roger and about how each will act. If they find unfamiliar words that might be linked to one of the two characters, they should place the word on the chart and define it, relying first on context clues to try to determine the definition and then checking their guess with the dictionary. (After they finish reading the story, students should be allowed to share their character charts in small groups and then collect the descriptions into a class list that is posted on a large piece of butcher paper, on the bulletin board, or any place that will accommodate a word wall. The character chart then becomes a kind of context-specific vocabulary list, with descriptive words and phrases that students can apply to their own story writing. A note: Vocabulary instruction is, very legitimately, frequently addressed as a major component of reading instruction. In this book, however, vocabulary instruction is addressed more specifically in "Warming Up with Word Play" and "Dialects: Different, Not Deficient" in Chapter 6.)

Seventh, ask students to read the story, or read it aloud as they follow, from the start to the turning point, in the paragraph that begins, "Sweat popped out on the boy's face" (Hughes, 1997, p. 256). Have them find a clue that prompts a focal prediction that Roger lives without parents or adult supervision. (You might ask them to answer the specific question, "What does he tell Mrs. Jones that seems to convince her that he is pretty much on his own?") Next have them discuss what impact Roger's disclosure has on what we think that Mrs. Jones will do to Roger. Have students directly discuss whether they are using focal or global clues—or both. Emphasize during this discussion how they are proving—as readers—the importance of using both focal and global clues when reading print texts.

Eighth, finally, have students finish the story, and discuss whether or not Mrs. Jones's actions were consistent with their predictions. Ask them to refer to their completed character chart and to the story itself to identify specific evidence that led to their predictions about how Mrs. Jones and Roger might act (which clues enabled them to make focal predictions as readers) and where they made decisions about how the story was going to turn out for Roger and Mrs. Jones. Ask students to volunteer to discuss how closely their initial predictions matched Hughes' story and how similarities and differences were produced. Then ask volunteers to create and perform role plays, putting Mrs. Jones and Roger together or letting each appear solo in scenes that occur outside of the story. For example, have them role play the scene that would occur if Mrs. Jones were ignored by a salesperson when she went into a department store intent on buying a new blouse; have them role play Roger's likely response if Mrs. Jones asked him to stay at her apartment after dinner and help her clean it. After the role plays, ask them to discuss how they knew what Roger and Mrs. Jones would do and say in the role play scenes to reinforce the benefits of making and checking predictions to help visualize characters and actions in a story.

Ninth, close the lesson by returning to the notions of focal and global predictions. Assess students' understanding of the concepts as they relate to careful reading by having them practice with one sentence: Have students look closely at the story sentence, "She didn't watch her purse, which she left behind her on the day bed" (Hughes, 1997, p. 257). Ask the students, "Which details in that sentence give information for a reader's focal predictions?" (The answer should be related to information about where the purse was in relation to Mrs. Jones.) And "Which details give the reader insights for making global predictions?" (Answers should refer to what kind of person Mrs. Jones has proven to be.) Ask a student to summarize the benefits of using clues that allow the reader to make moment-to-moment (focal) and longer-range (global) predictions simultaneously. Teach concepts that students do not know. Then evaluate their ability to employ effective reading skill by giving them a short story that they have not studied as a class, and ask them to write about or illustrate its main ideas.

Reading Words, Reading Worlds

As teachers of language arts in the middle grades, we must help students understand that reading skills provide the foundation for development of broader critical literacies that are essential for successfully making sense of the infinite kinds of messages that they receive in today's multimedia world. We must teach adolescents to use literacy skills, including reading, to differentiate between important and unimportant ideas, helpful and harmful information, reasonable and unreasonable conclusions, humane and inhumane recommendations, and uplifting and damaging credos. We must teach them to scrutinize print and nonprint media for words, intended meanings, and subtle but often potent messages.

Those students who develop the abilities to make these distinctions, those who can read words and the world with critical eyes, are able to achieve and rely on creating a balance between their personal responses and broader perspectives that they may have gained from an outside source. We are back once again, then, to the initial question that was posed in this chapter: Where does a teacher of middle school students begin when it comes to reading instruction? These are a few practical recommendations:

- Fill spaces with books, and allow all students easy access to them. Allow students to leave the classroom or media center with books as often as possible. Have them just read as a regular part of the curriculum, and devote instructional time as often as possible to directed individualized reading units.
- Spend time assessing individual students' reading achievement levels, and modify instruction and support for reading based on what you find to be true for each reader. In the language arts classroom, use informal reading inventories, silent reading, and think alouds for all students and modified reading miscue analyses with students who are struggling to read. The amount of time needed to perform these assessments sounds overwhelming, I realize, especially for those of you who teach in overcrowded classrooms, but it can and must be done. Spending time in reading assessment early in the year frees you to spend the bulk of the year engaged in appropriate instruction for all readers, unskilled and extraordinarily skilled alike. Include in the curriculum specific lessons to address reading skills including these potential trouble spots: decoding of words; constructing organizational frameworks for making sense of texts; recognizing cause and effect relationships; differentiating between fact and opinion; distinguishing between explicit and implied or inferred meanings; and determining the meaning of unfamiliar vocabulary words.
- Be sure to include books for which today's young adolescent readers have indicated a preference (use the Reading Interest Survey, Figure 4.1, so that you will be informed about your students' preferences each year). Middle school readers enjoy fantasy, realistic adventure, nonfiction, and collections of shorter works that promote positive human values. As their teachers, we need to get to know several of these ourselves so we can make convincing pitches when students ask for suggestions.
- Provide plenty of time for reading, and do not restrict students to serious texts that are difficult and challenging for them. Recognize that the more words students read, the more their fluency improves; therefore, balance the challenging texts with easier ones that appeal to readers because of subject matter or theme or escape or the potential for a fun literary experience.
- Give student readers credit for making sense of texts themselves, for creating meaning with the authors, and teach them to have confidence in their own readings. Then use their thoughtfulness as a vehicle for extending lessons of reading to the nonprint media that are so prevalent in their worlds, such as feature-length movies, television advertising, popular music and music videos, and magazines targeted toward teens.

This is a long chapter, but I hope that you understand that it has to be. Many cultures transmit their stories and their histories through oral language, and for them, oral literacy is as important as print literacy. But the ability to read well is necessary for success in our schools, and for most people today, personal, social, and financial success also requires the ability to read. Therefore, reading skills form a cornerstone of literacy instruction for the twenty-first century. Further, the ability to transfer reading skills to the task of reading nonprint texts, as we will explore in the chapters that follow, serves as the foundation for the multiple literacies required for success in today's society. Our goal is to help young adolescents become successful readers of print text and critical readers of the world around them.

Integrated Literacy Checklist

In this chapter, literacy skills in all of the language arts areas are integrated in the focus on reading.

Literature

Informal individual reading inventory: Each student chooses one fiction and one nonfiction piece from the set of easy, medium, and difficult texts provided by the teacher and then reads the two pieces silently before reading excerpts aloud for the teacher.

Silent reading/think aloud assessment: Each student reads a teacher-selected work of fiction silently and then engages in a think aloud to describe his or her reading and comprehension process.

Modified reading miscue analysis (for select students): Struggling readers read a short text for the teacher, who listens and marks miscues and mistakes to better assess the student's strengths and problem spots.

Popular literary texts: "All Summer in a Day" is mentioned as an example in the description of the initial assessment; "Thank You, Ma'am" by Langston Hughes (a traditional text) is used specifically in the model lesson; and *Make Lemonade* by Virginia Euwer Wolff (a contemporary adolescent novel) is referred to at length in the focal and global predictions lesson description.

Responding to passages for lessons on focal and global predictions: Students write and may be able to edit and revise responses to focal and global predictions and modify written responses based on insights exchanged by classmates during class discussion.

Speaking/Listening/Language

In a think aloud, students talk about their reading process while the teacher listens.

In the focal/global predictions lesson set, students share character charts in small groups and as a class.

Students create and perform role plays related to the focal/global predictions lesson set.

Media

Metacognition that is practiced and reinforced in the focal/global predictions lesson activity has direct transfer value for study of nonprint media.

Print/nonprint advertisements are used in an example to demonstrate how to test differences in readers' use of (and frequent combination of) efferent and aesthetic reading stances.

Students publish a class-created character chart as an extension of the focal/global predictions lesson.

Help for English Language Learners

Silent reading/think aloud assessment: Attention to processing of written English

Modified reading miscue analysis: An attempt to isolate some particular problem spots for English language learning readers, and to therefore provide direction for instruction

Focal and global predictions lesson: Gives readers practice in learning to distinguish between important and insignificant details, in establishing a purpose for reading, in learning and reinforcing metacognitive strategies for comprehension

Role play in lesson set: Allows English language learners to express themselves without being restricted by limited English

Other Instructional Activities **(Bunker, 1999)**

Visuals (charts, photographs, illustrations, objects, films, videos, and audiocassettes along with books) or gestures to make instruction meaningful;

Graphic organizers (teacher-created diagrams or pictures that show which ideas are main ideas, which are subordinate, which introduce important words, and so on);

Guided notes and story maps.

NCTE/IRA Standards

The material in brackets is not specifically addressed in the chapter, but the standard in general is addressed.

Standard Number One: Students read a wide range of print and nonprint texts to build an understanding of texts and of themselves [and of the cultures of the United States and the world]; to acquire new information; to respond to the needs and demands of society and the workplace; and for personal fulfillment. Among these texts are fiction and nonfiction, classic, and contemporary works.

Standard Number Three: Students apply a wide range of strategies to comprehend, interpret, evaluate, and appreciate texts. They draw on their prior experience, their interaction with other readers and writers, their knowledge of word meaning and of other texts, their word identification strategies, and their understanding of textual features (e.g., sound–letter correspondence, sentence structure, context, graphics).

Standard Number Ten: Students whose first language is not English make use of their first language to develop competency in the English language arts and to develop understanding of content across the curriculum.

Standard Number Eleven: Students participate as knowledgeable, reflective, creative, and critical members of a variety of literacy communities.

Standard Number Twelve: Students use spoken, written, and visual language to accomplish their own purposes (e.g., for learning, enjoyment, persuasion, and the exchange of information). (Farstrup & Myers, 1996, p. 3)

Works Cited

Allington, R. L. (2001). *What really matters for struggling readers.* New York: Addison Wesley Longman.

Bambara, T. C. (1997). Raymond's run. In *Choices in literature*, Silver. Upper Saddle River, NJ: Prentice-Hall, pp. 53–59.

Beers, K. (2003). *When kids can't read, what teachers can do: A guide for teachers 6–12.* Portsmouth, NH: Heinemann.

Bradbury, R. (1994). All summer in a day. In *Literature and language*, Red level (7). Evanston, IL: McDougal, Littell, & Company, pp. 123–129.

Bunker, M. R. (1999). Embedding ESOL competencies into the pre-service teacher education program. *Sunshine State TESOL Journal* Fall 1999: 21–29.

Clay, M. (1972). *The early detection of reading difficulties.* Portsmouth, NH: Heinemann.

Farstrup, A. E., and Myers, M. (Eds.). (1996). *Standards for the English language arts.* Urbana, IL and Newark, DE: National Council of Teachers of English and International Reading Association.

Faulkner, W. (1936). *Absalom, Absalom!* New York: Random House.

Flynt, E. S., and Cooter, R. B. (1998). *The Flynt/Cooter reading inventory for the classroom*, 3rd edition. Columbus, OH: Merrill/Prentice Hall.

Garan, E. M. (2002). *Resisting reading mandates: How to triumph with the truth.* Portsmouth, NH: Heinemann.

Goodman, K., Goodman, Y., and Hood, W. J. (1989). *The whole language evaluation book.* Portsmouth, NH: Heinemann.

Graves, M. F., Juel, C., and Graves, B. B. (2001). *Teaching reading in the 21st century.* Boston: Allyn and Bacon.

Hughes, L. (1997). Thank you, ma'am. In *Literature and integrated studies*, Grade Eight (originally published in 1958). Glenview, IL: Scott Foresman, pp. 255–257.

Irvin, J. L., Buehl, D. R., and Klemp, R. M. (2003). *Reading and the high school student: Strategies to enhance literacy.* Boston: Allyn and Bacon.

Jen, G. (1997). The white umbrella. In *Choices in literature*: Silver (8th grade). Upper Saddle River, NJ: Prentice Hall, pp. 45–50.

McQuade, F. (1980). Examining a grammar course: The rationale and the result. *English Journal 69*: 26–30.

Michaels, J. R. (2002). *Dancing with words: Helping students love language through authentic vocabulary instruction.* Urbana, IL: National Council of Teachers of English.

National Reading Panel. (2000). *Teaching children to read: An evidence-based assessment of the scientific research literature on reading and its implications for reading instruction.* Washington, D.C.: National Institute of Child Health and Human Development.

Owen, D. (1997). Lego. In *Choices in literature: Myself, my world*: Silver. Upper Saddle River, NJ: Prentice Hall, pp. 125–127.

Reutzel, D. R., and Cooter, R. B. (1999). *Balanced reading strategies and practices.* Upper Saddle River, NJ: Merrill/Prentice Hall.

Robb, L. (2000). *Teaching reading in middle school: A strategic approach to teaching reading that improves comprehension and thinking.* New York: Scholastic.

Rosenblatt, L. M. (1995). *Literature as exploration*, 5th edition. New York: Modern Languages Association (originally published in 1938).

Smith, F. (1986). *Understanding reading*. Hillsdale, NJ: Lawrence Erlbaum Associates.

Smith, M. W., and Wilhelm, J. D. (2002). *"Reading don't fix no Chevys": Literacy in the lives of young men*. Portsmouth, NH: Heinemann.

Stevenson, C. (1998). *Teaching ten to fourteen year olds*, 2nd ed. New York: Longman.

Strauss, S. L. (2001). An Open Letter to Reid Lyon. *Educational Researcher 30*(5): 26–33.

Tompkins, G. E. (2002). *Language arts: Content and teaching strategies*, 5th edition. Upper Saddle River, NJ: Merrill-Prentice Hall.

Vacca, J. A., Vacca, R. T., Gove, M. K., Burkey, L., Lenhart, L. A., and McKeon, C. (2003). *Reading and learning to read*, 5th ed. Boston: Allyn and Bacon.

Wilhelm, J. D., Baker, T. N., and Dube, J. (2001). *Strategic reading: Guiding students to lifelong literacy, 6–12*. Portsmouth, NH: Boynton/Cook Heinemann.

Wolff, V. E. (1993). *Make lemonade*. New York: Scholastic.

CHAPTER

4 Overflowing with Possibilities for Literature Engagement

Writing about literature.

Learning Lessons about Literature from Our Students

As prospective and practicing language arts teachers, we are the most fortunate folks on middle school faculties. Colleagues may pity us, since we tend to take home stacks of papers, student portfolios, and book projects to grade during our "free" time. We even pity ourselves, sometimes, because it is we who take the lion's share of responsibility for preparing every student for the reading comprehension and written composition demands of the standardized tests. Despite these challenges, though, the hours we spend with students in middle grades language arts classrooms can—and should—be filled with the enthusiastic, meaning-making languaging of young adolescents.

Literature study often provides the subject matter through which we invite our young adolescent students into conversations about the emotional, social, and global issues that are truly important to them. Through reading and studying a wide variety of short stories, dramas, poems, songs, magazines, novels, and nonfiction, our students begin to seek connections between their world and text worlds. They look for answers to questions about human nature that typically begin to emerge during young adolescence. Through literature, they strive to make sense of their world, to know it, and to identify their place in it. As their teachers, we have rare opportunities to listen attentively and learn from young adolescents, to provide the ears of a trusted adult for them. In our language arts classes, we have opportunities to manifest the "ethic of concern, self-responsibility, and compassion" (Giroux, 1997, p. 60) that is the heart of the student-sensitive integrated literacy pedagogy.

As teachers of middle grades language arts, our possibilities for integrating life and literature issues are almost unlimited. We can teach literature as a base from which to introduce attention to authors' literary art. We can use literature as a springboard for student writing. We can use literature as the subject matter for language study. We can present film and video interpretations of literature to teach critical thinking about how and why we render texts as we do. And just as important as these subject-area uses of literature, we can also draw on literature to address the issues and concerns that dominate young adolescents' thoughts and out-of-school conversations. The reading and classroom study of literature should provide a safe and healthy outlet for students who need to hear, talk about, and consider life issues and who are likely to benefit from exploring others' insights as well.

Literature Study and an Integrated Literacy Pedagogy

The kind of literature study that I promote in this chapter fits naturally into a student-sensitive integrated literacy pedagogy because it is compatible with the four core beliefs:

Belief One: Through literature instruction, we can honor students as individuals and as members of many groups, encouraging them to read to better understand themselves and to gain knowledge of others.

Belief Two: During literature lessons, we can focus on students' interests as humans and their strengths as thinkers and then gently nudge them to expand the capabilities and concerns that they carry into our classes when we first meet them. We can also encourage participation of students who bring different linguistic and cultural backgrounds into our classes through our decisions about tests and learning activities.

Belief Three: With literature as a focal point, we can encourage critical thinking across multiple literacies; for example, we can help students discover ways that readers work with authors to create meaning with print texts and ways that film viewers and film makers collaborate to make sense of stories told on film.

Belief Four: As teachers of literature, we turn to professional standards for guidance regarding appropriate texts and activities for middle school students in order to complement our own tastes and habits as eager and experienced readers.

A Plan for Literature Instruction

In this chapter, we explore issues related to literature instruction within a student-sensitive integrated literacy pedagogy. We begin with a discussion of the decisions we, as teachers, must make regarding what we consider to be "literature" and then we listen to middle grade students' ideas regarding reading and literature instruction. Next, we look at literature as a mirror, a microscope, and a telescope that readers can use to view their world more clearly and carefully. We then shift our attention to typical formats for organizing literature instruction and common text selection issues to highlight the significance of literature study within the middle grades language arts curriculum. From there, while still focusing on texts, we consider adolescent literature as a genre through which we can match our students' interests with artistic literary content. Then we see how two popular teaching formats, directed individualized reading and literature circles, can be incorporated into literature lessons. Attention to those strategies will be followed by consideration of the tricky issues of how to generate and sustain meaningful classroom discussions of literature and how to evaluate literary learning. We close the chapter with attention to a sample lesson set in which the popular adolescent novel *Shiloh* (1991) is presented within the framework of literature as a mirror, microscope, and telescope. This sample is followed by a list of the ways that the ideas of the chapter support an integrated literacy curriculum and a list of the NCTE/IRA standards that are addressed in the activities recommended in the chapter. The chapter closes with a list of strategies within the chapter that are particularly helpful for promoting the reading development of English language learners, and with notes on other strategies that promote the reading development among English language learners.

The Ways We Define Literature

In order to make decisions about how we will approach teaching and learning of literature, we need to start by considering how we define *literature*. The definition must support all of our thinking about how to select, teach, and evaluate literature and literature learning. In one camp, *literature* is treated as though it always needs and deserves proper noun status: Literature. In this camp, the leaders are the only ones who determine which works are worthy for reading by their minions. The camp leaders trust only themselves with answers about authors' intentions and readers' proper reactions. I have never enjoyed spending time in that camp. I believe that literature needs to be as broadly defined as readers' interests dictate. In my classroom and, I hope, in yours, the literature selection will include not only canonical and contemporary books, short stories, poems, and drama but also newspaper articles and editorials, print advertisements, letters, diaries, memoirs, self-help books and other nonfiction, magazines, job descriptions, instructions for removing stains, insurance forms, admission forms, cereal boxes, board game directions, Web site reviews, travel brochures, menus, soda bottles, and on and on.

I have not always felt this way. Like many of you, I was an English major in college, before deciding to add teaching credentials to my degree. I developed all of the traits of a literature snob: snubbing the trash novels that my friends took with them to the beach, turning up my nose at the junk magazines that I saw others absorbed in on airplanes. But teaching young adolescents taught me that literature does not have to be lofty. It has to be able to attract and satisfy a reader. I am now convinced that if we want our students to become lifetime readers, the best things we can do for them are these:

- Surround them with print and nonprint texts,
- Give them time to read,
- Allow them to respond,
- Pay intense, careful attention to their responses.

We can trust that, with their increased experience and confidence, and with our patience and support, our students will learn to separate the literary rubbish that they might come into contact with from the riches that they will discover.

In this chapter, I have chosen to stay away from the temptation to present a toolbox that includes all of the creative ways of teaching short stories, novels, plays, poems, newspapers, magazines, biographies, histories, essays, speeches, and so on that I have collected through the years. Instead, I have included a few specific teaching suggestions to illustrate the kind of thinking about literature instruction that a student-sensitive, integrated literacy pedagogy promotes. As you grow as a teacher, I urge you to continually reflect on your habit of mind, on the way you think about your instruction. As you reflect on your literature lessons and literacy instruction, remember that our teacherly thoughts should begin and end with attention to the primary subject: our students.

The Ways Young Adolescents Respond to Literature

Those of us who adhere to principles of a student-sensitive integrated literacy pedagogy have several good reasons to ground our curricula in literature study. First, there is some evidence that middle school students have more positive attitudes toward literature study than we might assume they will have, especially if we give them access to good reading materials and allow them to choose from those materials (Ivey & Broaddus, 2001). Second, middle school students are capable of recognizing the great paradox of literature: Some books lead them toward self-examination, while others allow them to escape their world for a time. They recognize, too, that they can turn to books to examine their own values and to explore their world from others' perspectives. Third, young adolescents can help us find books that address their current interests and that also nudge them beyond immediate concerns toward more challenging and sophisticated artistic presentations of issues and concerns characteristic of adolescents and also those that are universal.

Ivey and Broaddus (2001) found that middle school students are drawn to good books and that they enjoy free reading time and being read to by the teacher above other classroom reading activities. In another survey, Carroll and Gregg (2003) flesh out the picture of young readers even further: Look at how a representative group of young adolescents from across the country responded to direct questions about themselves as readers (the number represents the respondent's age at the time he/she answered the question):

Do you like to read?

"I like to read because when you read, it's YOURS!"	male, 11
"I like to read because it makes you think and takes your mind off things that bother you."	male, 11
"Reading makes me sleepy (yawn)."	male, 11
"I like to read because I use it as an escape from reality."	male, 12
"I love to read because you can let your imagination fly."	male, 12
"I love to read because it gives me new ways to perceive the world."	female, 13
"It takes me out of my everyday life into something so much more interesting."	female, 13
"I don't like to read very much because I think there are better things to do than sit on your butt and read."	male, 13
"I like to read to take up time."	male, 13

How would you describe yourself as a reader?

"I'm a fairly good reader, but I can't be distracted while reading or I don't comprehend anything."	male, 14
"I love to read, but not when I am forced to read a certain book in a certain period of time."	female, 14
"Talking about books helps [me] want to read."	female, 13
"You get to know what it is like being a teen and the hardships there are."	female, 12
"[As a reader] I'm very creative."	male, 14
"I'd rather read harder, more sophisticated books than books [targeted for] my age level."	male, 14
"I am serious about reading and I don't let anyone disturb me."	female, 13
"I LOVE IT! I imagine myself there. I am very attentive."	female, 14

(Carroll and Gregg, 2003)

Few of the approximately 3,000 middle school students who responded from across the nation to the Carroll and Gregg survey claimed to hate reading. However, many students did comment that they dislike the kinds of assignments and constraints that they have learned to associate with school-related literature study. One of our primary goals of literature instruction might be to eliminate the need for students to assume that pleasure reading can only occur when they choose a text and read it outside of school and that school reading always requires a set of instructional activities. This is the goal that we will work toward in this chapter. (See Figure 4.1. I invite you to use it with your students and then incorporate the results into your literature curriculum.)

FIGURE 4.1   Reading Interests and Preferences

Your Name _____
Your Age _____
Today's Date _____

Reading Interests and Preferences

Part One: Think about the kinds of books and stories that you like to read. Please place an X in the blank if you like to read books or stories about the topic that is listed. You can mark as many as five topics. If you can, also add the title of your favorite book in a particular category.

For example: __X__ animals   Shiloh Season

An important note: Please mark only the topics that you really like to read about as you read down the list. You are not going to get a grade for your responses. I want to know more about what you like to read so that when I make assignments in this class, and when I buy books for our classroom collection, I will be sure to have books that appeal to you.

_____ animals

_____ adventures (fiction—made-up stories)

_____ mysteries

_____ the supernatural

_____ sports

_____ growing up around the world

_____ home and family life

_____ slapstick humor

_____ settings in the past

_____ fantasy

_____ true adventure stories (nonfiction—not made up)

_____ history

_____ mystical romances (a romance that occurs in unusual circumstances)

_____ adolescent life

_____ search for personal values (fiction or nonfiction)

_____ social values (fiction or nonfiction)

_____ strange and unusual human experiences (fiction or nonfiction)

_____ growing from adolescence into adulthood

_____ science fiction

_____ elderly people

_____ middle-aged people

_____ wealthy people

_____ politics/government

_____ industry/business

_____ the troubles of marriage

(continues)

FIGURE 4.1   Continued

Part Two: Please write short answers to as many of the following as you can:

1. Do you like to read, or not? Please explain.

2. How much time do you spend reading every day, not counting school assignments?

3. What do you read when you read just for yourself (not for a school assignment)?

4. Which one of these is important to you when you are selecting something to read?

_____ Length (check one: I like short books and magazines _____.
I like long books and magazines _____.)

_____ Cover

_____ Subject of the book

_____ My friends like it.

_____ Title

_____ Author

_____ My teacher or the librarian recommended it.

_____ My parents like it.

_____ Another reason (please write the reason in the space):

5. Do you like books and stories better if they are about boys or girls, or does it matter?

6. Do you like fiction (made-up) books and stories or nonfiction (true) stories better?

7. What is your all-time favorite book? Why is it your favorite?

8. What is the best book you have read in the last year?

9. Who is your favorite author (if you have one)?

10. Please finish these five sentences:

I like to read when I _____ .

I like to read more than I like to _____ .

I like to _____ more than I like to read.

I think that the best books are ones that _____ .

The best time to read, for me, is _____ .

Based on the Carroll, Gregg Survey (unpublished, 2002).

Literature Study

It might be helpful, especially for beginning teachers, to think of literature and literature study in terms of looking at life from three different perspectives: in a mirror, through a microscope, and through a telescope. These different perspectives offer our students at least three very different views of people, the world, and life.

Literature as Life in a Mirror

When we think of literature as a mirror, we can use it to open up conversation on the issues that are presently at the forefront of our students' minds. In effect, we use literature to hold up a mirror to our students' worlds, so that they see themselves in the midst of others and thus they see that they have a place. Literature, used as a mirror, helps young adolescents feel less alone, less alienated, less distanced from others by virtue of the proof in print: Others have felt similar feelings, have experienced similar frustrations, have celebrated similar accomplishments. In student-sensitive classrooms, we need to provide students with the opportunity to read like we do—as if they are holding up a mirror to better see themselves and their place in the world. Literature is a mirror when we encourage students to put themselves into the text and to read with close attention to the actions, attitudes, and values of the individual characters who emerge from the pages. We also encourage students to consider the relationships among people, nature, and other elements that are part of the world of the text when they hold a mirror up to that world as if it were their own. For example, when students read "Raymond's Run," by Toni Cade Bambara (1997), they might imagine what their lives would be like if they had a mentally handicapped younger brother who idolized them. They might respond to a question such as, "How would I feel if my friends saw my handicapped brother hanging around me?" or "Would I be the kind of person who would laugh at Raymond, or who would help him learn to run?" When literature is a mirror, the reader looks closely at the text world as if it is her own world in order to construct meaning.

Literature as Life under a Microscope

When a reader looks at literature as if he were looking through a microscope, he determines what aspect of the text he will focus on and then examines that aspect carefully. He notes its attributes, its relationship to other parts of the text, and its contributions to the isolated element of the text, as well as to the whole organism of the work of literature. The reader who views "Raymond's Run" through the microscope might focus on protagonist and narrator Squeaky's claim, "I run. That is what I am all about" (Bambara, 1997, p. 56), to determine whether or not running proves to be the most important thing to her, after all. Through the act of isolating one text feature (such as Squeaky's attitude), the reader's role is not to look into a mirror but to examine small details carefully, to collect and analyze samples, and to draw conclusions based on what he finds. His conclusions may be restricted to the focal feature of the text (Squeaky's apparent attitude), or they might expand to touch on the bigger picture of the entire story (such as how seeing Raymond run alongside the track where she is competing influences her attitude).

Literature as Life through a Telescope

When a reader uses literature to look at life through a telescope, she shifts her focus further from herself and the text to consider a much larger view of the world. She may consider where she fits in the big picture as she observes it but the focus is not on herself. Instead, it is on the combination of things that contributes to the total picture. The property that allows literature to be a telescope allows us to use literary texts as a means of introducing students to others' views, perspectives, and concerns. In effect, the notion of literature as a telescope allows readers to transcend their lived-through experiences to interpret the world presented in the text with a broader frame of reference than the one they brought to the reading event. When reading "Raymond's Run" with a telescopic lens, for instance, a middle school student might ask questions about the following:

- Challenges faced by the author as an African American woman;
- Cultural significance of the description of Squeaky's family responsibilities;
- Importance of winning a running competition for a young African American girl who describes herself as "a little girl with skinny arms and a squeaky voice" (Bambara, 1997, p. 53);
- Reactions to those who have various handicapping conditions.

In a student-sensitive integrated literacy environment, the reading and study of literature from each of these different focal points give us, as teachers, and our students a common vehicle for considering actions, attitudes, values, and beliefs. They provide us with scaffolding that will work toward the goal of helping students develop the "ethic of caring" that will, as Henry Giroux (1997) notes, help young people "function effectively as critical citizens capable of self-determination, social responsibility, and individual compassion in the 21st century" (p. 67).

When literature is seen as a mirror, literature study should solicit personal reactions to and connections with the text. When literature becomes a way to examine life through a microscope, literature study should encourage comments on the text. When literature provides a way to observe life from the lens of a telescope, literature study should engage the reader in critical thinking and activities that extend beyond the text. It is because literature invites readers to react to and connect with, comment on, and extend beyond the text that it makes an ideal anchor for integrated language arts study.

Reacting to and Connecting with a Text When Literature Is a Mirror

Literature learning requires first that readers make personal connections with the world of the text. Connection is essential if the text is one like Gail Carson Levine's *Ella Enchanted* (1997), the modern-day fairy tale about a girl who was cursed with the gift of obedience until she had to fight for the prince, whom she loves. Connection is also essential when the text is like author and activist Toshi Maruki's nonfiction account, "Hiroshima No Pika" (1994), about one Japanese family's tragedy when the United States dropped an atomic bomb on their hometown in August 1945. And the connection needs to have at least two branches: One branch is personal and visceral, more involuntary than planned; the other branch is deliberate and has discernible roots in the text itself.

The first question that adolescent readers need to be asked, as they work their way through texts, whether they are reading as students or as people, is simply this: "What did you think?" Until they establish a personal, gut-level response to a text, no other meaningful connections will occur; literary learning will stall if there is no point of personal contact with the text. Frequently, the response we get when we ask middle school readers, "What did you think?" is, of course, "This is stupid!" or "This is sooooo boring!" Yet even these responses can help us determine a few things about the reader's experience with the text, and a quick preliminary assessment of their ability to read with comprehension takes no more time than to ask the second question: "Why?" Students who are able to make sense of the text will be able to give an answer to the "Why?" question, an answer that is grounded in the text itself.

Let's imagine that two students, after reading "Hiroshima No Pika," respond by claiming, "This is a dumb story." Yet one student, when asked the second question, "Why?" admits that he does not like the way that Maruki describes the torture of an innocent Japanese family during the World War II bombing. The other student, who had difficulty making sense of the text due to the unfamiliar vocabulary and lack of knowledge regarding the use of atomic bombs during World War II, hides behind his "It is dumb" response. This reader is unable to generate a text-rooted answer to the second question, "Why?" He therefore provides the teacher with a clue that he needs his teachers to keep a close eye on his reading. It is likely that he has chosen to cling to an unsupported comment rather than admit that he was unable to comprehend the text.

As readers, even experienced critical readers who are earning or have earned college degrees, I suspect that we have all experienced this lack of connection with a text at some point. At its worst, this lack of connection is manifest in an inability to comprehend. For example, I admit that I struggled to make any sense at all of the enigmatic opening lines of Chapter 6 of William Faulkner's *Light in August* (1972) during a number of rereadings:

> Memory believes before knowing remembers. Believes longer than recollects, longer than knowing even wonders. Knows remembers believes a corridor in a big long garbled cold echoing building of dark red brick sootbleakened by more chimneys than its own, set in grassless cinderstrewnpacked compound surrounded by smiling factory purlieus and enclosed by a ten foot steel-and-wire fence like a penitentiary or a zoo, where in random erratic surges, with sparrowlike childtrebling, orphans in identical and uniform blue denim in and out of remembering but in knowing constant as the bleak walls, the bleak windows where in rain soot from the yearly adjacenting chimneys streaked like black tears. (p. 111)

My initial, gut-level response to the poetic paragraph was an inarticulate, monosyllabic, "Huh?" Without even the most basic level of comprehension, I was unable to make any personal connection with the passage during several readings of it. Yet as a tenacious reader, and a fan of Faulkner, I kept trying. Finally, after reading the lines a few times, I was able to see the picture that Faulkner was painting. At that point, I calmly returned to the opening lines and was able to put them into the context of the chapters that had come before and make sense of them. At last, I was able to move beyond my initial reaction to a point from which I could marvel at the precision, power, and poetic impact of Faulkner's art.

This need for personal connection is not limited to fiction or poetic texts. How many of us have been frustrated by our inability to make sense of one page of a computer manual or the directions for enrolling in a new health insurance policy? Until we answer the two initial questions, "What did you think?" with a personal reaction, and the follow-up, "Why?" with a text-based response, we will not be able to go further in thinking about the text.

As important as these questions "So what did you think?" and "Why?" are as the starting point for encouraging readers to react to a text, we will be making a mistake if we are satisfied with answers at that point. Literature learning is just beginning when those questions are answered.

Commenting on a Text When Literature Provides a Microscope

Depending on our instructional goals, instruction that solicits comments on the literary text might entail asking students to connect with any of the following: the author's artistic use of language; the impact of the text on the reader's knowledge or attitudes; the development of discrete literary elements such as characterization, plot structure, theme, tone, voice, and setting, throughout the work; the significance of the writer and/or text within a tradition such as Southern writers in modern U.S. literature. If our instructional goals determine that we want students to explore their reactions to a literary piece, we might ask them to consider issues like the following: the feeling about the characters and/or situation that they have and are left with at the end of the work; the author's treatment of the characters in terms of stereotypes or real types and so on; frustrations or surprises regarding the outcome of the literary work.

Although its textual elements can be isolated for careful study when literature becomes the microscope through which we examine a text world and a reader's world, the rendering of a text cannot be accomplished through the study of its individual parts alone. Nor can any significance be ascribed to a text without attention to its impact on a reader. It is the reader who considers the interconnections of the individual aspects of a work of literature to compare, analyze, synthesize, and evaluate the effectiveness of both the individual parts and the impact of the parts when they interact together. In *Literature as Exploration*, originally published in 1938, Louise Rosenblatt posited her seminal statement of reader response, or transactional, literary theory: "A novel or poem or play remains merely inkspots on paper until a reader transforms them into a set of meaningful symbols" (1995, p. 25).

Rosenblatt also sounded an early alert about a potential pitfall related to looking at literature through the kind of lens that treats form as separate from content:

> Teaching practices and assignments should be scrutinized to make sure that students are not given the idea that the formal relationships in a literary work exist apart from, and are merely superimposed upon, something called the *content*. Much truer to the reality of both literary creation and literary experience is the sense of how organically interfused are these two phases of the work of art. (1995, pp. 47–48)

Does Rosenblatt's insistence on the organic nature of a literary work mean that we cannot help students see how individual literary elements contribute to the overall work of literature? Of course not. The point is that we should always return to the impact that the individual parts have on the whole literary work and experience and include the reader as one of those parts of the whole. (The section on focal and global aspects of reading in Chapter 3, called Teaching Reading to the Whole Class, may help clarify this notion that we can read with attention to the immediate details as well as with an eye toward the big picture of the text simultaneously.)

How might we accomplish this part-and-whole literature instruction in a middle grade's language arts classroom? How might we have students look at literary elements as separate aspects, but ensure that they fit the individual pieces into the context of the big picture as well? One popular activity is to have students consider the setting of a story and then change it and record the ways that a setting change affects the development of the plot and even the characterization.

For example, when students read *The Diary of Anne Frank* (dramatization by Goodrich & Hackett, 1994), they find that the setting, a secret hiding place in an Amsterdam warehouse and office building, is almost as strong a presence in the unfolding of the story as most of the characters are. Thus the drama is ideal for study of setting; students might be asked to take one scene and rewrite it, using a modern apartment setting, a school setting, and so on. Then they should trace the impact of a setting change on several of the characters and on several events in the plot. Discussion and small group questions might include ones such as these:

- How might Anne act differently toward Peter Van Daan if she had an opportunity to be further away from him, at least for part of each day?
- What would the adults' conversations and arguments sound like and focus on if they had separate living quarters?
- What kinds of items might Anne bring into her room if she were able to add personal touches? What would you bring to the room if you were in her place?
- Imagine that Anne had chosen another way of expressing herself. What forms might she have chosen? Write a sample passage as you think Anne would have written it. Have a classmate respond to your passage as if he or she were Peter or Mr. or Mrs. Frank. Do your writing in a notebook that you design to look like Anne's diary.

Notice that these literary questions and directions nudge students to develop the abstract thinking capabilities that characterize intellectual growth during adolescence, which we considered in Chapter 2.

Teacher Tameka King offers another strategy for helping students look at distinct literary elements, without losing sight of the whole. Her student-sensitive strategy increases her students' awareness of structure and interconnections in literature and also in life. She explains her intriguing and successful approach:

I teach the common literary techniques such as plot (rising action, tension, denouement, falling action), mood, characterization (protagonists and antagonists), and so on. One week, while my students were working to track the plot in Richard Peck's *Remembering the Good Times* [1985], it occurred to me that if they can recognize these techniques in literature, they might also be able to recognize what is going on in their own lives. Further, they will be able to see that they are writing their own story—their lives—and that they can still choose the outcome. One student, whom I'll call Shelby, came to me and said she was having a problem with her friend Tasha, who was acting distant. I asked Shelby to talk about the events as if she were tracking the plot of a short story and to put herself in the role as narrator and protagonist. As she analyzed the plot of her own story, she realized what she had done that could have caused Tasha's feelings to be hurt. She planned to change what seemed appropriate for the next scene of her story—an impending argument with Tasha—and to create instead a scene in which they could talk over their troubles and resolve them. I would like to have time to help all students develop their life stories, because I feel that when I put my student's needs as humans first, the lessons come almost naturally. (June 6, 2002)

In middle grades and high school classrooms, literature has long been studied as if it provides a microscope to examine the world. The challenge for those of us who are committed to a student-sensitive pedagogy, even when we want students to examine discrete literary elements, is twofold: First, we must remember that a work of literature is a living artifact—that it changes with each reader's rendering. Second, we must remember to recognize that the element that can never be isolated when we approach a literary text is the reader. The literary experience must be personally meaningful before it can become academically enriching.

Extending beyond a Text When Literature Becomes a Telescope

When readers use literature as a telescope through which they look into the world beyond the text, the text itself recedes from view. In the classroom, this can mean that literature instruction actively engages students in an exploration of ideas that have been, prior to their experience with a particular text, beyond their thoughts, outside of their field of vision. This telescopic perspective intrigues middle school students, who are eager to look beyond their current limits and to stretch their thoughts as they grow into their individual adolescent identities and develop their own values. This perspective also teaches students the value of thinking critically to seek connections. While the microscopic lens allows readers to find connections within the elements of a text, the telescopic perspective encourages us to find connections between all kinds of print and nonprint texts, whether they are written, verbal, or graphic representations.

Veteran teacher Anna Jordan provides an excellent example of looking at life through the telescopic lens of literature in an activity that she uses to enrich students' reading of Virginia Hamilton's *The House of Dies Drear* (1968), a novel that harkens back to the Civil War era and the Underground Railroad. Anna describes the "Life of the Coin" activity, which promotes an integrated literacy stance:

After students have read *The House of Dies Drear*, I invite a guest speaker who is a history buff to come talk with the class. This speaker brings coins from the Civil War era, and we pass them around for a few minutes, so that the students can hold, jingle, and admire them. Next, we ask all of the students to clasp just one coin tightly in their hands. We tell them to close their eyes and imagine answers to these questions:

Who else may have held that coin?
What might it have been used for?
What could have been bought with it? A slave? His freedom?

Could John Wilkes Booth have had it in his pocket when he shot President Lincoln? Could the president have been carrying it?

Of course anything is possible. Students become enthralled in the mysteries and the possibilities that they imagine surrounding the coins they are holding. This intrigue reinforces the tone for the mystery they encountered in the novel.

Students are hooked on the idea of finding out more about the coin and the era from which it came! After the guest speaker's presentation, the students and I brainstorm a list of topics that have emerged from the coin activity. Then they log onto the Web and research the coins and their actual value, the cost of slaves during the Civil War, the cost of "silence" as slaves escaped on the underground railroad, and other topics that enrich their background knowledge and enhance their reading of the novel. The Web-based resources that they discover become both expository and creative writing prompts. While they write factual essays about slave auctions, for example, their favorite writing assignment is to compose "The Life of the Coin" story, in which they tell where and with whom their Civil War coin has been.

Anna's "Life of the Coin" activity takes a work of literature and uses it as a telescopic lens through which students observe and explore life that extends far beyond the text. Clearly, it is an activity in which literacy skills are practiced—students engage in reading, listening, creative thinking, research, critical thinking, expository and expressive writing, and speaking. And the project is also an example of one in which literacy skills can be integrated across the curriculum; like the "Our Generation's Heroes" project, this one could be developed even further as a collaboration between the language arts and social studies teacher; the mathematics and science teacher could become involved, too, by leading students in the study of money values, metals and processes used to mint the Civil War money, and so on.

Making Good Choices as a Literature Teacher

It has been my experience that beginning teachers in middle schools are often more unsure about how to select texts and then to organize and pace literature instruction than are their high school counterparts. This difference is to be expected for several reasons. One is that the middle school literature curriculum is much less codified, much less stable, than is the high school curriculum. High school anthologies and courses are generally structured to reflect a common pattern: study of genres in ninth and tenth grades (with some American and world literature introduced in tenth grade), survey of American literature in eleventh grade, and survey of British and world literature in twelfth grade (Applebee, 1990, p. 39). Middle grades literature curricula might be organized around themes, genres, or even reading skills. The findings of Arthur Applebee's (1990) national study of English/language arts teachers and programs help us establish a baseline against which we can compare our own practices. Applebee reports that middle grades teachers prefer to organize literature instruction around the following:

Genres (71.4%),
Individual major works (65.7%),
Themes (54.5%),

Literature representing specific groups (35.5%),
Chronology (13.3%). (p. 56)

Further, he notes that in junior high/middle schools, short stories are the most popular form of literature, consuming over 43 percent of literature instruction time. Novels are the focus of 23 percent of instructional time, while drama receives 10 percent and poetry receives 8 percent of the time devoted to literature study. In contrast, in high school English classes, novels are the focus of 40 percent of literature instruction time, short stories receive 23 percent, poetry and nonfiction each consume about 10 percent, film or video receive 8 percent, and plays are allotted almost 5 percent of literature instruction time (p. 56).

Another common problem for many of us is related to our own habits as readers. As college or university students, we read the heavy texts that English majors prize: works by Thomas Hardy, Franz Kafka, Wallace Stevens, Eudora Welty, Albert Camus, Gabriel Garcia-Marquez, and on and on. Because of the time we spent reading and writing about these serious works, we legitimately question our own instincts when it comes to engaging in easier reads. We wonder if the critical judgments that we apply when reading the classics are valid criteria for judging the relative merits of literature that we teach to young adolescents.

A related concern has to do with familiarity with texts that adolescents can and do read. Have you visited a seventh grade classroom lately? Was it one in which bookshelves were filled with a wide variety of adolescent and young adult trade books (books that are sold to the general public, instead of school textbooks)? Did you notice J. K. Rowling's *Harry Potter and the Sorcerer's Stone* (1998), and the other Harry Potter books, which seem to have almost single-handedly convinced a generation of young adolescents that reading is an adventure, shelved alongside other works of adolescent literature that our students love to read, share, and discuss among themselves? Did you find that nonfiction works were tucked into the shelf, too, including the ubiquitous *Chicken Soup for the Teenage Soul* (and . . . *the Pet-Lover's Soul* and . . . *the Kid's Soul*)? In this classroom, were recent adolescent books sharing shelf space with the classics of adolescent literature, such as the perennially popular *The Outsiders* (S. E. Hinton, 1967), *Hatchet* (Gary Paulsen, 1987), *The Chocolate War* (Robert Cormier, 1974), and *The Crazy Horse Electric Game* (Chris Crutcher, 1987)? While you may not see books with which you are familiar as a reader among these, look closely; I suspect that you will see some familiar names among the authors. Gain familiarity by reading journals that focus on adolescent literature, such as *The ALAN Review*, published three times per year by the Assembly on Literature for Adolescents of the National Council of Teachers of English (ALAN). (You can find NCTE at www.ncte.org, and ALAN, including *The ALAN Review*, at www.alan-ya.org). Ask other teachers, school and public media specialists, and bookstore clerks about the books that are most popular among the middle grades readers in your community. Take time to read those books; within their pages, you will see the themes, issues, and concerns that are important to your students today.

And don't fret that you haven't a lot of spare time to read all of the newer additions to the adolescent literature genre. Although it is likely that you will be charmed by and therefore slowed down in your reading of some adolescent books, most adolescent novels and biographies/autobiographies are approximately 180 pages long and thus as adults, we can read one in a couple of hours or so. (There are several series, including the Harry Potter books and many science fiction titles, that are exceptions to this generalization about length; the fifth book in the Potter series is over 850 pages long in paperback, and many readers love it for its heft.)

A Closer Look at Adolescent Literature in the Middle Grades

Teachers and adolescents who dive into the adolescent/young adult literature genre are likely to discover that young adult literature is particularly appropriate for middle school readers for many reasons, including these ten:

1. Protagonists in young adult literature are most often teenagers themselves; middle school readers are attracted to stories that feature characters who are their age or slightly older and characters who speak in their language.
2. Problems that characters experience in young adult fiction and nonfiction often mirror problems that many adolescents experience, such as alienation, conflicts with parents, changing relationships with friends, pressure to do well in school and other activities, girlfriend/boyfriend disputes, and self-concept conflicts.
3. Characters are often placed in extreme situations, such as being alone after losing parents in a car crash, dealing with a friend's realization that he is gay, discovering that a sibling has a drug problem or a terminal disease, and living through a shipwreck only to awaken blind and alone.
4. Settings might be an "anywhere" school or neighborhood or a major part of the story.
5. One or two multidimensional central characters are well developed, while subordinate characters are left sketchier.
6. Readers can investigate others' responses to extreme situations while enjoying the comfortable distance that literature provides from the problems.
7. Poetry and short stories with a decidedly young, contemporary flair are included in the genre.
8. Factual information for teen readers who are interested in learning about health issues, historical events, famous athletes, popular entertainers, important scientists and writers, and so on are presented in nonfiction young adult books for today's teens.
9. Young adult books are typically shorter than the books that older teens and adults choose to read, and they move more quickly, with less attention to descriptive details than is typical of adult literature.
10. When teams of teachers include it in interdisciplinary thematic units, young adult literature can enhance instruction across the curriculum.

Notice that the first six characteristics on the list encourage readers to enter adolescent books as if they are holding up a mirror, looking under a microscope, and peering through a telescope.

See Figure 4.2 for a list of authors whose books I recommend for middle school language arts classrooms. Please add other authors' names as you discover them, and set aside

FIGURE 4.2   130 Popular and Skillful Contemporary Authors for Young Adolescents

I will resist the urge to list my favorite adolescent novels here but will note that there are many fine resources in which you can find reviews of books for young adolescents. Two journals published by the National Council for Teachers of English (NCTE) are among them. *The ALAN Review* is a journal devoted exclusively to adolescent literature; published by the Assembly on Literature for Adolescents of NCTE, each of the three issues published per year includes reviews of recently published adolescent books in a clip-and-file format. *Voices from the Middle* is an NCTE journal devoted to teaching language arts in the middle grades; it includes reviews of adolescent books written by teenagers. The International Reading Association publishes an additional resource: *Journal of Adolescent and Adult Literacy* frequently has articles about adolescent literature and includes the annual Readers' Choice book winners listing. Boynton/Cook Heinemann, Greenwood Press, Scarecrow Press, Scribner's, and Christopher-Gordon Publishers are among the publishing houses that have series or titles devoted to teaching young adult and adolescent literature and books on individual writers and themes.

The 130 contemporary writers listed here have proven to be popular among young adolescent readers—and their parents and teachers. The list does not include authors whom you would be likely to find in the traditional middle school canon; intead of adding names such as Jack London, Mark Twain, or even Harper Lee, I have attempted to gather the names of authors who are currently having an impact in the field of young adult and adolescent literature.

I have added a parenthetical note regarding the kind of writing that they are most known for though the tag is not meant to be a complete descriptor. For more information on these authors, please see the Scribner's *Writers for Young Adults* series (four volumes, 1997; 2000), edited by Ted Hipple.

Joan Aiken (realistic fiction, historical fiction, humor)
Lloyd Alexander (fantasy)
Maya Angelou (autobiography, poetry, memoir)
K. A. Applegate (fantasy—Animorphs)
Sandy Asher (realistic fiction)
Avi (historical fiction, adventure, humor, horror, realistic fiction)
Joan Bauer (humor and realism)
Marion Dane Bauer (realistic fiction)
Jay Bennett (realistic fiction and mystery)
T. Ernesto Bethancourt (realistic fiction, science fiction, mystery)
Francesca Lia Block (magical realism)
Judy Blume (realistic fiction)
Robin Brancato (realistic fiction)
Sue Ellen Bridgers (realistic fiction, families, social issues)
Bruce Brooks (realistic fiction)
Eve Bunting (historical fiction, realistic fiction)
Betsy Byars (realistic fiction)

Michael Cadnum (realistic fiction, medieval settings, poetry)
Alden Carter (realistic fiction)
Aidan Chambers (realistic fiction, linguistic and stylistic distinction)
Alice Childress (realistic fiction, urban settings)
Vera and Bill Cleaver (realistic fiction)
Brock Cole (realistic fiction)
Christopher and James Lincoln Collier (biographies, historical fiction, nonfiction)
Hila Colman (realistic fiction, social issues)
Caroline B. Cooney (realistic fiction, horror, family fiction)
Robert Cormier (intrigue, realistic fiction)
Sharon Creech (realistic fiction, families)
Chris Crutcher (sports settings for realistic fiction)
Karen Cushman (medieval settings in fiction)
Paula Danziger (humor, realistic fiction)
Terry Davis (realistic fiction)
Lois Duncan (psychological novels, mystery)

FIGURE 4.2 Continued

Paul Fleischman (historical fiction, poetry, realistic fiction)

Adrian Fogelin (realistic fiction, social issues)

Paula Fox (historical fiction, realistic fiction)

Russell Freedman (nonfiction)

Michael French (historical fiction)

Nancy Garden (realistic fiction, social issues)

Leon Garfield (eighteenth-century England settings with adventure)

Jean Craighead George (ecological adventures)

Mel Glenn (poetry)

Bette Greene (realistic fiction, social issues)

Adele Griffin (realistic fiction, families)

Lynn Hall (family, dogs, and horses in fiction)

Virginia Hamilton (realistic fiction, folklore)

Jim Haskins (biographies, nonfiction)

Nat Hentoff (realistic fiction, social issues, nonfiction, autobiography)

Karen Hesse (historical settings for realistic fiction, families)

S. E. Hinton (realistic fiction)

Will Hobbs (realistic adventure, environment)

Isabelle Holland (realistic fiction)

Monica Hughes (travel, historical adventure)

Mollie Hunter (fantasy, Celtic lore)

Hadley Irwin (realistic fiction, social issues)

Lou Kassem (middle school settings, realistic fiction)

M. E. Kerr (realistic fiction, social issues, autobiography)

David Klass (realistic fiction, social issues, sports, families, environment)

Norma Klein (realistic fiction, social issues)

Ronald Koertge (realistic fiction, family and social issues)

Gordon Korman (humor)

Trudy Krisher (social issues, realistic fiction)

Kathryn Lasky (realistic fiction, social and environmental issues)

Ursula K. LeGuin (fantasy, social action, short stories)

Anne C. LeMieux (realistic fiction, fantasy, family and social issues)

Madeleine L'Engle (fantasy and time travel, morality)

Robert Lipsyte (realistic fiction, urban settings)

Lois Lowry (utopia/dystopia, historical, realistic fiction)

David Lubar (slapstick humor)

Chris Lynch (humor, realistic fiction, social issues, sports)

Margaret (May) Mahy (realistic fiction, supernatural)

Kevin Major (Newfoundland settings for realistic fiction, historical fiction, humor)

Carol Matos (historical fiction)

Harry Mazer (realistic fiction)

Norma Fox Mazer (realistic fiction, families, short stories)

Anne McCaffrey (fantasy)

Milton Meltzer (biographies, history, social issues)

Carolyn Meyer (realistic fiction with social issues, nonfiction)

Gloria Miklowitz (realistic fiction, social issues)

Nicholasa Mohr (Puerto Rican culture, historical fiction, short stories)

Kyoko Mori (realistic fiction, anomie)

Walter Dean Myers (realistic fiction, urban settings, social issues, Vietnam war)

Donna Jo Napoli (realistic fiction, humor, fantasy)

Phyllis Reynolds Naylor (realistic fiction, families, humor)

Joan Lowery Nixon (mysteries, historical fiction)

Naomi Shihab Nye (poetry)

Scott O'Dell (historical fiction, sea settings, dogs)

Zibby O'Neal (realistic fiction, families)

Katherine Paterson (realistic fiction, families, faith)

Gary Paulsen (realistic adventure, historical fiction, survival, dogs)

Richard Peck (realistic fiction, intrigue, autobiography, poetry)

(continues)

FIGURE 4.2   Continued

Robert Newton Peck (realistic fiction in rural and past settings, families)

Susan Beth Pfeffer (realistic fiction, family relationships)

Rodman Philbrick (realistic fiction, future fiction, horror)

Christopher Pike (Kevin McFadden) (horror)

Randy Powell (realistic fiction, sports, families)

Phillip Pullman (historical fiction, realistic fiction, fantasy)

Ann Rinaldi (historical fiction, realistic fiction)

John H. Ritter (baseball, social issues)

Sara Ryan (realistic fiction with social issues)

Cynthia Rylant (realistic fiction in Appalachian settings, autobiography, short stories)

Louis Sachar (fantasy, realistic fiction)

Graham Salisbury (realistic fiction with historical and sometimes exotic settings)

Neal Schusterman (realistic fiction)

Sandra Scoppettone (realistic fiction with social issues, mystery)

Quida Sebestyen (realistic fiction, families and faith)

William Sleator (fantasy, autobiography, exotic settings)

Gary Soto (realistic fiction with urban settings, poetry, short stories)

Jerry Spinelli (realistic fiction, humor)

Suzanne Fisher Staples (international and multicultural settings, realistic fiction)

Shelley Stoehr (realistic fiction, social issues)

Todd Strasser (realistic fiction, historical fiction, humor)

Mark Talbert (realistic fiction, families)

Mildred D. Taylor (realistic fiction with historical settings)

Theodore Taylor (realistic fiction often with exotic settings)

Joyce Carol Thomas (realistic fiction, poetry, short stories)

Rob Thomas (humor in realistic fiction)

Julian F. Thompson (realistic fiction, social concerns)

Stephanie Tolan (realistic fiction)

Ann Warren Turner (poetry)

Cynthia Voigt (realistic fiction, families)

Will Weaver (sports, rural life, realistic fiction)

Barbara Wersba (realistic fiction)

Robert A. Westall (WWII and sea settings, realistic fiction, fantasy)

Carol Lynch Williams (realistic fiction, social issues, families)

Rita Williams-Garcia (realistic fiction in urban settings, African American experience)

Virginia Euwer Wolff (realistic fiction, family relationships, social issues)

Jacqueline Woodson (realistic fiction, social issues, short stories)

Laurence Yep (fantasy, autobiography)

Jane Yolen (realistic fiction, fantasy, folk tales, biography, humor, nonfiction)

Paul Zindel (realistic fiction, social issues, humor)

---

shelf space for works by the authors whom your students designate as their favorites, too. Your list should grow to include both the newest and the time-tested names and should lead students directly to their books.

Also see Figure 4.3, which provides themes around which student-sensitive literature study can be arranged, so that literature can provide a dependable curricular anchor for the literacy classroom.

FIGURE 4.3   Themes for Literature Study in Middle School Classrooms

While working in middle school classrooms during the past twenty years, I have found these ten theme topics, and the sample themes listed by category, to be productive ones around which to organize literature-based literacy units in middle grades classrooms. These themes reflect the interests and concerns of contemporary teens (see Chapter 2 for more information on these). They also allow for connections across the language arts, and across subject disciplines, and therefore allow for integrated instruction.

Environment: Treating the Earth Gently; Truth and Consequences—Our Impact on the Environment; What the Future Holds; We Belong to the Land

Families: Family Relationships; Changes in Family Relationships; Significance of Home; Where Did My Parents Go?; What Do They Expect from Me?; Independence: How Long Do I Have to Wait?

Friends: Finding a Place in the Group; Changes in Friendships; Intergenerational Friendships; Multicultural Friendships; Following the Crowd and Standing Out from the Crowd; The Value of Loyalty; How Far Would You Go for Your Friend? Is Sex Next?

Music and Movies: What "Entertainment Today" Looks Like in Our School; Music and the Teenage Experience; Television and Movie Stars: Reality vs. Appearance; That's Reality?; Our Media Role Models; My Music Will Tell You Who I Am

Sports: Sport as a Metaphor for Life; Talent and Determination—Which Is More Important: Winning or Playing the Game?; The Connection Between Coaches and Athletes

Self: Who Am I?; Finding My Self, Finding My Way; You Should Have Known Me When; My Family and Me; My Friends and Me; Where I'm Going; My Dreams; Body Image: How Healthy Is Mine?; Why Am I Different?; Moving Out, Moving On; All I Ever Wanted; Listening to My Heart

Taking Risks: Risky Behaviors; Accepting Challenges; Survival; Standing up for What Is Right; Setting High Goals; When Teens Do Drugs and Alcohol

Travel: Different Places; Different Times; Follow Me; The Perfect World

Values: This Matters to Me; What Counts Most; Keeping Our Promises; In Control; The Courage to Change

Violence: Moves and Motives of Young Gangsters; Could It Happen at This School?; Teens as Victims: Protecting Ourselves; Outlets for Anger

Implementing Literature Instruction

Making Time for Just Reading

Understandably, in today's schools that are driven by accountability measures and standardized testing, many among us have grown skeptical about the wisdom of devoting instructional time to just reading. Yet we know that life for middle school students begins to be extremely busy, and in their busyness, time for just reading is diminished. During afterschool hours, many young adolescents begin to participate in group meetings, sports, social interactions (in person, on the telephone, and on the Internet), and even some part-time jobs.

We need to provide time for students to experience and enjoy just reading during the school day. If we do not build that kind of time into curricula, we do a disservice to all of the young adolescents who have not developed the habit of reading for pleasure.

Richard Allington reminds us that the pleasure many of us take for granted—settling into a book we enjoy—requires time. A fifth grader who is an average reader can silently read approximately 200 words per minute. Therefore, a young adolescent can be expected to read Cynthia Rylant's *Missing May* (1992), which has about 12,000 words, in approximately four hours. A young adolescent can be expected to read Paulsen's *Hatchet* (1987), which has about 50,000 words, in approximately eight hours (Allington, 2001, p. 37). Evidence is strong: students who reported spending more time reading in and out of school than their classmates earned higher reading scores in grades tested (fourth, eighth, and twelfth) (Allington, 2000, p. 26; Anderson, Wilson, & Fielding, 1988, in Allington, p. 26).

Allowing students to choose reading texts from a large selection of books, magazines, newspapers, and other print materials improves the chances that students will do the quantity of reading that is necessary in order for them to develop fluency and comprehension. If we always expect our middle school students to read common texts with the whole class, we ignore one of the most common and most difficult classroom realities that preservice and beginning teachers must learn to address: The individual young adolescents who fill our classrooms read at many different levels. A five-grade reading range is common. For example, in a seventh grade classroom, we can expect to have students who read on the level of fifth, sixth, seventh, eighth, and ninth graders. When our classrooms include students with learning disabilities, particularly those related to processing print, or some physical disabilities, particularly those related to vision, the reading performance range may be even greater. When our classrooms include students who are English language learners (ELL), we may experience a greater reading range as well. In this case, we must determine whether or not the student who is an ELL is a competent reader in his or her home language so we know how to proceed with reading instruction in English. The directed individualized reading strategy provides the essential ingredients that many literature lessons and units omit: time, diverse texts, and student choice.

Directed Individualized Reading

When I recommend addressing these realities with directed individualized reading (DIR), I know that I am not alone. Arthur Applebee found that, in a national sample, 59 percent of middle school teachers and 38 percent of high school teachers were using directed individualized reading (DIR) approaches in literature instruction (1990, p. 42). I will admit up front that the DIR unit is my all-time favorite practice for immersing students in the reading and study of literature. During the two- or three-week DIR unit, students spend the majority of their class time reading books or other print texts that they select from the texts made available to them. They take about five minutes at the end of each reading session to add notes to their reading log, showing how many pages they read at that session and recording the main gist of those pages. This log may help them identify gaps in comprehension early enough to reread portions for self-initiated clarification, to seek help from you, or to choose another book. Some teachers also require that students add a minimum number of vocabulary words that are new to them, with page number and sentence in which the new word occurs, as well. You will check with every student during an impromptu writing chat a few days after everyone has settled into a book or other print material for the DIR.

As a student finishes reading each selection (those who read quickly may finish a book every few days; others will read only one book during the unit), he will sign up for a book talk with you. He will leave you a copy of his book to peruse the night preceding the talk, so that you can familiarize yourself with its key elements. Before the scheduled talk, you will skim the book and jot down some details; notes on the plot, setting, main characters and their relationships, and themes will be useful as prompts if the student is initially reluctant to talk as the authority on the book. These notes will also reduce your work the next time a student wants to talk with you about that same text.

During the book talk, the student will be the expert and will teach you, an interested listener, about the book he has recently finished. The unit ends with two or three days during which all students present their favorite (or only) completed book (or alternate text) to the class, using one of a wide variety of response options. Each student is evaluated on the reading log, the book talk, the presentation. You might also build in a challenge factor that is a weighted portion of the final evaluation. Unlike the accelerated reader program, in which books are assigned a difficulty level without regard to the reader, you will look at your notes on the student as a reader, and, in conjunction with the student, determine a book's challenge factor in terms of that specific reader. With the DIR, there are no multiple choice questions, no long, dry essays. There are, instead, readers sharing the gems they find when they act like people who read. Please see Figure 4.4 for tips on how to set up DIR in your classroom. Figure 4.5 is a list of possible responses to reading that you will want to keep handy, especially during your first few years of teaching.

I have used the DIR strategy successfully in middle school, high school, and even college classrooms, and I am convinced that it is a hit with readers for two reasons: (1) students choose what they'll read, and (2) students choose how they'll respond to what they read. Further, this is one strategy that accomplishes what so few can: it individualizes instruction. Readers can select books that are easy or challenging for them (and earn more credit for pushing themselves toward books with higher degrees of difficulty than they have previously read independently). For this reason, it is an excellent choice for classes when they include English language learners and special needs students. It is also an activity that can be tweaked to fit a number of instructional aims. For example, you can use the DIR to support theme-based instruction: If you want to complement students' study of David Klass's *California Blue* with a DIR unit that continues the theme of "Treating the Earth Gently," you will fill the room with fiction and nonfiction books, newspapers, magazines, and other resources that are devoted to environmental issues. You can use the DIR to support genre-based instruction, as well. If you are introducing modern poetry, you will fill the room with as wide a variety of books, magazines, and software that include samples of modern poetry as possible. The possibilities are virtually limitless.

Literature Circles and Book Clubs

If you are unable to devote two or three weeks to just reading during a DIR unit, I have another suggestion: literature circles or books clubs. I highly recommend the literature circle or book club approach, especially for theme-based, topic-driven, or genre-specific instruction.

FIGURE 4.4   Directed Individualized Reading

Setting up the DIR

1. Stock your room with books, borrowing from colleagues and the media center and soliciting contributions from students and parents.
2. Choose four or five books from the classroom collection and read short excerpts from them as "book hooks." Be sure that the books you use are different in style, theme, topic, language, and so on, since the purpose of the book hook is to show students they will interest everyone within the classroom collection.
3. Set up accordion-style student folders that students will use throughout the weeks of the DIR. Before you distribute them, put two things in each folder: (1) multiple copies of the reading log sheet, with space for students to write their name, the book title, and three columns that they will fill in every day: The Page I Started on Today, The Page I Ended on Today, What I Read about Today; (2) one sheet of paper that has the partial statement, "This is who I am as a reader:" printed across the top. Students will finish this statement during the first day of the DIR unit. (The ambiguous nature of the partial statement works to students' advantage; some will list all of the books they have ever read; others will describe their reading strengths or weaknesses; some will note that they hate reading. In the act of finishing the statement, though, each will define him- and herself as a reader.)

Conducting the DIR

1. Book Pass: On Day One, arrange all student desks or chairs in a circle. Put one book from the classroom collection in each student's hands. On your signal, they will have two minutes to survey the books in their hands, scanning the first few pages, reading the back cover, examining the cover illustrations, and so on. At the end of two minutes, tell them to stop. Allow one minute for them to write the title of the book they have surveyed. If it is of interest to them, on the next signal, have them pass their book to the person on their right. Repeat the two-minute survey process. At the end of approximately thirty minutes, students will have looked at ten books, some of which they may never have picked up on their own. This activity is valuable because it increases enthusiasm for reading, demonstrates the value of looking at a wide range of choices, and ultimately reinforces the fact that readers will be making personal choices during the DIR.
2. Daily Reading: The majority of each class period should be devoted to silent reading. After a few days, some students will be scheduling book talks with you, and these can be conducted in a reading corner so that others will not be distracted by them.
3. Daily Reading Logs: Reserve the last five to ten minutes of class time for students to make entries in the daily reading logs, and to schedule their book talks.
4. Mid-Project Book Chats: As the teacher, you will circulate to each student and talk very informally and briefly with him or her about the book, using the log as a conversation guide. These chats are not scheduled like the more formal book talks; instead, they are designed to help you identify any potential problems (if a student has chosen a book that she cannot comprehend but that she continues to struggle through, for example, and to allow you to gauge students' enthusiasm for reading books that they have selected).
5. Book Cards: Each student, on completion of each book (or story, etc.), completes a book card, a large index card that contains this information: book title, author, year of publication, a brief summary of the book, and a rating on a scale of 1–5, with 1 as "Don't Waste Your Time!" and 5 as "You NEED to Read This One!" with a brief explanation.

FIGURE 4.4 Continued

6. Book Talks: After making the book card, the student signs up for a book talk, to be held the following day, and then gives you her book so that you can take it home and skim it, taking a few notes on major literary elements. During the talk, the student is the expert on the book; you will use your notes only if conversation drags or the student is too nervous to begin. End the talk by determining, with the reader's input, the challenge factor of that particular book for that reader, using a scale of 1 (easy) to 5 (very difficult).

7. Presentation: Reserve a few class periods for the presentation of book projects. (See Figure 4.5. For the presentation, students should choose the book that they liked best, if they completed more than one, and everyone will do a presentation of a project on one book (or story, etc.).

   Implement student evaluations of project presentations that include a line where the student indicates whether or not he is interested in reading the book that was presented.

Evaluating a DIR

Use the following, weighing each as appropriate for your goals and your students' abilities:

> Book chat
> Reading logs
> Book card
> Book talk
> Project and presentation
> Challenge factor

Thanks to Terry C. Ley, Professor Emeritus, Auburn University, for sharing DIR strategy with me many years ago.

In the version of literature circles that I like best, you will collect five or six copies each of five or six books that in some way address a common theme (or topic or genre, depending on your instructional goals). Students are able to choose one of several books that present a common theme (or topic or genre). Then they meet to read and work with others who have chosen that book. When finished with the book and following some group conferences, they report on the theme (topic, genre) as it is developed in their group's book. For example, if the theme for the unit is "Changes in Family Relationships," you might allow students to group themselves by selecting from among these book choices:

> Sharon Draper's *Tears of a Tiger* (1994), which shows how Andy's parents try to deal with, yet ultimately misjudge, the depth of their son's depression after he is responsible for his best friend's death in a drunk driving accident.

> Sue Ellen Bridgers's *Permanent Connections* (1987), in which a teen who is used to living in the big city learns a lot about his own strengths and needs when he is forced to spend time in the North Carolina mountains with his father's odd family.

> Randy Powell's *Run if You Dare* (2001), in which a teen boy watches his father self-destruct and must learn to let him go.

> John H. Ritter's *Over the Wall* (2000), in which a teen baseball player explores the impact of the Vietnam War on his relationship with his distant father.

FIGURE 4.5   100+ Literature Response Possibilities for You and Your Students

Use these ideas yourself, when you want to introduce a new book to your students, and share them with your students so that they can respond to books they read using one of the following strategies.

Remember that the kind of introduction you give for a book can become a model for the students' response to that book. For example, if you create a montage that reflects a protagonist's inner conflicts and use the montage to introduce the book, your students might decide to create a montage to show another character's conflicts, actions, or relationships, and so on when they complete the novel.

I have found it useful to insist that during the school year, students complete a minimum of one response project from each category. In addition, I have found it useful to stipulate that they have to prepare a minimum of one written, one dramatic, one technology enhanced, and one visual response project during the year. This requirement encourages students to explore expression in modes that they normally do not rely on, and in some cases, introduces a student to a modal strength that he was unaware he possessed. (I still remember the shy, stuttering, trembling Danny C. rise to the occasion and absolutely shine when he dramatized a passage from Jack London's "To Build a Fire" for his eighth grade classmates.)

A. CHARACTERS
 1. Discuss how the main character is like/unlike you or people you know.
 2. Pretend you are one character and introduce the other characters to your class.
 3. As an interior decorator, how would you decorate the main character's bedroom? Why? (Write a description, draw it, use pictures from magazines to create a poster, etc.)
 4. Invite three people who are famous today to a dinner party with the characters in the book. Write or role play their conversation.
 5. Make and illustrate a time line of the events in the life (or a day, week, month, year) of the main character.
 6. Make up five interview questions for the main character, with answers. "Stage" the interview with the help of someone from the class.
 7. Pretend you are Oprah, Phil Donahue, Riki Lake, or any talk show host. Have the character(s) of your book as your guest(s) and your classmates as the audience. (You may want to prepare the audience by reviewing the characters' roles in the book and even by sneaking questions to them.)
 8. Imagine you are a movie director. Which actors would play the characters in the book? Why? (You might want to promote your movie by creating a poster to go with it, using pictures of the actors who are starring in your movie version of the book.)
 9. Create a PowerPoint slide show or Web site that depicts the trials and joys that the character lives through in the book (temporal and/or geographic settings, social situations, and so on can be focal points here). Add voices, animation, video clips, etc. if you wish!
 10. Create a "WANTED!" poster for a character in the book.
 11. Write a personal ad that the main character might send to the newspaper seeking a friend.
 12. Write a newspaper help wanted ad that the character might respond to and explain why.
 13. Explain how the main character changes during the book.
 14. Present a tableau of a powerful event or turning point in the novel. Have audience members describe the expressions of each character who is represented in the tableau.

FIGURE 4.5 Continued

B. SETTING

1. Make a map or a model that shows where the book's action occurs.
2. Compare, in writing or with a drawing or model, your own town (or school or house) with the town (or school or house) that is the setting of the book.
3. Change the time during which the book is set; if it is in the present, try sending it back or forward in time 100 years, for example. Use the Web if you need to engage in research, but be sure to check the validity of your sources. Prepare a PowerPoint slide show that describes the effects on the story (plot and characters) that the change would have.
4. Create a Web-based or PowerPoint map game in which clues from the book help your friends move from one screen to the next.
5. On a poster board, make a larger-than-life-sized newspaper front page, referring to events and settings from the book. Be sure to add photographs and/or drawings to catch readers' eyes!

C. AUTHOR

1. Write to the author and explain your reaction to the book. Be sure to give details about what you liked, what you have questions about, etc.
2. Write to the author and explain why you will recommend this book to friends who are your age.
3. Stage a mock interview with your author, preparing five questions and answers, and ask a classmate to help you role play the interview. Videotape the interview and present it to the class as if it were part of a television special on famous writers.
4. Pretend you are the author and talk to the class about which part was the most fun to write, which was the most difficult, and describe the other books you have written.
5. Pretend that you are the author. Make a list of the writers who have had an influence on your style of writing. Record your list and explain them to an audience as if you are a guest on a talk radio show.

D. PAST and FUTURE

1. Describe what you think happened in the lives of the characters or in the setting before the book begins.
2. Describe what you think would happen to the characters and/or setting after the book ends.
3. Rewrite the ending of the book.
4. Discuss why the book would or would not have been popular in your grandparents' school days.
5. Describe the parts of the book (setting, characters, plot, etc.) that would be difficult for someone to understand if he or she found the book 200 years from now.

E. THE BOOK and YOU

1. Compare this book with another that you have read. Perform your favorite scenes, but shift the characters from one book and put them into the scene of the other book.
2. Describe an experience you have had that was similar to one you read about in the book. Was the outcome also similar? Explain.
3. Create a magazine advertisement or create and videotape a television advertisement for the book and present it to your class.

(continues)

FIGURE 4.5 Continued

4. Write a poem that expresses your response to the book or to one of the characters' actions and thoughts.
5. Write an acrostic poem, using the letters of a character's name or the book title to begin each line, and include references to the book.
6. Make a television script for your favorite scene in the book. Have your friends help you dramatize the scene (and videotape it, if possible).
7. Make a thumbprint book of your book (dip your thumbs in paint and then stamp them on paper; add identifying elements—a bow tie, a skirt, etc.—and captions under each).
8. Make a mobile, using a coat hanger and string and either drawings or pictures and words you cut from a magazine, that represents the book's characters, setting, plot, and so on.
9. Write a letter to your best friend and explain why you are sending him or her this book and why you think he or she should read it.
10. Make a crossword puzzle that can be solved by using clues from the book; have a friend try it.

F. LANGUAGE
1. Make a small dictionary that will help readers of the book deal with its unusual words or uncommon subject matter (especially helpful for science fiction and books about specialized subjects).
2. Make a list of superlatives and discuss how each applies to your book.
3. Rewrite your favorite portion of dialogue, changing the characters' dialects to different ones; for example, change a teenager's slang into Shakespearean, or give a character from New York a Southern drawl.
4. Find and record at least ten powerful and interesting similes and metaphors related to the book or to one aspect of it.
5. Rewrite one scene using a different narrator, perhaps a minor character, to describe it.

G. OTHERS (add your own ideas here)

(Many of these ideas are borrowed from Nancy Mavrogenes, "101 Ways to React to Books," *English Journal*, May 1977, pp. 64–66, an oldie-but-goodie article that I have kept in my teaching file for years!)

Caroline Cooney's *The Face on the Milk Carton* (1990), in which a teen discovers that she is not the child of the people who have raised her, and is reluctantly removed from her home and reunited with her birth family.

The students who discuss common texts will learn that consensus about the literary work is not necessarily required. One of the benefits of the literature circle/book club approach is that it allows individuals to create and retain their own readings, while it provides them with access to a group of others with whom they can bounce around ideas.

Literature circles/book clubs promote the idea that time spent talking about books is valuable. Within the literature circles/book clubs, members can discuss issues in the readings that attract their attention, confuse them, aggravate them, and so on. They can also be places in which members write, in journal entries, letters, or even lists, about their responses to books and then explore those responses within the safety of their small group. Within the literature circles/book clubs, students might raise questions to see how other readers make sense of portions of text that confuse them or ask classmates for input against which they will compare their rendering of a text. They might act out a scene in order to try to better know how the characters within it interact, what their motivations are, and so on. Because the discussions and choices regarding activities to explore and clarify readings are typically student generated in classroom literature circles/book clubs, students who participate are likely to feel that they have joined what Frank Smith (1988) calls the "literacy club."

After spending time in their literature circles/book clubs, some groups might choose to present their book to the class as a group. We can encourage them to choose from a wide selection of possibilities for sharing individual and group responses to the book read; some possibilities include dramatizing key scenes, reading aloud their journal entries and other book-related writing, creating visual aides to represent their sense of important issues in the book, and presenting their interpretations of the book to the class in the format of a panel of literary experts. The point here is that literature circles/book clubs allow us to step away from the center of instruction to encourage our students to be people who read. With literature circles/book clubs, we can help our students learn to establish and trust their own purposes for reading and discussing literature, to be directed by their own needs to know, their own interests, their own curiosities about their own and others' ideas and responses. For a more thorough discussion of literature circles, please see Harvey Daniels' *Literature Circles: Voice and Choice in the Student-Centered Classroom* (1994) and *Literature Circles: Voice and Choice in Book Clubs and Reading Groups* (2002).

Discussing The Cay *during literature study.*

Discussion and Evaluation in Literature Instruction

Before moving into a sample lesson set in which an approach for conducting another kind of literary experience, whole-class instruction of a book, is presented, I need to take a detour to address two issues that commonly cause teachers, especially beginners, great frustration. One is the issue of how to create and sustain an effective, informative, helpful class discussion. The other issue is how to evaluate students' literary learning.

Leading Literature Discussions

One of the most difficult tasks a new teacher faces is conducting what appears, when written in her lesson plan, to be a simple job: "Have a class discussion on . . . ." Often the scene is similar to one that occurred recently, while I was observing a student teacher during his first attempt at leading a literature discussion with a group of eighth graders. The students had been reading Christopher Paul Curtis' funny yet poignant *The Watsons Go to Birmingham—1963* (1995). They had just finished reading the scene in which a church in Birmingham, Alabama, was bombed and four little girls who were attending Sunday School were killed. The protagonist, Kenny, fears that his baby sister, Joetta, is among those injured or killed, but she is not; she later shows up at their grandmother's house, unharmed. Careful readers will notice that Kenny is led to think that Joetta was injured or killed because he sees small black shoes in the rubble—the same kind of shoes that Joetta was wearing when she left for Sunday School that morning.

> STUDENT TEACHER: So what happened here?
>
> STUDENT ONE: The church blew up and Kenny's sister got hurt, but then she walked home.
>
> STUDENT TWO: She did not get hurt, Kenny just thought she did, and he freaked out.
>
> STUDENT ONE: If she wasn't hurt, why was Kenny thinking she was dead?
>
> STUDENT THREE: I don't get it. Why did the church blow up, anyway? Was it storming outside?
>
> STUDENT TEACHER: Storming?
>
> STUDENT THREE: Well, there was a lot of noise and commotion going on.
>
> STUDENT TEACHER: What was really happening here, though?
>
> STUDENT TWO: I would've run away as fast as I could.
>
> STUDENT ONE: Yeah? Would you have left your baby sister there?
>
> STUDENT TWO: She wasn't even there.
>
> STUDENT TEACHER: So what is going on in this scene, anyway?

The student teacher was successful in getting three students to engage in conversation, but he was unable to get them to work toward zooming in on an answer to the question that he asked. He returned, three times, to the same question, but was not able to use it to encourage deeper thought about the scene. Eventually, he moved away from his original question and asked, "How would you feel if you were in a church that blew up?" and "What would you do if you thought somebody in your family was inside?" Several students who had not spoken before brought up references to the families of victims of the terrorist attacks on September 11, 2001. At that point, the discussion took on a personally meaningful nature. Finally, the student teacher asked the class to think about the bombing as it must have appeared to Kenny, and to look back into the book to see what Kenny saw in an effort to determine how he felt. Eventually, he was able to probe their responses enough to help them make sense of the scene; they generated an understanding of it when they paid closer attention to the clues that author Curtis gives his readers.

Despite its slow start, this student teacher's lesson went more smoothly than another I witnessed a student teacher struggle through recently, as she was preparing to teach Theodore Taylor's *The Cay* (1969/2002):

STUDENT TEACHER: Does anyone know what a "cay" is?

STUDENT ONE: It's a letter—hij*k*lmnop.

STUDENT TEACHER: Not that K, another one, spelled cay, c-a-y.

STUDENT TWO: That's like OK.

STUDENT TEACHER: No, that is still the letter K. I am thinking of a word that has to do with the ocean and islands and coves.

STUDENT THREE: Well then why don't you just tell us what it is, since you are thinking of it?

In this episode, the student teacher is trying to follow the familiar advice: introduce literature by tapping into students' prior knowledge. However, the situation left her feeling defeated by her students. The problem was that with her singular focus, she seemed to be expecting students to read her mind. They were not fooled into believing that she was encouraging a discussion or conversation; they knew that she already had "the" answer in mind, and were impatient that she share it with them. Leading class discussions of literature is much more difficult than it appears to be.

Below are four models, presented by scholars of literature instruction who write from their own experiences as teachers. Hynds's model is an effective student-sensitive method for engaging an entire class in personally significant discussions of literature. She encourages teachers to model and solicit statements, not only questions, since statements about texts reflect thoughtful engagement with literature. Dias's model begins with the teacher reading to the entire class and then moves into students reading and rereading and discussing the text in small groups. In this model, students delay crystallizing their ideas about the text until they have read it several times and have listened to others' ideas. Finally, small groups present their ideas to the whole class. Probst's "Five Kinds of Literary Knowing" (1992) encourages readers to be guided by five different questions as they make sense of a text or an experience; the questions are concerned with the self, others, the text, the context, and the meaning-making process itself. Like Probst's "Five Kinds of Literary Knowing," Langer's (1995) idea of envisionment building offers us a model that extends beyond discussion of literature, per se, to a construct for thinking about all meaning-making activities. She uses the word *envisionment* to refer to "the world of understanding a person has at any point in time," "what one knows, how one feels, and what one is after . . . what the individual does and does not understand" (p. 9).

Susan Hynds's Guidelines for Whole-Class Literature Discussion (1992)

1. First, examine your own questioning practices to determine whether or not your teaching philosophy and instructional goals are reflected in the kinds of questions you ask. Often, we tend to stick with literal-level comprehension questions even when we claim to value students' use of literature as a means of exploring their own feelings, assumptions, and values. Our questions should reflect our philosophy and goals.

2. Use questions only when there is a genuine need to know; learn to listen and discover what can be learned in the "deliberate appreciative silence" (p. 97). Begin discussions by making a thought-provoking statement, or by asking students to give statements as their responses as readers or to make statements that connect two students' points. For example, students might have jumped into a discussion of *The Watsons Go to Birmingham—1963* if they had been encouraged to respond to a provocative and controversial statement by their teacher, such as "The children of our society have always been protected from the ugliness of racial prejudices."

3. Teach students to ask questions of each other, not just of you, the teacher. Aim for real discussions instead of recitations (p. 93).

4. Encourage students to explore and discuss their own (even idiosyncratic) readings, instead of always working toward consensus, to "nurture self-assured interpretation, rather than blind dependence on teachers or study guides" (p. 97).

Patrick Dias's Suggestions for Whole-Class and Small-Group Literature Discussion (1992)

1. Distribute copies of a poem or a short excerpt from a work of literature that the class is reading and then read the selection aloud. In the next twenty-five minutes or so, conduct the other steps of the lesson sequence.

2. Solicit students' questions about any unfamiliar words and allusions, and answer those questions with literal meanings (thereby leaving students to make their own connections with figurative meaning possibilities).

3. Have one student read the passage aloud to the whole class, while you listen for any stumbling point; if necessary, have another student read the passage aloud one more time.

4. Have students get into groups of four to five members. Each group should designate a reporter who will focus the group's attention, and who will report to the whole class. No one writes. Diaz recommends that students talk but not write throughout this activity. When students write their responses, they tend to crystallize their ideas. When they talk, they continue to develop their ideas and to be open to others' views.

5. Within each group: One member reads the passage aloud again. Each member of the group gives an initial response, with no comments from the group. (Note that at this point, even after hearing the passage at least three times, there is no expectation that the students understood it, only that they have some kind of response.)

6. After all members of the group have given an initial response, they can begin to discuss their responses. They may find that they need to reread closely.

7. The group will decide on which comments they will report to the whole class and which can be discarded. If their discussion fails, they should reread the passage.

8. Each group reporter makes an oral presentation, unaided by notes, to the whole class.

9. The entire class rereads the passage once again.

Our role as the teacher in this kind of literature discussion is one of "providing information students need, of urging and encouraging, of generally managing the process" (Dias, 1992, p. 146) and of selecting texts and evaluating learning and growth.

Robert Probst's "Five Kinds of Literary Knowing" (1992)   Probst provides us with a framework for leading readers beyond their initial responses to texts (or other problems in which they work as meaning makers). He encourages us to help students learn to read with an eye toward what the text reveals about self, others, the text itself, contexts, and the meaning-making process:

1. Knowing about Self: Students learn to "reflect up aspects of [their] own lives evoked by the transaction with the text" (Probst, 1992, p. 63). For example, in discussing *The Watsons Go to Birmingham—1963*, students might enter a conversation about the text by first discussing their own experiences with racial prejudices and hatred. Such a discussion will not be directly or exclusively connected to the novel, but it opens the door to give students easy access into the novel by bringing their personal attention to one of the book's major issues.

2. Knowing about Others: Through discussion of individual interpretations, questions, and responses to a literary text, our students can learn about others' perspectives. Probst recommends the use of a four-part reading log to encourage students to learn about others' perspectives. On a sheet of paper with four columns, one student (a) writes notes on a selected portion of a text and then (b) writes a response to that portion. That student then passes her log to a partner, who (c) adds a comment about what appears in the first two columns. The second student then returns the log to the original writer, who reads the classmate's comment and (d) writes a reply. These logs would provide solid resources on which to build a substantive class discussion.

3. Knowing about Texts: With this focus, students learn to consider "how texts work upon them, controlling and directing them, either intentionally or inadvertently" (p. 69). While warning against the implication that there is one right way to make sense of any work of literature, Probst recommends that we help students look for patterns, artistic style, images, phrases, words, and so on that influence their responses as readers.

4. Knowing about Contexts: At this point, Probst recommends that we help readers understand that their reading is influenced by the "context in which reader and text come together"

(p. 71). Probst suggests that we ask readers to think about how the text would be different if the context of reading were different. For example, when discussing *The Watsons Go to Birmingham—1963*, we might ask students to consider what would happen if Kenny, the protagonist and narrator, were from a family that never had fun or laughed together. They might be asked to consider, too, how they would read the book if they had been a friend of one of the little girls who was killed in the church bombing, which is described in the novel. This kind of thinking helps readers learn to attend carefully to the text as well as to their work as meaning-makers when they engage in languaging as readers.

5. Knowing about (Meaning-Making) Processes: This stance is one in which readers learn to think metacognitively about what they can do to enter and experience texts. Probst recommends that we have students engage in an activity that is similar to the "Silent Reading/ Think Aloud" that is described in Chapter 3; Students describe how they make sense of a text and discuss their processes with each other. One goal related to this stance is to help students broaden their repertoire of strategies for making sense of literary texts.

Experience with each of these kinds of literary knowing enables readers to develop their understanding of the importance of the transaction between the reader and the text and the essential nature of the reader's active participation in making sense of the text.

Langer's Envisionment Making   Langer (1995) encourages us to promote a literature class environment in which "questions are part of the literary experience" so that "sense making in literature is open-ended and inquisitive, in search of new horizons" (p. 58). In her view, literature discussions should contribute to "developing understandings" and exploring "the uncertainties and hunches [students] bring with them and consider other possibilities and perspectives as a result of interacting as part of the group" (p. 59). Her view is consistent with an integrated literacy pedagogy because it emphasizes students' contributions as individuals and as group members. Further, Langer calls for "multiple perspectives":

> as a way to help students reflect on ideas that did not initially come to mind, as a way to confront his own ideas more reflectively (and more analytically) in comparison to or in conflict with others, as a way to develop interpretations based on particular points of view, and as a way to gain sensitivity in response to perspectives that are not their own. (p. 59)

Langer's model points us toward four stances that can help students (and us) reflect on meaning-making processes. One is "being out and stepping into an envisionment," in which the readers work to "gain a sense of what the work will be about" (and may revise earlier predictions when there is evidence that they were not on target). The second is "being in and moving through an envisionment." When readers choose this stance, they bring their own personal knowledge to bear on the text and make sense of it in light of the knowledge and background that they bring to it, along with the information provided by the author. The third possibility is "stepping out and rethinking what one knows," a stance that Langer describes as "essentially different from the others" because readers use their experience with, and understanding of, the text as a resource that helps them understand better the world that exists beyond the text. The fourth stance is "stepping out and objectifying the experience," during which readers step back from a text and their experience with it, analyze the reading event, and evaluate both their reading and the text itself (Langer, 1995, pp. 16–19).

None of these four models requires that the teacher predetermine the meaning of a text for students. None of the four requires that all students must create identical renderings of a particular text. Neither does any offer a 100 percent guarantee that students will become active participants during discussions of literature. Each does, however, provide ideas regarding potential places to start literature discussions.

Matching Goals for Literature Instruction with Evaluation of Growth in Literary Understanding

The first question we need to ponder regarding evaluation of literature learning is this: "What does it mean to *know* a work of literature?" Think of the possible answers to this question. What are the implications for approaches to measuring learning that these varied answers suggest? Some teachers argue that readers know a work of literature when they can:

- Recall the plot, characters, setting, themes, mood, tone, and point of view.
- Identify its place within the larger body of literature, or within an era, genre, author's canon, and/or realm of social influence.
- Comprehend the text on focal and global levels, using the author's cues and clues in conjunction with his or her own knowledge and experience.
- Feel a personal connection with elements presented in the text.
- Discuss the literary work as it compares and contrasts with other artists' expressions of ideas.
- Move from reading into taking some kind of action.

Perhaps an answer to the question about what it means to *know* a work of literature lies in a combination of these possibilities. The point here is that the stance we take regarding what it means to *know* literature should inform our efforts to teach literature and then to evaluate growth in literary learning. And that stance must be apparent in our instructional goals if it is to inform our evaluation of student learning.

Three teachers with whom I have worked, one beginning and two experienced, expressed these overarching goals for their literature instruction:

TEACHER ONE: "Students will develop an appreciation for a work of literature."

TEACHER TWO: "Students will enjoy reading."

TEACHER THREE: "Students will be able to analyze texts in terms of literary elements and appeals to readers."

The goal statements these teachers provided are a bit amorphous and thus difficult to measure. Nevertheless, the first two represent the teachers' desire for students to engage in a personally meaningful and pleasurable literature event. The third combines reading skills with literary experience. These are all worthy goals. A problem arises, though, when these same teachers discuss their methods for evaluating students' literary growth in these ways:

TEACHER ONE: "I give my students a quiz before we discuss every chapter of a novel, to be sure that they have read the assignment. All of the quiz grades add up to one test grade."

TEACHER TWO: "My students have to write character descriptions and plot summaries of every story and book we read. That is how I know whether or not they were able to understand the author's meaning."

TEACHER THREE: "I give a test at the end of each story; it has quotes from the book, and students have to match each quote to the character who said it and explain the significance of the quote in the story."

Notice that none of these teachers has designed evaluative strategies that are consistent with their overarching goals for literature instruction. These teachers are representative samples; we often teach with one focus and test with a different one. The mismatch does a disservice to our students, because it ignores what they have learned and fails to tap into their connections to, or feelings regarding, the literature that was studied.

If we want our middle school students to become lifelong readers, we need to focus our efforts on helping them learn to enjoy the act of reading. Literature study is not an appropriate venue for requiring that they memorize long lists of character and place names, literary terms, or minutiae about authors. Instead, it should be the venue in which students are encouraged to probe their initial reactions to texts, to clarify their reasons for responding as they do, to investigate the source of the personal connections they make with a text. With these student-sensitive goals in mind, how might we measure and evaluate our students' literary growth? Here are some ideas that you might develop to suit your needs and purposes.

Evaluating Literary Growth When Looking into a Mirror   Ask students to engage in a role play, having them perform as if they are the characters from the literary work that they have read. Place those characters in situations that are, according to the class, important in your school. For example, if they have just read *The Diary of Anne Frank* (dramatization by Goodrich & Hackett, 1984), and one focus was prejudices, characters could perform as Anne and Miep, bringing their perspective to a race-related incident that recently occurred in your school, for example. The characters must stay true to the literary depiction of them, in terms of attitudes and other attributes. This activity will demonstrate how well your students understand the literary characters and also allow them to continue developing personal connections with the text.

Evaluating Literary Growth When Looking under a Microscope   Instead of assigning a traditional test on the completion of a story, drama, or novel, you might ask students to rewrite a scene, changing one significant literary feature, such as the point of view. You might also have them respond by writing about the topic, characters, or setting, using a genre that is different from the work studied. As a response to *The Diary of Anne Frank*, they might write a poem as if Anne were writing it; or a letter from Otto to his wife. Visual art or songs could be created as a response to poetry, in order to help students demonstate which parts of the poem they used to make sense of the whole. If they have read Langston Hughes's "Mother to Son" (1987) for example, you might ask them to choose a work of visual art or a popular song that the mother would be likely to give, or sing to, the son whom she addresses in the poem. These kinds of evaluative activities give you evidence of students' literary growth; more important, perhaps, they allow learning to continue throughout the evaluation period.

Evaluating Literary Growth When Looking through a Telescope   When you have studied literature as if it were a telescope for exploring life beyond the text, evaluation options are almost limitless. Students might take the topic that is a focal point and create a series of television public service announcements or advertisements about that topic. For example, those who have read "Raymond's Run" might develop a public service announcement about the benefits of regular exercise, or their community's recreational opportunities. Those who have studied "Mother to Son" might develop a series of announcements about adult and family literacy programs that are available in the community; they might even create billboards that could reach adults who have limited print literacy.

An obvious yet essential point is this: Evaluation does not have to mean formal, traditional objective and essay testing. Formative evaluation should occur continually in classrooms that are devoted to literacy building. As teachers, we need to be close enough to students to be able to identify when they need our help and to distinguish those moments from those in which our presence is an intrusion. Summative evaluations in student-sensitive integrated literacy classrooms should be designed in ways that allow students to demonstrate what they have gained as a result of time spent in the study of literature. These evaluations should enrich students' literary encounters. New learning rarely happens while a student takes an objective test; new learning does, however, occur when the student performs, analyzes, extrapolates, and extends texts for evaluation.

A Sample Lesson Set

Teaching *Shiloh*

In order to demonstrate ways that literature can be viewed as a mirror and as microscopic and telescopic lenses, I have developed the following sample set of lessons. They are recommended to accompany whole-class reading and study of *Shiloh* (1991), the first novel in Phyllis Reynolds Naylor's Shiloh trilogy. *Shiloh* (1991) is followed by *Shiloh Season* (1996) and *Saving Shiloh* (1997). These poignant novels feature Marty, a poor boy who lives with his family in a rural mountain community, and Shiloh, the beagle dog he treasures. The trilogy appeals strongly to young adolescents who enjoy the adventure, suspense, and insights into growing up that Naylor embeds in the stories. I recommend using the first book, *Shiloh*, as a whole-class reading, so that those who especially like Naylor's art can choose to read the two other books in the series during free reading, a DIR unit, or outside of school. I hope that you will find ways to modify these sample lessons to apply them to the books that you teach in your middle grades language arts classes.

The Shiloh ***Trilogy***   *Shiloh* (1991) is the novel in which readers first meet 11-year-old Marty Preston, his family, and Marty's beagle puppy, Shiloh. Marty narrates the story from his perspective as the son of loving, poor parents in West Virginia. Shiloh, though, comes at a steep price. The beagle puppy originally belongs to Judd Travers, a heartless and unscrupulous character who beats, chains, and almost starves his dogs to death, believing that the best hunting dogs are desperately hungry and raised to be mean. Shiloh runs away whenever Travers tries to take him hunting. The puppy takes refuge with Marty, who hides and protects him in a secret pen as well as he can. When Shiloh is attacked by another dog in the secret pen, Marty has to reveal to his father that he has been hiding the dog and sharing his own food with the puppy. Despite the fact that Mr. Preston had told Marty that the family could not afford a dog, he lets Marty take Shiloh to the local doctor, who happens to be a neighbor.

As the puppy recovers, the entire Preston family becomes attached to it. Readers feel Marty's dismay and anger when Judd Travers suddenly reappears, demanding the return of the dog he had beaten and nearly starved to death. Marty offers Travers a deal; he will do yard work for Travers as barter for the puppy. But when Travers tries to back out of the deal, Marty has to resort to blackmail to get Shiloh.

In *Shiloh Season* (1996), the tension between the Preston family and Judd Travers mounts, but when Travers is in a bad accident, it is Shiloh who alerts the family and leads them to save Travers's life. Marty tries to befriend Travers; *Shiloh Season* closes with a scene in which Marty takes Shiloh to visit a recuperating and lonely Travers. The friendless man gently pets the dog he once kicked and cursed.

In *Saving Shiloh* (1997), almost the entire town is beginning to turn against Travers and accuse him of a man's murder; nevertheless, Marty and the Prestons continue to extend kindness to him. Their efforts are repaid when Travers is able to rescue the dog from drowning in a swollen and cold river. Throughout the trilogy, Naylor maintains a constant tension surrounding the question of whether or not the nasty Travers will try to steal or harm the dog or the boy.

The strategy of introducing an author and encouraging students to read more of the author's work independently is one that paid off for beginning teacher Hannah Gerber. She explains:

> The majority of my (eighth grade) students will read only if the material is short and has an interesting cover. One of the favorites last year was one of Walter Dean Myers's books; I had a class set of twenty copies and students shared them. Reading this novel led a few students to read Myers's *Monster*, and to present a project on it for their classmates (one created a scrapbook for the character, one did a brochure advertising the book, for example). When I thought about how the whole-class reading influenced their choice of a book for free reading, I realized that if you can grab a student's attention with one author, then you start a chain reaction.

Reading *Shiloh* as a Mirror

"My Reactions" Journal: Tracing Personal Encounters with Literature   As teachers, we can take advantage of the fact that readers make personal connections with literature by asking them to carefully answer the following kinds of questions.

How do you feel about the story [*Shiloh*]? Why do you feel that way?

What parts of the story [*Shiloh*] do you remember most vividly? Why is that?

Did the story [*Shiloh*] remind you of anything that you have gone through while you have been growing up?

Did the story [*Shiloh*] remind you of anything else that you have read about or seen on television or in a movie? How was this story [*Shiloh*] different?

Were there any parts of the story that you did not like? If so, why? How might you change that part so that you would be happier with it?

Before we move beyond response-eliciting questions, I want to add a quick note about our practices related to seeking students' personal reactions to literature: Notice that none of the suggested questions elicits a yes/no answer. Instead, each asks the reader to delve into his or her response and probe the reason for that response. This form of questioning is beneficial because it promotes critical thinking. It also helps us, as teachers, distinguish between students who have comprehended the story, and can thus answer the questions, and those who were unable to make sense of parts of it. We need to remember that, especially when our classes include English language learners, it is essential that we ask students to explain their responses and reactions fully and, when possible, critically. If we allow students to give us monosyllabic answers without probing further, students can use "yes" and "no" as screens behind which they hide lack of comprehension and thus lack of understanding.

To help students chart their evolving responses to *Shiloh* (or any short story, drama, or novel), you might assign a "My Reactions" journal. In this journal, students keep their initial responses to each chapter (or to each portion that they read at one sitting, during one class period, and so on). You can encourage them to use a double-entry format by splitting their paper down the center with a line. On the left-hand side, they write page numbers and quotes from the book, or brief explicit details, for passages that caught their attention. On the right-hand side, they write why the passage caught their attention. When they complete the book, they can return to their initial responses and look for responses that (1) were especially potent, (2) remained consistent throughout the novel, or (3) changed as the novel progressed. They can then use these identified responses as a resource for writing an essay in which they trace their experience as a reader of *Shiloh*. This kind of response-fueled essay is important for young readers because the process of writing it demonstrates to them that their job as a reader is to interact with the book, to examine personal connections. It also demonstrates to them that you are interested not only in other experts' interpretations of the book and descriptions of the impact of the book but that you want to know about the impact on your students, as individuals and as members of the classroom community.

Tableaux to Tap into Personal Response   There are many poignant scenes in *Shiloh* that small groups of students could dramatize. One effective method, as suggested by Purves, Rogers, and Soter (1995) in *How Porcupines Make Love, III*, is the creation of tableaux, or frozen scenes. To create tableaux, students work in small groups to identify a significant scene. Then instead of performing the scene with movement and dialogue, they get into place and, on the count of three, freeze the scene. The audience contemplates the tableau and discusses what the characters and the scene reveal. For example, students might freeze the scene in which Marty finds that Shiloh has been badly injured by another dog. Marty's facial expression and posture, the distance between Marty and his father, and the position of his mother in the scene could offer audience members a wealth of images to consider. After seeing the tableau, the audience can begin a rich discussion of text-related issues such as Marty's values, his desire to keep the puppy and all that it entails for this poor family, and his relationship with his parents. The actors of the tableau can be called on to explain why they chose particular positions, what they hoped to emphasize through their choices, and so on.

Reading *Shiloh* under a Microscope

***"Dogabulary": A Lesson on Figurative Language and Connotations in* Shiloh**   Marty refers to Shiloh with affection throughout the novel. However, your students will know that expressions that use the word *dog* are not always terms of endearment. Ask students to brainstorm informal expressions and compound words in which *dog* is used. After they create a list and record it on the board, ask them to determine (1) which of those expressions uses *dog* in a literal sense and which uses it figuratively (be sure to review what *figurative language* means if they need a reminder). (2) Ask which of those expressions carry positive connotations and which carry negative ones (be sure to explain or remind students what *connotation* means, using a positive and a negative example from the class-generated list). Students can take turns investigating and reporting on the intended meanings, roots of the phrases, possible reasons the phrases have become popular, and situations in which they have heard, or are likely to hear, the phrase or word. If your students have trouble getting started with their list, you might help them by providing a few of these:

> Doggone it!
> It's a dog's life.
> Dog days
> Hot dog! (used as an exclamation)
> Hot dog (used as a food item)
> Dog tired
> In the doghouse

You can extend this focus on figurative language and connotations for a class period this way: Draw and cut out twenty or thirty dog profiles of varied sizes and shapes. Use different shapes and colors of poster board or construction paper for increased visual appeal. Students each take a profile and write one of the words from the class "dogabulary" on the front and literal and figurative translations of the expression on the back of the profile. They can then present their profiles to the class and decorate the classroom walls with them. You might even have them create a line of the dog profiles along the wall, as if the animals are walking across the room.

Going to the Dogs: Intertextual Connections   Students can conduct research on different breeds of dogs and then determine which types of dogs would be the most appropriate companions for the characters they have met in other stories and books that they have read throughout the year. For example, if students have read Bambara's "Raymond's Run" (1997), they might decide what kind of dog they recommend as a pet for Raymond. If students have just read Curtis's *The Watsons Go to Birmingham—1963* (1995), they might decide on a breed that they would recommend for the weird Watson family, or pair individuals in the family, such as Kenny and Joetta, with just the right dog. A group might dramatize a scene in which Kenny asks for a golden retriever while Joetta begs for a prissy toy poodle. Another might create a "Top Ten Reasons Why Byron Should Not Be Allowed to Have a Puppy" list, based on what they learn about him in the novel.

Students' matching of dogs with owners could be presented through poster-sized illustrations, comic book creations, role play, letters from the characters that describe their new pets to fictitious friends or members of the class, and so on.

Reading *Shiloh* through a Telescope

Stepping into Social Action   Students are likely to raise questions related to the treatment of dogs in their communities or in society in general as they read any of the *Shiloh* books. Some will be outraged about the treatment of hunting dogs. Others will be appalled at the abuse dogs suffer when their owners beat, starve, or utterly neglect them. Still others may become concerned about the overpopulation of unwanted puppies, and some will raise questions about how today's puppy mills treat dogs before selling their puppies to pet stores, for example, as well. Each of these stances, and others that the students define, can become the basis of a social action project.

For example, students who object to the treatment of dogs in puppy mills might form a group and begin gathering actual information on industry practices associated with breeding dogs for commercial profit. Students need to think carefully about their assumptions and then critically examine them from several perspectives, including the perspective of those who engage in the practice that the students oppose. They might ask themselves, for example, What are the benefits of raising dogs this way? This activity will increase the chance that students who object to hunting will base their objections on a well-informed foundation. Once they have gathered, analyzed, and synthesized information, they can pursue opportunities to publicize it.

Students who are concerned about overpopulation of unwanted puppies might visit the local humane society and collect information on how they, as students, can help officials spread information about spaying and neutering pets. They might ask animal control officials to speak to their class, produce newsletters for their neighborhoods, create and distribute window or bumper stickers, and so on.

Regardless of the cause that draws the attention of students as individuals or groups, students who engage in social action projects must be willing to find ways to take their work into their communities, or bring their communities into the classroom. (See Carroll, 2000, for more ideas related to dogs and boys in adolescent literature.)

Integrated Language Arts Checklist with a Focus on Literature

In this chapter, literacy skills in all of the language arts areas are integrated in the focus on traditional and contemporary literature.

Reading Skills

Directed individualized reading unit: Students have an opportunity to use interest as well as readability level as a criterion for the texts they choose to read and to which they will respond; all students select texts that appeal to them based on individual criteria or in terms of a required focus.

Choice: Students are able, at times, to select efferent or aesthetic stance when reading and interpreting texts.

Writing

Reading interests and preferences survey: Students write short responses to voice their opinions as people who read, not only as students who are given reading assignments.

Shiloh lesson set: Many of the suggestions for teaching *Shiloh* involve writing; examples include the "dogabulary" project, the My Reactions journal, and the social actions project.

Directed individualized reading unit: Students are able to select response activities, including several that require writing, after reading each text in the DIR unit.

Speaking/Listening/Language

Directed individualized reading unit: Students may choose from spoken response project options for the DIR project and will listen and may respond to class-mates' book response projects.

Reading interests and preferences survey: Students might discuss survey responses in small groups, and might form reading circles based on shared interests, for some activities.

Group discussion ideas from Hynds, Dias, Langer, and Probst relate to the integration of speaking/listening/language.

Media

Shiloh: Many of the novels for young adolescents that are recommended in this chapter, including *Shiloh*, are available on audio tape, and some of the novels and other texts are also available on educational or commercial videotapes. Reluctant readers, students with learning disabilities, and English language learners, in particular, will benefit from the complementary use of audio tapes with literature lessons.

Projects: Students can select media-based projects when they respond to texts in the DIR units, as listed in Figure 4.4.

Help for English Language Learners

Directed individualized reading unit and 100+ Possible Responses: ELL reader is able to select print texts in first language, if available, and is encouraged to read fluently, quickly, and accurately, for pleasure as well as for development of reading skills; ELL reader is encouraged to read English texts that are high interest, low readability.

Many of the activities suggested in this chapter incorporate visual images and small group work, both of which lend support to the ELL student. The recommendation that accompanies the description of the "My Reactions" journal regarding the kinds of probing questions that we ask students to answer also addresses the need for teachers to be able to gauge ELL students' actual comprehension levels.

The common and recommended practice of teachers reading aloud to middle school students, especially when students have a copy of the text to follow, reinforces language learning.

An extra few notes regarding working with ELL students while teaching literature: In *The CALLA Handbook: Implementing the Cognitive Academic Language Learning Approach* (1994), ELL experts Anna Uhl Chamot and J. Michael O'Malley recommend that teachers determine students' "background, interest, concerns, and prior experience," including, most importantly, the "level of literacy in their native language, because students' prior knowledge and skills can be applied to reading and writing in English" (p. 293). They also recommend that teachers of ELL students use "observation, discussion, and shared experiences" to identify themes that are "meaningful to students and that lend themselves to developing a literature and composition unit" (p. 293).

The following are among criteria that Chamot and O'Malley suggest we use when choosing literature that we will ask ELL students to read and study:

Choose well-written, high-quality stories.

Select texts that are authentic, not rewritten.

Include a variety of genres, such as fables, folk tales, stories, and poems.

Include texts that reflect or represent students' home cultures and cultures that are unfamiliar to all students in the class.

Organize the texts according to themes that are of interest to students.

Use the literary themes "as springboards to writing." (Chamot & O'Malley, 1994, p. 294)

They also list a series of specific activities that invite students who are English language learners to participate as meaning makers during classroom study of short stories and novels, including these:

> Use prereading to help students tap their prior knowledge about the topic or theme of the text.
>
> Lead students through a preview of the story by drawing attention to the title, illustrations, and headings, or by skimming the story to predict its main gist.
>
> Help students establish and articulate purposes for reading the text.
>
> Read the story aloud to the class, while all students follow, or identify skilled readers to read it aloud in small groups while the other students, including ELL students, follow and periodically check their comprehension by making predictions and so on.
>
> Have students engage in self-evaluation of their understanding and comprehension, using a checklist or rating scale on which they note their ability to make sense of the vocabulary, to comprehend at the literal level, to use inferential comprehension, and so on. (p. 299)

NCTE/IRA Standards

Standard Number One: Students read a wide range of print and nonprint texts to build an understanding of texts, of themselves, and of the cultures of the United States and the world; to acquire new information; to respond to the needs and demands of society and the workplace; and for personal fulfillment. Among these texts are fiction and nonfiction, classic, and contemporary works.

Standard Number Two: Students read a wide range of literature from many periods in many genres to build an understanding of the many dimensions (e.g., philosophical, ethical, aesthetic) of human experience.

Standard Number Three: Students apply a wide range of strategies to comprehend, interpret, evaluate, and appreciate texts. They draw on their prior experience, their interactions with other readers and writers, their knowledge of word meaning and of other texts, their word identification strategies, and their understanding of textual features (e.g., sound–letter correspondence, sentence structure, context, graphics).

Standard Number Four: Students adjust their use of spoken, written, and visual language (e.g., conventions, style, vocabulary) to communicate effectively with a variety of audiences and for different purposes.

Standard Number Five: Students employ a wide range of strategies as they write and use different writing process elements appropriately to communicate with different audiences for a variety of purposes.

Standard Number Six: Students apply knowledge of language structure, language conventions (e.g., spelling and punctuation), media techniques, figurative language, and genre to create, critique, and discuss print and nonprint texts.

Standard Number Seven: Students conduct research on issues and interests by generating ideas and questions, and by posing problems. They gather, evaluate, and synthesize data from a variety of sources (e.g., print and nonprint texts, artifacts, people) to communicate their discoveries in ways that suit their purpose and audience.

Standard Number Eight: Students use a variety of technological and information resources (e.g., libraries, databases, computer networks, video) to gather and synthesize information and to create and communicate knowledge.

Standard Number Nine: Students develop an understanding of and respect for diversity in language use, patterns, and dialects across cultures, ethnic groups, geographic regions, and social roles.

Standard Number Ten: Students whose first language is not English make use of their first language to develop competency in the English language arts and to develop understanding of content across the curriculum.

Standard Number Eleven: Students participate as knowledgeable, reflective, creative, and critical members of a variety of literacy communities.

Standard Number Twelve: Students use spoken, written, and visual language to accomplish their own purposes (e.g., for learning, enjoyment, persuasion, and the exchange of information). (Farstrup & Myers, 1996, p. 3)

Works Cited

Allington, R. L. (2001). *What really matters for struggling readers.* New York: Longman.

Applebee, A. N. (1990). *Literature instruction in American schools.* Report Series 1.4. Center for the Learning and Teaching of Literature. Albany, NY: State University of Albany and the U.S. Department of Education, Office of Educational Research and Improvement, and the National Endowment for the Arts.

Bambara, Toni Cade. (1997). Raymond's run. In *Choices in Literature: Myself, My World* (Silver). Upper Saddle River, NJ: Prentice Hall, pp. 52–60.

Bridgers S. E. (1987). *Permanent connections.* New York: Harper.

Canfield, J., Hansen, M., and Kirberger, K. (Eds.). *Chicken soup for the teenage soul.* New York: Health Communications.

Carroll, P. S. (2000). Going to the dogs: Dogs, owners, and loyal connections in books for adolescents. In J. Kaywell (Ed.). *Adolescent literature as a complement to the classics*, vol. IV. Norwood, MA: Christopher-Gordon, pp. 47–68.

Carroll, P. S., and Gregg, G. P. (2003). National survey of adolescent readers' interests and preferences. Unpublished research data.

Chamot, A. U., and O'Malley, J. M. (1994). *The CALLA handbook: Implementing the cognitive academic language learning approach.* Reading, MA: Addison Wesley Longman.

Cooney, C. B. (1990). *The face on the milk carton.* New York: Bantam Doubleday.

Cormier, R. (1974). *The chocolate war.* New York: Bantam.

Crutcher, C. (1987). *The crazy horse electric game.* New York: Greenwillow.

Curtis, C. P. (1995). *The Watsons go to Birmingham—1963.* New York: Dell.

Daniels, H. (2002). *Literature circles: Voice and choice in book clubs and reading groups.* York, ME: Stenhouse.

Daniels, H. (1994). *Literature circles: Voice and choice in the student-centered classroom*. York, ME: Stenhouse.

Dias, P. X. (1992). Literary reading and classroom constraints: Aligning practice with theory. In J. A. Langer (Ed.). *Literature instruction: A focus on student response*. Urbana, IL: NCTE, pp. 131–162.

Draper, S. (1994). *Tears of a tiger*, New York: Simon & Schuster.

Faulkner, W. (1972). *Light in August*. New York: Vintage. (Originally published by Random House, 1932.)

Giroux, H. (1997). *Channel surfing: Race talk and the destruction of today's youth*. New York: St. Martin's Press.

Goodrich, F., and Hackett, A. (1994). *The diary of Anne Frank* (dramatization). In *Literature and language*, Green level (8), pp. 495–568. Evanston, IL: McDougal, Littell.

Hamilton, V. (1968). *The house of Dies Drear*. New York: Scholastic.

Hinton, S. E. (1967). *The outsiders*. New York: Scholastic.

Hughes, L. (1997). Mother to son. In *Choices in literature*, Bronze. Upper Saddle River, NJ: Prentice Hall, pp. 95.

Hynds, S. (1992). Challenging questions in the teaching of literature. In J. A. Langer, (Ed.). *Literature instruction: A focus on student response*. Urbana, IL: National Council of Teachers of English, pp. 78–100.

Ivey, G., and Broaddus, K. (2001). Just plain reading: A survey of what makes students want to read in middle school classrooms. *Reading Research Quarterly 36*(4): 350–377.

Jordan, A. (2002). Personal conversation, Tallahassee, Florida, June 6, 2002.

King, T. (2002). Personal conversation, Tallahassee, Florida, June 6, 2002.

Klass, D. (1994). *California blue*. New York: Scholastic.

Langer, J. A. (1995). *Envisioning literature: Literary understanding and literature*. New York: Teachers College Press; and Newark, DE: International Reading Association.

Levine, G. C. (1997). *Ella enchanted*. New York: HarperTrophy.

Maruki, T. (1994). Hiroshima no pika. In *Literature and language*, Gold level. Evanston, IL: McDougal, Littell, pp. 396–399.

Naylor, P. R. (1991). *Shiloh*. New York: Aladdin.

Naylor, P. R. (1996). *Saving Shiloh*. New York: Aladdin.

Naylor, P. R. (1997). *Shiloh season*. New York: Aladdin.

Paulsen, G. (1987). *Hatchet*. New York: Simon & Schuster.

Peck, R. (1985). *Remembering the good times*. New York: Delacorte.

Powell, R. (2001). *Run if you dare*. New York: Farrar, Straus & Giroux.

Probst, R. (1992). Five kinds of literary knowing. In J. A. Langer (Ed.). *Literature instruction: A focus on student response*. Urbana, IL: NCTE, pp. 54–77.

Purves, A., Rogers, T., and Soter, A. O. (1995). *How porcupines make love*, *III*. White Plains, NY: Longman.

Ritter, J. H. (2000). *Over the wall*. New York: Philomel.

Rosenblatt, L. M. (1995). *Literature as exploration*, 5th ed. New York: Modern Language Association.

Rowling, J. K. (1998). *Harry Potter and the sorcerer's stone*. New York: Scholastic.

Smith, F. (1988). *Joining the literacy club: Further essays into literacy*. Portsmouth, NH: Heinemann.

Taylor, T. (1969/2002). *The cay*. New York: Yearling.

Wolff, V. E. (2001). *True believer*. New York: Atheneum.

5 Overflowing with Ideas: Writing as Students, Writing as People

Polishing writing.

The first thing that we all need to remind ourselves about written composition is this: Writing is always personal. This fact does not change, regardless of the writer's age, experience, topic, or purpose. When I write a note to ask my colleague if I can borrow one of her books, my writing is personal. When I jot a note to the UPS driver to ask that a package be left on my back porch, it is personal. When I send an email reply to a prospective student's inquiry about our English Education program, it is personal. The writing of this book is hugely personal because whatever we put down on paper or on our computer screen is part of our

thoughts, a part of who we are. We cannot separate the thoughts from the person who com-
poses them.

When working with adolescents, we must remember that every piece of student writing carries a part of the student with it. Even when time constraints and lackluster efforts
frustrate us, we should never treat a student's writing as if it is a lifeless artifact or a problem
that needs to be dissected. In much the same way that the act of speaking tells the listener
something about the speaker himself or herself, writing says something about the writer,
regardless of the subject or genre, the style or tone, that appears on the page.

The writing process movement in the last quarter of the twentieth century shifted the
paradigm for writing instruction from a focus on the final product to a focus on how writers
arrive at that product. Thanks to this movement, few of us who have taught adolescents
would consider the familiar scenario that follows to be an example of effective writing
instruction:

> The teacher walks into her classroom and announces: "OK, class, I have your descriptive
> essays to return to you at the end of the period today. Your next writing assignment is to
> compare and contrast two of the leading characters in "Flowers for Algernon" and *Of Mice
> and Men.* Your comparison/contrast essay is due Friday. You may begin now."

Where does this scenario miss the mark as writing instruction? It confuses making a
writing assignment with teaching writing. The teacher indicates nothing about a connection
between the descriptive essay writing and the new assignment. From the writers' perspectives, the pieces are totally independent entities. Worse, she gives no indication that she will
help the writers generate ideas, draft their ideas, revise their work, polish it, or prepare it as
a final product. Instead, she tells them to write. This is a subtle yet crucial point for us to
understand.

Writing Workshops and an Integrated
Literacy Pedagogy

In today's middle grades language arts classrooms, we are much more likely to find a version
of the writing workshop, often based on the format that Nancie Atwell has popularized in
In the Middle (1987, 1998), than the kind of assign-wait-collect-grade approach described
in the short scenario above. In contrast to writing instruction that is packaged in one-size-
fits-all wrappers, students in writing workshop classrooms have the freedom to find and use
strategies that work best for them. The kinds of differences between a traditional writing class
and a writing workshop class can be seen in an example that demonstrates how student writers choose to engage in prewriting, or "percolating" (p. 55).

In traditional writing instruction, a teacher might require that students turn in an outline of an essay as evidence that they have engaged in prewriting before they actually compose the essay. The teacher in that class has probably spent time teaching the rigid form of
a topic outline, and thus he expects each student to use the outline as a means of generating

ideas for the essay. (His expectation is problematic in itself, since those of us who write know that outlines are usually fairly ineffective as a means of generating ideas; more on page 142, in the section called, "Where Is Your Outline, Young Lady?")

In contrast to this one-size-fits-all-writers approach, the workshop model allows students freedom to choose and use prewriting methods that best suit them. Some might prefer to write a list of ideas related to a topic as a means of generating ideas for an assignment, while others prefer drawing diagrams such as webs or maps to generate ideas that are related to each other and to the paper topic. Still others might choose to sit quietly and let thoughts float through their minds, while one or two are likely to find that they generate ideas best when they are moving, and thus they will choose to engage in prewriting while they take a short walk around the school grounds. The writing workshop model allows students to explore all of these possibilities, often through ten-minute mini-lessons devoted to the introduction and practice of each. It also allows students to choose, from among the options, the methods that are most helpful for them. The point is that no one set of steps, no one formula works for all of us. One of our goals in the student-sensitive integrated literacy pedagogy is to help students find what works for them and to use what works for them—not because we want them to use one method instead of another, but because one method is more effective, for them, than another. With this goal in mind, we help students establish functional writing processes that they can carry with them from assignment to assignment, class to class, and which they can modify as needed, instead of insisting that they adhere to practices that actually interfere with their progress (Calkins, 1986).

Writing Workshop Format

The writing workshop model is consistent with the beliefs on which the student-sensitive integrated literacy pedagogy is grounded:

Belief One: Students are both individuals and members of many groups. In the writing workshop model, students move through composing processes at their own individual pace, spending as much or little time prewriting, drafting, and revising, for example, as they need, to prepare their written compositions. They also work as members of small groups and of the classroom group, collaborating as peer editors and responding as readers to classmates' writing.

Belief Two: Our specific students' interests and needs are of primary concern as we develop instructional goals and plans. In the writing workshop, students identify and develop their strengths as writers and work to improve their weaknesses. Their teacher and their peers assist them by providing input about the effectiveness of their writing.

Belief Three: We must draw on a broad definition of literacy. In the writing workshop, students are able to take advantage of multiple definitions of literacy as they fine-tune their skills as writers. For some, this aspect of the writing workshop will mean that they create or write about texts that are not commonly included in the middle school curriculum. For example, they might compose advertising copy for commercials about a new brand of skateboards, information about extracurricular activities that will be added to the school Web page, or a review of an area marching band competition. These assignments, along with the more traditional ones, such as writing expository essays, character sketches, poems, and so on, help students learn about expanded definitions of literacy. The assignments give students an opportunity to explore the relationship between audience, format, author's intention, and message as they consider what twenty-first-century literacy includes and requires.

Belief Four: We need to rely on professional standards, in addition to our own intuitions about and observations of our specific students, in order to set appropriate goals and plan appropriate activities. When we implement a writing workshop format, we must develop a set of logistic rules to hold student-writers accountable for progress, to ensure that students are developing skills beyond those that they had when they began our classes; we must be example, coach, and ultimately, in many cases, the judge of our student-writers' work. We benefit from other teachers' advice about how to juggle all of these responsibilities and from taking time to reflect on what our students—as individuals and as members of the class group—need most and how we can provide that for them.

Developing Writing Instruction

In thinking through specifics regarding what teachers need to know to teach middle school students to become writers, I have reflected on the aspects of writing instruction that caused difficulty for the middle school students whom I taught and the questions that I faced as their teacher. For students, the aspects of writing instruction that were most troublesome boiled down to two. One problem was the classroom setting itself. All writers have different needs regarding noise, temperature, seating, procedures, and so on. For some, the classroom itself was not conducive to writing. The other problem involved learning to use the writing process as a mode of thinking about personal, academic, and social issues. A related problem rests within the writing-as-thinking issue: Some students were preoccupied with correctness at all stages of their writing; they had learned to proceed as safe writers, to equate good with error free; their efforts to avoid mistakes often resulted in flavorless and voiceless writing.

My two big questions were these: First, "How can I organize writing instruction in such a way that students understand that writing is a tool not only for academic uses, but for personal and social purposes, too?" And second, "How can I match my instructional goals with fair, useful evaluation of students' growth as writers and their literacy growth in general?" Addressing these difficulties and questions provides the framework for this chapter. Specifically, we consider the look, feel, and focus of a middle school classroom with an eye toward creating a writing workhop environment for writing (one in which grammar, usage, and mechanics are integrated into writing instruction). The section is followed by one in which we consider the different phases of the writing process—prewriting, drafting, revising, polishing, and publishing—individually (although we know that they occur recursively, not one at a time), with ideas for helping students get involved in each phase. Next, we examine the literacy teacher's tasks in regard to writing assignments, assessments, and evaluations. In this section, I introduce a framework that presents writing instruction from three perspectives: personal goals, social goals, and academic goals. By using these perspectives, we can keep the needs and interests of our young adolescent students in mind as we make decisions about writing instruction. Assessment and evaluation are presented with ideas about the differences between assessing writing and using writing to assess learning of content, as well as various strategies for evaluating students' writing, including portfolios and rubrics. This section ends with a look at related issues, "When a Test Requires Writing" and "When Students' Writing Is What Is Tested." The chapter concludes with a description of the "A Picture Is Worth a Thousand Words" project in which sixth graders became nature photographers and writers. Some of the sixth grade students' own words are included. The chapter closes with a summary of the ways that the ideas of the chapter support an integrated literacy curriculum, suggestions that are especially helpful for teachers of English language learners, and a list of the NCTE/IRA standards that are addressed in the chapter.

Establishing a Writerly Environment: The Look, Feel, and Focus of the Classroom

A group of preservice teachers generated the following list when I asked them to identify the personal necessities they need to write a letter, a paper for class, or any other piece that would require more than a couple of minutes of concentration:

> complete silence
> white noise
> instrumental music
> a favorite CD playing
> a television on in the same room
> a room that is cool but not cold
> a lamp instead of an overhead light
> subdued lighting
> windows and a lot of sunlight
> total isolation from friends and family
> a clean room
> clutter
> at least six pens on the desk
> yellow legal pad
> a PC and a keyboard that clicks a lot
> time to think and doodle
> food to munch on
> something to drink
> an idea about what I am going to say, start to finish
> a cat nearby
> a place to sit in the middle of the bed or on the floor
> a desk that has nothing on it but paper
> a (close) deadline

We laughed about the conflicts within our class set of requirements (from complete silence to the noise of a television, a clean house to clutter, pencils to keyboards). Then I asked them to review our list and scratch through any item that is not usually provided for adolescents in the classroom. The significantly reduced list that remained looked like this:

> yellow legal pad
> a desk with that nothing on it but paper
> a (close) deadline

We talked about what the winnowed-down list suggests about how we treat students when we want them to be writers, and about the amount of control over their environment that students-as-writers are able to exert. Our conclusion was that we tend to treat students who write as students, not as people who write. We concluded, too, that our real goal is to help young adolescents think of themselves as people who write instead of embodying the more restrictive definition: students who write. We began then to seek ways to give middle school students some control over the classroom environment so that they could find out what they require to do their best prewriting, drafting, revising, polishing, and publishing.

We have to be realistic here. First, we must recognize that even the most devoted teacher can do little to control the noise outside of his classroom (sounds from the air handler, the lawn mower, the intercom system, and other loud noises seem to conspire to add an undertone of noise in school buildings). Next, we must realize that since our student writers' personal necessity lists are as varied as their lists of favorite snack foods, we will not be able to provide every student with his or her necessities at all times during in-school writing assignments. However, there are ways that we can build choice and flexibility into our classrooms. Following are a few areas on which you and your students might expand.

The Look

Writing All Around.   Students usually enjoy seeing their own writing and that of their classmates on display in the classroom. In addition to posting final, formal, graded papers, display other student writing, too. Perhaps some of your students like to write poems and songs; if so, encourage them to post their work on a Creative Genius bulletin board. Reserve a Read all about It section on a wall or bulletin board so that students can post written schoolwork that they want to show their classmates, whether the work was written for language arts or for another subject. One teacher responded to a student suggestion that she allow them to use one white board as a Message Swap board; on it, students wrote notes to their friends who would be coming into the classroom during a different class period; typical messages ranged from reminders of band practice after school to requests for help with algebra homework. The only rules for that board were that the messages had to be positive and could never be demeaning to anyone, and that if anyone wrote obscenities, the board would be closed for business. For an entire school year, seventh grade students lived up to their teacher's expectation that they would treat the board and each other with respect. This activity could easily be modified to take advantage of electronic means for communication, such as a class listserve or Web message board exchange.

I have always enjoyed preparing a set of posters on which I display writers' quotes about writing. In recent years, I have relied most heavily on quotes by authors of books for adolescents. It is a good way to introduce students to these authors' names. Figure 5.1 provides quotes that address the question, "How do you go about doing your writing?" I hope you can use these quotes as a starter set for your own collection (each is from an interview or article published in an issue of *The ALAN Review*, NCTE's journal on adolescent/young adult literature).

FIGURE 5.1 Writers for Adolescents on Writing

I open a secret place in myself, a room sensitive to everything I see or hear or think about. The room has a screen door which filters a little. Big blocks of misspent days can't get through but light can and does, music can, poetry can, the expression of a friend's eyes, a phrase of speech, an anecdote can. Gradually this room fills up, the furnishings of a life haphazardly crammed into the corners and against the walls. One day I approach my word processor. There is a yearning that pushes me to that familiar place, a room uniquely mine where I am surrounded by sayings and books and photographs. I wish I could describe what happens there. The only words I have are "discovery" and "revelation" and they fail miserably to define a creative act, a moment secretly longed for and worked for, that suddenly bursts open with tremendous energy. You are suddenly courageous and hopeful but there is fear in it, too, and the risk of failure. You know you are paddling a canoe against an ocean tide; and yet, on the swells, you are visionary and honorable and heady with creation. So you write.

Sue Ellen Bridgers (Fall 1995, pp. 3–4)

Through language we can tell the truth, and hear the truth spoken, just as we can be deceived. Sometimes it's a painful realization: we can be lied to. As I write I think of myself as putting my eye under oath, so that what I write is the truth about my characters. . . . The details are what matter—they are the experience.

Michael Cadnum (Winter 1999, p. 6)

If I had to characterize the core of my writing process, I'd describe it as making connections . . . Connecting small graphic symbols into groupings which carry meaning . . . Connecting words into ordered strings which hopefully compound the meaning . . . Connecting sentences until the constructs of language are as laden with meaning as I can make them—ideas, events, symbols, all connected to character—the whole hopefully forming a conduit for human meaning, leading to a reader, the final connection.

Anne C. LeMieux (Winter 2000, p. 11)

I have to trick myself into writing a novel—and the trick is to convince myself that I'm not actually writing one. . . . When I'm at the typewriter (or driving the car or waiting in a supermarket line) and all the time thinking of characters, I am conscious of letting them come and go, allowing them to do all sorts of things. Some have staying power, others drift off. Some are not anticipated but arrive and stay around. . . . I don't think of them as characters in a structured novel I am writing but simply as people I'm watching grow and change. I don't sit and tell myself that I must write five or ten pages by noontime. I go to the typewriter to find out, say, what is going to happen today. . . . finding out is the peculiar joy I encounter when I'm writing, although that same finding out sometimes leads me astray and costs me countless pages that are eventually discarded.

Robert Cormier (Winter 1980, p. 31)

(continues)

FIGURE 5.1   Continued

With each of my novels, I've begun from a single image. Long before I start scratching around for a story, there's that image so full of promise and so laden with emotion.

Will Hobbs (Fall 1994, p. 5)

The only way to learn to write—or really to finish a written work—is to write consistently, and that means writing when you don't feel like it. At eight in the morning . . . I am not in the mood to write. I would rather do anything else. By nine every morning I feel sorry for people who do anything else for a living.

Dean Hughes (Spring 1983, pp. 10–11)

My journal is my "safe," the place where I can protect and save the tender shoots of new ideas, the broken pieces of my life, the sometimes awesome heights of my spirit. On the other hand, I truly dislike writing in my journals and notebooks. I don't like the effort of it, the loss of time grudgingly devoted to it, the feelings of "why am I doing this? I'll never read it again," the self-consciousness of assuming I have anything important to record. . . . I'd rather be working on a novel, an article, a short story; I'd rather be reading or running or boating or fishing or renting a video, for cripes sake. But somehow I know there is gold dust in the air. Sometimes I breathe this dust, and ideas form. Ping, ping. Little gifts popping in my mind, my spirit. . . . a journal, a notebook , is simply a personal safe with a combination lock on it. And writing in it is my way of capturing the single most important gift a writer has: notes on how it FEELS to be human.

Graham Salisbury (Winter 1999, pp. 22 and 24)

There is a point in writing when I feel as if I have reached the crest of a hill. The journey's end may still lie a long distance away, but it is now all downhill. As part of that momentum, it almost seems as if the characters have a life of their own and begin telling me what they would do.

Laurence Yep (Spring 1992, p. 8)

I became a novelist, and novelists are chronic collectors of Scenes from Life. . . . To fuel our fiction we poke through our earlier experiences and observations like so many wastebaskets, looking for words, foraging for phrases.

Richard Peck (Spring 1997, p. 3)

Where do I get my ideas? The same place you do. Seriously. I'm convinced that everyone has tons of ideas each day. They pop up unbidden in the mind like targets in some sort of cerebral police firing range. They rarely shout for attention. The trick is learning to notice them.

David Lubar (Spring 1999, p. 6)

(All citations are from issues of *The ALAN Review*, NCTE's journal on adolescent/young adult literature, and are cited in an article that I wrote for *English Journal*, " 'Learning to Notice,' and Other Broad Thrills," January 2001).

Arranging and Organizing Space.   The posters, along with displayed student writing, can help establish a tone that announces, "This is a classroom where writers write." The organization of desks, tables, and other work spaces, as well as a system for keeping track of in-process papers and supplies, will also contribute to the feel of the classroom as a writer's place. Middle school students usually enjoy sitting together at tables and with their desks facing each other in small groups as they prewrite, revise, and polish a piece of writing. It is at these stages that students, as writers, benefit from easy access to their classmates' readings of and reactions to their work. However, when they are drafting a piece of writing, students benefit from sitting alone, undisturbed. In order to accommodate this need for two kinds of writing spaces, I suggest that you arrange the classroom into at least three areas: a draft zone with several desks in rows or a semicircle to accommodate writers who are in stages that require them to work independently, a brain cluster area with a large table or desks facing each other (depending on what is available in your school) that allows students to solicit input from classmates about their writing and publication plans, and a small one-on-one corner that serves as the place that the student meets with the teacher for planned or impromptu writing chats. This corner is essential. It can be the same location that the teacher moves to in order to conduct individual reading assessments (see Chapter 3) and participate in directed individualized reading (DIR) book talks (see Chapter 4). Students should feel free to approach you and request that you come with them to The Corner when they need your advice, and you can invite a student to join you there when you notice he or she is stuck or needs encouragement to keep moving with his or her writing.

The Comfort Zone.   Writers need to feel comfortable in their space in order to do their best job. Help your students define and articulate what *comfortable* means to them, in the physical sense of the term, and try to find ways to accommodate them. It may mean bringing in some sets of headphones for those who need quiet when they compose; it may mean adding an old couch or bean bags to a corner of the room for those who prefer to write while seated somewhere besides in a student desk. For some, it could require decorating the classroom with a few small lamps or live plants; for others, it may mean adding quiet background music, at least during some writing assignments. When we take time to ask students what they need in order to do their best writing, then respond to their answers, we treat them with respect as writers.

The Feel

The notion that inexperienced writers need to be able to take risks to develop their skills and talent has become cliché for a reason: It is true. Students need to be able to set their guardedness aside when they are learning to write. They need to feel free to experiment with words, emotions, styles, topics, directions, formats, and perspectives to find out where their strengths lie as writers.

Our job as student-sensitive teachers is twofold in this respect: on one hand, we need to recognize that some of our students will be reluctant to move beyond their comfort zone when we ask them to write in ways that they have never before tried. On the other hand, we must accept our responsibility to introduce our students to as many different forms, topics, styles, choices as possible, and to have them tinker, as writers, with all of the possibilities.

We cannot allow a student to settle into a singular comfort zone and build it around herself like a cocoon—to choose to write only five-paragraph expository essays when asked to respond to literature, for example. We are obligated to help them explore options and then support them as they hone their talents in one or more choice categories.

A specific example emerges from the "A Picture Is Worth a Thousand Words" project that is offered as a sample of writing instruction at the end of this chapter. Sixth grader Wally (a pseudonym) had never composed a poem at all, he claimed, and certainly had not written one on wildlife. A reluctant writer, he was easily able to convince himself that he "can't write nature poems." Wally carried his attitude and expectation with him into the wildlife photography and writing project, hoping that his teacher, Ms. Graham, would let him write a report on the topic he had chosen for this assignment: alligators. After all, he had shown some competence when writing a report on bats earlier in the year. But Ms. Graham insisted that he try to compose a poem. She showed him a few models and even suggested that he might try a concrete poem, in which descriptive words are arranged in the shape of his subject, an alligator (see Milner & Milner, 1999, p. 153). Nudged slightly beyond his comfort zone, but with the knowledge that he had authority over his topic, Wally ultimately turned in this poem:

> *Powerfully pushing itself through the water,*
> *The alligator stalks, unafraid.*
> *Its body is surrounded by clear, cold water.*
> *Its legs are hidden by green lily pads;*
> *Its body is sprinkled with green scales.*
> *Hungry, strong, and fearless,*
> *Its swift body glides to the surface*
> *And it eats a turtle.*
> *This outburst disturbs the peaceful elegance*
> *Of the river.*

Along with the poem, Wally now has a new addition to his self-definition: nature photographer and poet. While we must be especially sensitive to students' attitudes toward writing, since writing is always personal, we cannot allow that sensitivity to protect them from trying to improve their skills and increase their talents.

Giving Students Choices.   Where can we allow choices so that students can determine when and how they will take risks as writers in our classroom? A group of preservice teachers recently suggested the following areas to accommodate student choice:

Writing Form (or Genre) and Length: Allow students to choose whether or not they will use an essay, poem, story, or letter form when they respond to a work of literature, for example, and the length of their response, on occasion.

Writing Topic or Theme: Often our goal in writing instruction is to have students practice a form or style to develop a particular kind of skill. In these cases, we should strive to give students choices regarding the topics and themes that they will use. The activity that some experts refer to as *copy change* is an example of how students benefit from a blend of structure and freedom: In this activity, students take an existing text and rewrite it, using their own topic or theme but following the syntax of the published version word for word. For example, in the lyrical and compelling short adolescent novel, *The Tiger Rising* (2001), Kate DiCamillo, author of Newbery Honor Book *Because of Winn Dixie* (2000), writes this passage:

> His father read the note from the principal slowly, putting his big finger under the words as if they were bugs he was trying to keep still. When he was finally done, he laid the letter on the table and rubbed his eyes with his fingers and sighed. The rain beat a sad rhythm on the roof of the motel. (DiCamillo, 2001, p. 26)

If my goal is to emphasize the power of figurative language, I ask students to point out the simile and the personification in the passage, to copy and change the author's words, and to underline their own examples of simile and personification. A copy-change version might look like this:

> Her sister unwrapped the surprise from her boyfriend proudly, keeping her blue eyes on the box <u>as if it were bubbles</u> she did not want to burst. When she had completely finished, she set the box on the dresser and wiped her eyes with her palms and smiled. The <u>moon danced a little jig</u> in the corner of the room.

Since the object of this activity is to teach students syntactic dexterity, it is an ideal place to allow students to choose their own topics or themes.

Where Writing Will Be Done: Be flexible so that students have opportunities to experiment with writing in locations outside of the classroom. I recommend that you use some creative writing assignments as vehicles for having students identify writing sites for themselves. For example, arrange for a write site walkabout, in which students leave the classroom and go another location as a class (I have found the media center, school computer lab, and an outside lunch area to be good choices). Once they are at the location, students list everything they see, hear, feel, and smell there, in columns. When they return to the room, class members work alone or in small groups to compose descriptions of the location, using their senses chart, and they close their description with an explanation of why they would or would not return to that location as a write site in the future.

Deadlines: Give students options, on at least some assignments, with the due dates for preliminary and final drafts. Remember that some middle school students like to write at a leisurely pace and take advantage of the opportunity to write outside of class and that others will need help learning to manage their time to take advantage of an extended deadline. Another deadline-related concession is to allow students input in determining what happens when someone fails to turn in a draft or final paper on the due date.

How Responses Are Given: Give students choices regarding how they will solicit and deliver input about writing assignments. These are some response instructions that you can share with middle school students: (1) Write a short letter to the writer after you have read her work, telling her what you liked, what left you cold or confused, and what you would do if it were your paper and you were interested in making it even better. (2) List five to six of the words that stood out most in the writer's work (they might be key terms, or they may have merely caught your attention because of the way they were used, your lack of familiarity with them, and so on), and comment on at least three of them. This shows the writer exactly which words you are tuning in to as a reader of his work. (3) Use a reader-response form to comment on your classmate's writing (see Figure 5.2). (4) Read your classmate's work aloud and make comments into a tape recorder as you read. Give the tape to your classmate. Let her listen, and then switch roles with her.

This list of choice categories is by no means exhaustive; there are many other areas in which student choice can be incorporated into the student-sensitive integrated literacy

---

FIGURE 5.2   Peer Reader Response Form

Author and title of the written work: **Your name:**

A note to the reader before you respond:

As a reader, you might come across words or phrases or sentences that you think are outstanding—they might make you laugh out loud or bring tears to your eyes. They might also help you understand a point because they are so clear and precise. The writer will need to know about the kinds of effects his or her writing is having on you, the reader. Here are some of the words that our class has identified as helpful in making positive comments about our classmates' writing (copy some words and phrases from the class-generated list here):

You might also come across words, phrases, or sentences that you just can't understand, even after you try a few times. When you do, the writer needs to know about those spots, too. If something gets in your way of understanding the writer's words, then he or she will want to work on that spot to make the writing clearer for you—and for other readers. Here are some of the words that our class has identified as helpful in making suggestions for improvements in classmates' writing (copy some words and phrases from the class-generated list here):

Remember that by participating as a peer reader, you promise to give your classmate the best helpful advice and comments that you can.

Peer Response Form

1. These words and phrases really stood out for me when I read this piece of writing:
2. You did a really good job of
3. One word in your writing that best sums up what I think the whole piece is about is
4. I was confused when I read this part:
5. Are there other words that you could use here?
6. Here is what I would do if I wanted to try to make this piece of writing even better:
7. When I finished reading this, I felt like
8. If you turned this piece in just like it is, I think you'd get a grade of ___ because

curriculum when writing is the focus. I encourage you to start with this list and to ask your middle school students what needs to be added to it.

The Focus

Many of us attended schools in which composition instruction was synonymous with traditional school grammar instruction. In those years, grammar instruction consisted of three areas of emphasis: grammar lessons (identifying parts of speech and parts of the sentence), usage instruction (learning rules that keep correct and incorrect utterances and written passages separate and that demonstrate control over issues such as subject–verb agreement and clear pronoun–antecedent references), and mechanics (surface features such as punctuation, capitalization, and spelling). The emphasis on these elements of language was a visible part of the institutional upholstery that lay over concerns with students' ability to express their ideas in writing. For those of us who taught in the period that preceded the process movement, students' writings were artifacts. We plopped their paragraphs, essays, and poems down on classroom tables and dissected them, word by word or sentence by sentence. Of course, before we could dissect students' writing, we had to kill it. My own experience as a student includes the lovable and curmudgeonly Mr. Pearson, who insisted on grading an essay with an F if it contained a single tiny error, and who warned that we would not do well in life if we were unable to demonstrate the proper use of troublesome word pairs such as *continual* and *continuous*, *shall* and *will*, *compliment* and *complement*.

Others of us attended schools in which teachers had decided to put traditional school grammar instruction on hold while professional linguists debated structural and transformational models of grammar, and textbook publishers joined in the debates. Instead of diagramming sentences, the students in these classes may have created picture collages to complement (thank you, Mr. Pearson) their free verse poetry. Regardless of our background in grammar instruction, we must acknowledge that we will be expected, by a large segment of the population, to teach grammar. I am convinced that the most reasonable solution to keeping our focus on helping students develop their skills and strengths as writers, even when addressing the expectation that we will teach grammar, is to integrate grammar, usage, and mechanics instruction into our writing lessons.

I have to admit that there were some benefits to teaching writing with an emphasis on traditional school grammar for beginning teachers. When I first taught eighth grade, I took comfort in knowing that I could fill fifty minutes of class time with grammar exercises. This sense of comfort was especially rewarding whenever the mere thought of asking students to generate their own writing, to read and respond to literature, or to practice their oral language skills was too much for me. Teaching students to identify proper nouns or to underline the subject once and the predicate twice was clean and safe. Those kinds of lessons brought occasional order to my usually chaotic classroom.

The problem, of course, was that the only benefit that came from teaching composition with an emphasis on traditional school grammar was an occasional increase in my own comfort level and sense of classroom control. Students did not learn to connect the grammar exercises from the Warriner's *English Grammar and Composition* books to their needs as writers of English. The grammar lessons that I taught did not create in students an enthusiasm for the miracles of humans' innate ability to use language, for its quirks, its power, its promise. If anything, the time we spent in traditional grammar study, in those preprocess movement days, caused my students to push away—or sometimes run away—from trying to improve their use of written language.

Finally, after I learned how to manage a class without loading them down (in order to keep them quiet) with useless parts of speech worksheets or endless sentence part identification handouts, I began to reflect on my goals for grammar instruction. And finally I began to wonder if it were possible to integrate grammar instruction into the teaching and learning of composition.

What Is Grammar?

As Constance Weaver points out in *Teaching Grammar in Context* (1996), the definitions that are incorporated into middle and high school textbooks typically treat grammar one of two ways: as either a description of the parts of speech and parts of a sentence, to show "how different kinds of words in a language combine into grammatical structures, or syntax" (p. 1), or as a list of "prescriptions or rules for using language" that includes attention to correct punctuation, subject–verb agreement, and educated style (p. 2).

But few of us are satisfied with these definitions, because neither time spent teaching descriptions nor lessons devoted to the prescriptions translate directly into improvements in our students' writing. What we need is a more useful definition of *grammar*, and we can turn to psycholinguistics for just that. From psycholinguists, we learn that *grammar* actually refers to the internal structure of a language. We learn, too, that we all have an understanding of the internal structure of the grammar of our language. If you aren't sure I am right, try this simple experiment:

Read the following sentence and answer the questions that follow it:

Kli woggle nurt dev quirly glim.

What is the subject of the sentence? (Did you answer *woggle*?)

What did the subject do? (I bet you chose *nurt*.)

What word describes *glim*? (You selected *quirly*, didn't you?)

As speakers of English, none of the words in this sentence is familiar to us. Nevertheless, because we know our grammar, we know that *woggle* is the subject, since it is in the subject slot, that *nurt* is in the verb slot, and that *quirly* modifies *glim*. Still not convinced? Here is another simple experiment:

Read this sentence and try to make sense of it:

Of soda drank can one he.

We know all of the words here, but do not recognize the sentence as an English construction. No one who speaks English as a native speaker would produce that arrangement of words and expect it to be read or heard as a sentence. Even if we do not know how to describe the distorted syntactical order, we know it is wrong. However, we also know that if we rearrange the words, it becomes a sentence that we would be likely to generate: "He drank one can of soda." Again, this experiment demonstrates that we have a sense of English grammar not because we are taught it directly but because we are speakers of it.

When we define *grammar* as "the internal structure of a language," we use a definition that enables us to play with language, to marvel with our students at its acrobatic capabilities. When we view grammar as the internal structure that allows us to make sense of strings of words, we can experiment with conventions and expectations, with new ways of using words and structures; we can investigate social and political realities regarding why some forms of language—and thus some language users—are privileged, while others are not. With this kind of focus, grammar instruction can inform and enrich our composition lessons and our languaging.

My recommendation is that we work toward a compromise in definitions that will allow us to combine grammar and composition lessons with instruction in usage and the mechanics of our language. The goal associated with this recommendation is to help students tune in to their existing knowledge of how grammar works and to develop their sense of how to use language more effectively for their purposes as writers. We need to recognize, and help students understand, that their written language can be modified for different purposes and contexts, and that what is construed as appropriate and correct for some contexts will be read as incorrect or bad English in others. (We will also consider this issue in the section "The Language of Power: Dialects in Spoken Language," in Chapter 6.)

To create a blend of grammar usage and mechanics instruction, I suggest a framework for ongoing integrated instruction that has five parts. My suggestions are influenced by the work of Constance Weaver, who advocates integrating grammar lessons into writing instruction, and of Rei R. Noguchi, as proposed in *Grammar and the Teaching of Writing: Limits and Possibilities* (1991). Noguchi's less-is-more approach for teaching grammar and usage is based on two principles. One is that instruction should focus on a common problem: students' lack of understanding about what makes a complete and finished sentence, because it is that problem that generates a host of errors, such as fragments and run-on sentences. The second is that instruction should focus on the problems that meet the dual criteria of occurring frequently and of being status markers. Status marking errors are the ones that carry social consequences. Lack of subject–verb agreement and the use of nonstandard verb forms like "clumb" instead of "climbed," for example, are perceived by listeners or readers as an indication that the speaker/writer is not well educated. This perspective allows us to move smoothly into the sociopolitically charged subject of language privilege and dialects. But first, let's explore some ideas about grammar and mechanics instruction for the middle school curriculum from this two-pronged perspective: Sentence Sense and Sentence Savvy.

Sentence Sense

One way to integrate grammar usage and mechanics instruction into the broader context of languaging during composition instruction is to begin with a focus on sentence sense. Students should first learn to identify complete sentences and to identify capitalization and punctuation that signal beginnings and ends. Literary texts can be used as resource material here, but note, too, that in order to have conversations about sentences, students will need to understand the concepts of subjects and verbs. Your ability to communicate with students will be enhanced if your students understand the terms that refer to sentence structures, such as subject, predicate, dependent clause, and independent clause.

After they have learned about these essential parts, ask students to review a set of word groups that you prepare for this purpose, in order to identify those that break rules for proper sentence structure. Ask them to explain how the word group deviates from the conventional rules and the effect of that deviation. Your prepared collection should include an abundance of fragments (word groups that are missing a subject or verb and thus are not yet sentences). It should also include run-ons (word groups in which one complete and finished sentence—or independent clause—is joined to another complete sentence, with no punctuation between them). Writing by middle school students is often replete with these problems; thus, your students' papers might be useful resources for this focus.

Once students can distinguish between complete and finished sentences and other word groups, have them turn to samples of their own writing and identify and then repair fragments and run-ons where they find them. As a metacognitive extension of this activity, ask students to discuss their tendencies as writers by answering this question: "What does your writing show you about your 'sentence sense'?" See Figure 5.3 for more ideas regarding grammar and usage topics that can be integrated into writing and literature instruction for middle school students.

Sentence Savvy

In order to move from a focus on problems to attention to pizzazz, start with a focus on clarity of expression. Students sometimes mistakenly equate loquaciousness with effectiveness, sesquipedality with eloquence. (Did you notice how awkward that sentence seems?) Help student writers gain control of their writing through a continuing focus on clarity. Show them examples from newspapers and fiction that highlight the value of using the right word in the right place and the barriers created by excessive ornamentation, even when it is used in a controlled way by a professional writer.

Clarity

One simple speaking/writing activity that will help students practice clarity is to have them work in pairs to dictate opinion statements, stories, requests, and so on to each other. The writer's partner reads aloud the dictated language. He notes any words, phrases, or constructions that are unclear or distracting for him and either eliminates or rewords those. The speaker/writer then takes the written copy and crosses out or rewrites any remaining portions that she realizes could interfere with her ability to get her point across. This activity can be repeated, with modifications, after students have learned to use more sophisticated structures, such as subordinate clauses. It can also be modified during literature study as a way to closely examine how published authors construct their sentences.

FIGURE 5.3   Teaching Sentence Sense

noun (proper and common)
pronoun
verb (action and being)
adjective
adverb
preposition
conjunction

phrase
clause (independent and dependent)

sentence structure
subject
predicate
direct object
subject complement
sentence fragment
run-on (or fused) sentence
subject–verb agreement

standard English verb forms for regular and irregular verbs
verb tense for regular and irregular verbs

period
question mark
exclamation point
comma
semicolon
quotation mark
apostrophe

For a step-by-step description of how you might organize grammar and usage instruction in your middle school classroom, I recommend that you read Melissa J. Engel's contribution to the "Middle Talk" column, edited by Elizabeth Close and Katherine Ramsey, in the March 2001 issue of *English Journal*. Engel's essay is an extended answer to a student's inquiry, "What will labeling the parts of speech ever do for me?"

Syntax

Once they can express themselves clearly as speakers and writers, students will enjoy becoming syntactic acrobats. We can teach them, through professional examples and by scanning their own writing, about the effectiveness of changing their sentence length and inverting sentences when they want to add emphasis. We can show them what pretentious language is and help them learn to avoid it through an emphasis on clarity of expression. We can play with dangling and misplaced modifiers by presenting sentences such as "Walking down the street, the clock rang three," and Michael Pierce's headline, "Two Sisters Reunite After 18 Years in Checkout Lane" (see Chapter 6, "Warming Up with Word Play"), to explore the kind of impact that placement of phrases can have on meaning in their speaking and writing. Grammar and usage instruction is most meaningful when it is integrated into instruction that draws on students' actual speaking and writing as a resource.

Grammar and Language

Many teachers will find that the most convenient time to introduce lessons the on intricacies of the parts of speech, such as pronoun–antecedent agreement and comparative and superlative adjective forms, is within the context of teaching sentence savvy. The assumption that drives this practice is that, while students are involved with careful study of their own speaking and writing, they are receptive to lessons that help them discuss their work accurately and efficiently. Peer response groups can be more productive and efficient, for example, when language about language is used and understood: It is easier for a group member to suggest that her peer add "powerful verbs" to improve a story than to recommend, "more of the kinds of words that show action in a strong way." And yet those group members might profit more from examples than from labels. The responder might recommend the following: "I'd say something like 'The troop crashed its way through the thick woods,' instead of the milder version that you used, 'The troop walked through the thick woods' so that readers can see that it was not easy going for the troop."

Goals

Another concern that we, as teachers, must reconcile before we plan instruction revolves around how much instructional time we should be willing to devote to traditional grammar instruction. Does the student who generally understands nouns and pronouns need to know definitions for each of the following types, in order to improve his writing: proper noun/common noun; noncount noun/abstract noun; indefinite pronoun/personal pronoun; intensive pronoun/reflexive pronoun; interrogative pronouns/demonstrative pronouns, for example? While I believe that time spent teaching the vocabulary of grammar is valuable for most students, we need to remember that teaching students to use words associated with grammar is a means to more efficient communication about language use. It is not the goal itself. Helping students use language to make sense of their world is our overriding literacy goal. See Figure 5.4 for more ideas regarding grammar and usage topics that can be integrated into writing and literature instruction for middle school students.

In all of these examples, the focus of writing instruction remains on helping students use written language to express themselves clearly, appropriately, powerfully. Even when we incorporate grammar, usage, and mechanics instruction into the teaching of writing, we must remember that those lessons are a means to an end, not the end itself. The real focus, as demonstrated in the sections that follow, should remain on helping students become writers.

FIGURE 5.4   Teaching Sentence Savvy

coordination
subordination
parallelism
misplaced and dangling modifiers
shifts in tense
pronoun case
comparative and superlative adjective forms
pronoun–antecedent agreement
pronoun reference

shifts in point of view
active and passive constructions

vocabulary and the right word choice*
idioms
clichés
slang and jargon
pretentious language, doublespeak, inflated phrases
figurative language
spelling
use of troublesome word pairs (for example: who/whom, lie/lay, will/shall,
   compliment/complement, affect/effect)
adding emphasis through a combination of short and long sentences, sentence endings, inverted
   sentences, and punctuation

dash
hyphen
parentheses
ellipsis
abbreviations
writing numerals

*Please note: Vocabulary instruction is a topic that deserves a great deal of attention in and of itself, and I regret that I am not able to address it here. However, I can recommend two books that do give vocabulary instruction its due: Judith Rowe Michael's lively and intriguing *Dancing with Words: Helping Students Love Language through Authentic Vocabulary Instruction* (NCTE, 2001), and Camille Blachowicz and Peter J. Fisher's interdisciplinary focused *Teaching Vocabulary in All Classrooms*, 2nd edition (Merrill Prentice Hall, 2002).

The Writing Process

In discussing the major challenges she faces when teaching writing, veteran teacher Althoria Taylor speaks about a particular issue: "When students are no longer afraid to put down ideas on paper, I want to make sure they have the 'staying power' to complete their writing. Many times, students do just enough to complete the assignment; I always find myself asking them for more." In order to teach students to use various writing processes to their advantage, we need to convince them that writers follow a path that looks more like a bowl of spaghetti than a straight line, that their tendency to think in spontaneous bursts can aid them as they generate and play with ideas. At the same time, we need to help them learn that their overflow of ideas and energy must be kept in check when their goal is to communicate through writing. We need to show them that they can, as writers, take two steps forward, one step back, one sideways, and two on their hands, if that is what is required in order to get their ideas onto paper, and then how to refine and polish them.

The writing process model that I prefer, because it emphasizes how momentum builds as the writer works, includes five parts: prewriting, drafting, revising, polishing, and publishing. This model of writing is particularly compatible within a workshop setting like the one that Nancie Atwell recommends (1987, 1998) and that we have considered. Some students will spend the majority of their writing time in the prewriting stage, trying to generate ideas from which they will choose and delete as they draft. Others will prewrite and draft hastily in order to spend time with re-visioning and revising their work. Still others will rush the entire process in an effort to publish before their classmates are finished drafting. Although the stages of the process often overlap, and with the exception of publishing are virtually inseparable, we benefit from looking at the five stages separately in order to understand the interplay between them.

Prewriting

This is the stage during which ideas are generated. I have found that talk is the finest vehicle for prewriting; students enjoy brainstorming as a class and watching their ideas fill a chalk- or white board, or the overhead projector sheet, or the computer screen. Other practical strategies for prewriting include listing and paired listing, looping, and creating cluster diagrams. Some of you might choose to think of this stage using the term *percolating*, which writing specialist Tom Romano prefers. Romano borrowed the term from teachers and theorists John Mayher, Nancy Lester, and Gordon Pradl (1983). He then expanded it to denote all the thinking about a writing assignment that occurs before the writing of the piece actually begins. This period of thinking might include "brainstorming and mapping activities that generate ideas and information, the drawing of diagrams or pictures, the jotting of notes, impressions, or trial lines—in short, anything done in relation to the piece of writing aside from producing a draft or revising one" (Romano, 1987, p. 56). He likes *percolating* more than *prewriting*, since be believes that *prewriting* refers only to activities that "take place only before the first draft is begun" (p. 55). *Percolating*, by contrast, "occurs during the entire writing process," whenever writers talk about their ideas, sit back and reflect on their drafts, reread their words, walk away from the desk and let ideas settle, and so on (p. 55). Because *prewriting* is the more familiar and common term, however, I choose to use it here but with the understanding that we can prewrite even in the middle of the composing process, since it is the kind of thinking that we use to generate more ideas.

Listing and Pair-Listing. *Listing*, when used as a prewriting activity, merely involves first having students list all the terms that they associate with a particular topic. As they write, ask them to skip two or three lines between main items so that they will have space to add supporting items under the main ideas. For example, if I want to begin an essay about the pets I have treasured, I could start with a list that looks like this:

- Bunky
  Found on roadside
  Black and tan
- Snoopy
  Chased chipmunks
- Rocky
  Riding in bike basket
  Kidnapped and ransomed
  Running bases at ballgames
  Almost blind and hobbling
  Always happy

The listing helps me realize that I have more to say about Rocky than about the other two dogs, so I narrow my focus to Rocky, and continue generating ideas associated with him. Later, if I found I could get nowhere by writing about Rocky, I would return to my original listing and try other promising items.

Pair-listing is a collaborative variation of listing. It involves asking students to create a list of words that they associate with a topic and then to read the list and circle the three items that they believe are the most interesting. From there, they pair up with a classmate whose job it is to identify the most compelling of the three items, and to discuss that one item with the list writer. After the pair discusses the chosen item (and then switches roles so that each member receives input regarding his list), the writer begins to expand on that item in writing. In this variation, the prewriting act of listing is complemented by direct discussion among peers. This is a particularly good collaborative strategy to use when English language learners are among the students in our language arts classes. It gives those students an opportunity to try out their use of English in a low-risk setting and to receive immediate and focused feedback from peers about the effectiveness of their use of English, thus promoting both social and academic language growth.

Looping and Cluster Diagrams. *Looping* is a similar prewriting activity that starts when students write a journal entry as a preliminary exploration of a topic. After the focused freewrite, they read their entry, circle what they believe to be the most significant line of the entry, and begin writing their paper from that sentence.

A fourth idea that can be applied for almost any writing task is the creation of a *cluster diagram*. A cluster diagram is simply a graphic representation of words as they relate to a topic. To create a cluster diagram, write the name of the topic in an oval in the center of a page, and then write words that you relate to the topic, putting them in circles surrounding the topic. Draw a line from the circled word to the topic at the center to demonstrate a direct connection from the added word to the center word. Some or all of the circled words might generate their own related words; add other words around the circled words, and again use lines to draw direct connections from the added words to those to which they are most closely connected. The connections do not have to be obvious to anyone but the writer. The writer will decide which connections to pursue when she uses the diagram as a tool in the drafting stage.

Each of these simple prewriting activities can be used to introduce a topic theme that will become the focus of study. For example, in preparation for reading *The Tiger Rising*, students might choose listing, pair-listing, or cluster diagramming to explore the questions, "What kinds problems might exist in father/son relationships?" "How do parents demonstrate love for their children?" "What qualities do we hope to find in our friends?"

I recommend giving students many opportunities to try as wide a variety of graphic and other prewriting strategies as possible, so that they will have several choices to pull from when they transfer the prewriting lessons to other assignments. We cannot know which strategy will have the best results for each student. I confess to my classes that I can only do prewriting while on a long run; the physical exertion seems to generate writerly thinking for me. It is imperative that we provide myriad prewriting options if our goals include helping students find what works best for them as individual writers.

Where Is Your Outline, Young Lady? In traditional writing instruction, prewriting, if practiced at all, almost always meant the preparation of an outline of the essay or report that would be produced. I have not included the outline in this brief discussion of simple but effective prewriting strategies because, despite its value when used to check for cohesion and internal organization in a draft of writing, an outline is not usually the best tool to select when the goal is to generate a collection of ideas. Except when the broadest definitions are used, the construction of an outline requires that for every topic introduced, a minimum of two supporting details must be added. Yet we know, as writers, that we do not always proceed from main to subordinate ideas and relationships, that one idea may bring forth three more while another rests on its own, and so on. When we write, we need to have a vase filled with ideas, so that we can choose which ideas to keep and to discard as we compose. We do not limit our choices before we begin the actual writing of a piece. My recommendation regarding outlines is that we encourage student writers to use them during revision, when they are checking for organization, internal cohesion, substantive topic development and support, and logical flow. Used in that way, outlines are helpful tools.

Sounds of Silliness. In *Activities for an Interactive Classroom*, Jeff Golub describes one of my favorite ideas for encouraging students to explore their creative senses, an activity he calls "synesthesia" (pp. 56–58). The success of this activity depends, at first, on students' willingness to play with words. As they play, they build confidence that they can spin and twist ideas; this confidence then translates into their willingness to try their hands as writers. Here is how synesthesia, the writing activity, works: Begin by soliciting answers from students to a series of simple questions about the way things sound, feel, taste, appear, such as these:

What does a fire engine sound like?
What does tree bark feel like?
What does apple pie taste like?
What does a class of kindergarten students look like?

From there, ask questions in which the associations between the subject and the sense are less obvious, such as these:

What does happiness sound like?
What does silly feel like?
What does laughter taste like?
What does envy look like?

At this point, students are likely to have begun exploring possibilities that, prior to the exercise, they had not considered. Have them form small groups. Then give them more odd pairings like the following, which a group of preservice teachers borrowed from Golub and took into a seventh grade classroom (samples of the seventh graders' responses are added in parentheses):

What does the color green feel like? ("a football field"; "money")
What does pain look like? ("a hospital room"; "my brother's black eye")
What does a wish look like? ("stars"; "a kid staring into a candy store")
What does sadness smell like? ("old clothes"; "nursing homes")
What does thunder look like? ("a Greek god"; "the bowling alley")

Finally, give them pairs of items to compare or contrast, using adjectives like *louder, tastier, happier, friskier, deeper, funnier, harder*, and ask them to create new ways of expressing relationships; after they answer the questions, ask them to explain why they answered as they did:

Which is softer, velvet or a whisper?
What is happier, a lamp or a window?
What is tastier, summer days or high grades?

By answering these kinds of questions and generating their own pairing, students warm up their creative juices; they see that they have interesting ways of seeing the world, interesting ways of expressing themselves. With those realizations established, they are ready and able to write.

Starting with Ourselves.   Many middle school students are reluctant to write because they feel they have nothing to say about a topic, or they assume that whatever they have to say will not be of interest to their (adult teacher) reader. In their inventive book, *Teaching Adolescents to Write: The Unsubtle Art of Naked Teaching* (2003), Lawrence Baines and Anthony Kunkel address this issue by helping students find topics or themes about which they are willing to write. One theme that had proven fruitful for attracting students' interest is "growing up."

(Remember in Chapter 2 we discussed the fact that the key questions of adolescence are "Who am I?" and "Where do I fit in?" This theme takes advantage of their natural preoccupation with their own lives and development by having young adolescents raise questions about how they became who they are at the present.)

Drawing on rhetoric and composition theorist James Kinneavey's aims of writing (expressive, persuasive, informative, and literary) and modes of writing (descriptive, narrative, evaluative, and classificatory) Baines and Kunkel (2003) create a matrix in which aims and modes are combined to produce sixteen kinds of writing activities, with companion writing assignments, each of which is related to the theme of growing up. The blending of expressive aim and descriptive mode, for example, may lead to an assignment in which the student is asked to describe a photograph of a person from two perspectives—the person who took the photograph and the person who is in it. The blending of the literary aim and narrative mode, for example, results in an assignment in which the student writes a short story that includes a dialogue in which two people, the narrator and an adult observer, discuss an important event in the narrator's childhood. Students, particularly those who feel lost when asked to respond to vague prompts, such as "Describe your childhood," benefit from the kind of structure that Baines and Kunkel build into their approach.

During the language-rich three-week Growing Up project, students are asked to discuss and write about the following questions and to elicit responses from peers:

> What were you like as a kid?
> What are your top ten thrills of childhood?
> What piece of music best represents your childhood?
> What was your neighborhood really like, and what were the people in it like?
> What was a typical day in your life as a child like?
> What was an important event in your life as a child?

Reluctant writers benefit from having some sense of direction when they face blank pages of paper. The discussions that occur in class before they are asked to write about the questions provide some ideas that they might put on paper; the personal theme around which all of the questions are placed gives students a point of reference; the nature of the questions themselves allow students to be authorities as they write answers; the students' unique voices and accounts of their idiosyncratic experiences during childhood contribute to the building of a classroom community, one in which everyone's background is treated with respect. The Growing Up project, with its emphasis on a variety of writing aims, modes, and assignments, is an excellent example of how we can engage even reluctant writers in our middle school classrooms. (See Baines & Kunkel, 2003, p. 17–41, for a full description of the project, including the films and music, poems and essays, and speeches and other quotes that they used when teaching the Growing Up project, as well as samples of students' writing that emerged from the project.)

Drafting

During this stage of the writing process, one that is of necessity tangled with prewriting, writers work to put thoughts on paper. Our challenge here is to help students tolerate what experienced writers know: Drafting is chaotic and messy. Ideas do not emerge in neat order and beautiful garb. We need only enlarge and post a copy of one of our recent efforts—a report or letter or other piece of writing, in different draft stages—to show students the truth of this reality. Yet many adolescents will still assume that "real writers" automatically produce polished writing, because they are used to reading texts that are revised, edited, and published.

Tour of Ideas. Preservice teacher Andrew Young introduced this idea for story starters to his classmates. We were amazed not only with the funny results also but with the way the activity quickly gave us a place to begin writing a short story. Here is the activity:

First, pass out blank sheets from a sticky pad to every student in the class. (If you don't have sticky pads, you can use notecards and tape, but note that middle school students do enjoy the novelty of writing a class assignment on sticky notes.)

Next, ask them to write an answer to this question on one of the sheets, and to keep their answer secret: "What is something funny about you that only your best friends or family know?" They should write no more than a sentence and might even write just a phrase; they should not write their name on the sheet. Examples of the comments that were generated when the class of preservice teachers tried this activity include these: "I have a collection of Pez dispensers that I keep in a dresser drawer in my dorm room"; "My nickname really was 'Bubba' until I came to college."

Then ask them to write an answer to this question on the other sheet: "What is something funny about you that no one knows?" Again, their answers should be only one sentence or less, and they should be kept secret. The writer's name should not be on the sheet. The group of preservice teachers wrote comments that include these: "I like to eat grapes while sitting on the floor of the shower," "My first kiss was with the guy who eventually became my stepbrother."

After they have written responses to the questions, have them go to the chalkboard/white board, or any blank space on the classroom wall, and post both of their sheets of paper there. There is no need to put the sheets in any kind of order; the only requirement is that each one is easily visible.

When each person's sheets are posted on the wall or board, have students do a "tour of ideas." Expect a lot of noise at this point; students will be curious about what is written on each slip of paper that is posted. After everyone has read all of the ideas, they should return to their seats. Then call them to the wall or board a few people at a time; their job at that point is to remove the idea that most grabbed their attention and take it to their seat with them.

Finally, when everyone has taken a compelling idea from the wall, tell them that they are to use the words on the sheet in the first line of a story that they are going to write. Then let them write.

Graphic Organizers. Anna Jordan, who has taught teachers about writing instruction for several years in the Miami (Florida) Writing Project, suggests the use of graphic organizers to help students feel a paired sense of freedom and structure as they draft their writing:

> At this age, students are ready to find their voice, so one of our goals must be to provide them with opportunities and freedom to write while helping them maintain some sense of order and organization. That's tough. Graphic organizers really have helped my students, and I tai-

lor them to match assignments. As they write, I have students return many times to the orga-
nizer that they completed as a prewriting exercise This touchstone helps writers keep the
topic in mind while allowing for more freedom in getting to their destination. (June 6, 2002)

Examples of popular graphic organizers include informal outlines, time lines, Venn diagrams,
and character circles or sociograms. See *Reading and the High School Student: Strategies
to Enhance Literacy* by Irvin, Buehl, and Klemp (2003, especially pp. 90–96, 151–156, and
178–180) for specific examples of effective graphic organizers that readers can use with
expository and expressive texts.

All in Good Time.   To help students understand that drafting is only part of the process, not
the end of it, teach them how to separate the act of getting ideas onto paper from the act of getting them exactly like they want them. This activity works to help them see the difference
between getting ideas down (drafting) and getting them right (revising and polishing). Ask
students to take a list or cluster diagram that they have created during a prewriting activity,
and give them exactly five minutes to write about the items on the list/diagram. Remind them
that they are to write sentences but that they should not stop to think about their spelling, capitalization, and so on. At the end of five minutes, ask them to stop and count the number of
words they generated. Have four or five volunteers announce their word totals, and jot these
on the board. Then tell students that they will have five more minutes. This time, they are to
take one phrase, clause, or sentence from what they have just written and use it as the starting
point for a new piece. Again, remind them to stop for nothing, and that their job at this point
is to see how much they can get down on paper in five minutes. Again, stop at five minutes,
ask students to count their words, and have volunteers report and record their results on the
board. The final step of this activity is an essential one: Ask students to discuss what they
think this activity demonstrates about getting ideas down, or drafting.

It is imperative that students finish this activity with the knowledge that drafting is a
means of making ideas visible and that it does not require that the ideas are perfectly stated
or organized. Yet it is also important that they understand that there is no writing equation that
states: More words are always preferable to fewer words. They need to learn that when they
generate a larger number of words, they are providing themselves with a greater number of
choices from which they will pick when they refine the piece of writing. They will have more
words to keep, perhaps, but also more to discard. This strategy teaches them to use drafts as
if they are beachcombers: After collecting a bucket filled with ideas, they pour them out
where they can look at them carefully. Then they can begin to separate the junk from the treasures that they will keep, organize, arrange, polish, and eventually give to others. It is the separating, organizing, and arranging that constitutes the next stage in the writing process:
revision.

Revising

Veteran teacher Mark Shapiro speaks for many teachers:

> I have found that teaching writing is more an exercise in helping students organize rough drafts
> of their thoughts in a clear, meaningful way rather than stressing that they develop their
> ideas using one strict method or another. (June 6, 2002)

One of the most common complaints that I hear from middle school teachers regarding writing instruction is this: "Students don't want to take time to revise their work. They assume that their first draft is their best effort." Lately, too, I have heard this legitimate complaint: "For our state writing test, students get a prompt, then have only 45 minutes to prewrite, write, and edit their work. After they have practiced for that kind of forced and timed writing and have taken the test, they are more convinced than ever that writers don't take time to revise their work, that initial drafts are enough."

It may be more difficult to convince our students that they need to practice revision than it is to convince them to practice any other stage of the writing process. We have to teach them the value of taking time to re-vision their work if we are to have an impact on their use of revision as writers. The question then becomes this: How do we help middle school writers organize their thoughts, comb through their rough drafts and distinguish between jewels and junk, prioritize main and subordinate ideas, eliminate and add, and perform the other tasks of revision?

Use Your ARMS! Former teacher of middle school and English education professor Susan Nelson Wood teaches students to "use their ARMS," with ARMS serving as an acronym for **A**dd, **R**emove, **M**ove, **S**ubstitute. To use their ARMS, students work in small revision groups of three or four students. The first thing that they do is read each member's piece of writing and then write a one-sentence summary of it and a one-sentence response to it. Each student then reads aloud the three or four sentence-length summaries and responses he collects from his group members. No one is allowed to comment on the summaries or responses because the intention of this activity is to give quickly each group member a stake in the discussions that will follow. Next, each group member takes her own piece of writing and reads it silently, with an eye toward the A of ARMS: what she might add. She jots notes on her paper, then moves on, rereading three more times, each time with a singular focus on one kind of revision: remove, move, and substitute, adding notes on her paper with each rereading. After all the group members have reread their writing four times and have made notes, they share their revision ideas with their group members and ask for input. Since all members of the small group have read and invested some time into each piece of writing, this stage is usually quite productive. After "using their ARMS," the students resubmit their now-revised pieces of writing to their group members for another reading. The ARMS strategy is simple yet elegant; it gives students a general sense of what they need to look for during revision, and elicits the support of a peer response group. The specific nature of the rereadings makes this strategy particularly appropriate for use with students who are English language learners. It gives those students an opportunity to focus on one particular task related to a piece of their writing at a time and an opportunity to receive peer feedback on their work within the safety of a small group.

Peer Response Groups. Peer response groups, in which writers exchange papers, read them quietly, and offer specific feedback, offer another solution here. However, there are some issues that we need to consider before sending middle school students to small groups with the charge of talking about each other's writing. First, students this age typically do not like to criticize their classmates' work, whether the work is written, performed, spoken, or presented in other ways. Particularly in middle school classrooms, where students' self-esteem is largely dependent on how they think their peers view them, we need to take time to teach students to be kind, gentle, reliable, thoughtful, and constructive critics of others' work.

One way to establish the kind of atmosphere that will allow for this kind of response group is to elicit students' ideas regarding the specific kinds of comments they might give to each other during small group sessions in which writers read their work aloud for their classmates. Have students brainstorm a list of ways to say "This is good" and "This part needs work," and record the list that they generate. Distribute a copy of the list to each student for reference during peer response group time in the future. This list may be especially helpful for English language learners, since it will provide them with some readily available terms for discussing their classmates' work.

Writing Chats. Another suggestion is to fine-tune peer response groups by spending time modeling the kinds of critical comments that are helpful and hurtful. Set it up this way: Ask a student volunteer to play the role of writer while you perform in your role as teacher. Set two desks in front of the class; sit in one and ask the volunteer to face you in the other. During the first role-play, model a positive writing chat with the student, first asking the kinds of questions you would ask the writer to find out what he thinks about his work, and what plans he might have for improving it. Give the writer time to make comments on the work before you add your suggestions. (It is important to allow the writer to have the first words about his writing, since the author is the authority regarding his work). Then make one or two direct and specific suggestions, with the focus on the piece of writing, not on the writer. Be careful to help students identify subtle messages here. For example, "You are such a good writer because of how you used the adverb *coincidentally* here in the first paragraph" makes a judgment about the writer, not only the work. On the other hand, "You strengthened the first paragraph when you used *coincidentally* there" focuses the remark squarely and solely on the piece of writing. Be sure to voice both strengths of the paper and areas in which it can be improved.

Next, ask the same volunteer to role play a negative writing chat session with you. As the teacher, model the kinds of destructive and unhelpful comments that you want students to avoid. For example, tell the writer, "This part is really stupid because it doesn't make any sense," "I don't like this part since it is supposed to be funny but it isn't," and "I knew I wouldn't like this since I don't like you."

Follow up by having students discuss the differences in the two writing chat sessions by distinguishing between the helpful and destructive comments. Ask the volunteer to report how he felt during each session. Then ask students to generate a class-composed list of pointers for responding to their peers' work on an individual basis and in small groups, with an emphasis on protecting the feelings of the writer while helping her improve her skills and talent. Make copies of this list and distribute it as a writing talk guide. It can be used much as the peer reading response form that was introduced in the previous section, about establishing an appropriate classroom environment for writing (see Figure 5.2).

Reading Aloud. Beginning teacher Tresha Layne has uncovered a slight twist on the set of issues related to the use of peer response groups for writing instruction. Tresha, who works with academically talented middle school students, has found that students are able to respond to the problems in their peers' writing but don't see their own weak areas. In order to address this problem, she asks students to read their writing aloud to her, one at a time. She finds that, "When they hear that their writing sounds silly or just not quite on target, they generally smile and work on correcting the problem." Although having every student read aloud is time consuming, it is a useful practice to continue through the process of writing two or three papers. After students have learned to listen for their problem areas, Tresha shifts the task to peer response groups; each student reads her paper aloud to a group of peers. Peers know that they must wait for the writer to answer "what works" and "what does not work" about the paper she has just read aloud before they verbalize suggestions for revision.

It is worth noting here that the revision stage should deal with the big picture of a piece of writing: its sound, flow, feel, and fit. Questions that are appropriate for consideration during revision include those that deal with whether the organization, language, style, voice, and details achieve the writer's aims and speak to the intended reader of a piece of writing. The focus during revision, even while drafting continues, is on the impact of the piece in general, the piece as a whole. In contrast, when the writer turns his attention to the spelling of a single word, the rightness of a particular phrase, the construction of an individual sentence, he is moving into the polishing stage of writing.

Polishing

Teachers of middle school students are notorious for spending writing instruction time with the polishing stage, which many refer to as editing. (I prefer the term *polishing* because I believe that it distinguishes what happens at this point better than does the more commonly used *editing*.) It is here that the surface is cleaned, shined, corrected. It is here that grammar or, more often, the usage and mechanics of English are checked and irregularities are corrected. And it is this part of the writing process that even our most creative and talented students sometimes dread, because they have come to associate only error-free writing with good writing. They feel pressure to produce correct papers, even if in the effort to write within the boundaries of correctness they delete all parts of their work that do not exemplify safe syntax, acceptable style, predictable organization, and pedestrian language. Veteran teacher Cheryl Kopec Nahmias acknowledges the tension that the editing stage often produces when she says, "One of the major challenges to teaching writing is providing useful, timely feedback to students and balancing grammar/usage instruction with comments on content and style" (June 6, 2002).

The challenge here is to find ways that we can help students polish their work, while at the same time avoid making the mistake of putting so much emphasis on correctness that we create student writers who are afraid to try new voices, styles, words, structures, forms. Jan Graham, who conducted the "A Picture Is Worth a Thousand Words" project that is presented at the close of this chapter, explains how she combines direct instruction and student-sensitive mini-lessons to address surface features of students' writing:

> I don't think it is valuable to spend too much time drilling students on spelling, grammar, and punctuation. Lessons that work best are those where students use their drafts as the "texts"; they revise and then edit while integrating the "rules" for usage. I can then take advantage of the "teachable moments" that come along—answering questions about rules when students are unsure about how to handle them. The beauty of this strategy is that I am answering their questions at the time that they really need answers, so instruction is occurring in a meaningful context." (June, 2002)

She goes on to lament that this approach has limited application: "When classes have thirty-five or more students in them, there is little time for the kind of differentiated instruction that is necessary if I am able to really give each student what he or she needs" (June 6, 2002).

Whether used by writers who are working individually or those who are part of a writing response group, there are some questions that a writer can answer to identify areas that need polishing, once his revising is fairly complete. Please note, though, that most students will do a significant amount of polishing even while drafting their ideas for the first time. (See Figure 5.5.)

To identify those who are stymied by correctness, look for students who

- Are unable to start writing because they "don't know what they are going to say" (they may be fearful of making mistakes and thus taking refuge in inaction);
- Stop to erase and respell words before they can continue with a sentence;
- Cannot make some notes for an upcoming paragraph before they "fix" the first one;
- Use the cut and paste features of the computer before they compile more than a sentence or two in succession.

FIGURE 5.5   Polishing Your Writing until It Shines: Questions to Ask Yourself before You Finish

Your name and the title of your piece of writing: _____

_____

1. ____ I read my piece of writing aloud, then fixed any places that sounded awkward.
2. ____ I am happy with the way the ideas flow from one to the next in this piece of writing.
3. ____ I really like these words and phrases:
4. ____ I could probably improve this part before I finish:
5. ____ I checked to be sure that all of my sentences are complete and that I have not written any run-ons.
6. ____ I checked to be sure that I used capitalization at the beginning of sentences and with proper nouns and adjectives and that I used punctuation to end each sentence.
7. ____ All of my sentences have subject–verb agreement (if the subject is singular, so is the verb that goes with it, and if the subject is plural, so is its verb).
8. This is what I want someone who reads my piece of writing to know about why I wrote what I wrote:

9. I hope that anyone who reads this piece of writing feels this way about it:
10. ____ I am pleased with my effort on this piece of writing.

Note that self-evaluation questions 5–7 deal with surface features, also called the mechanics of writing, or usage problems. Please refer to Chapter 6, "Practicing Listening, Speaking, and Languaging with a Purpose," for a discussion of how to address mechanics in spoken and written language use.

These students are likely to benefit from further practice in separating prewriting, drafting, and revision from polishing. It may even be helpful to teach these students to actively disengage the inner filter in their minds, the function that checks for correctness and obstructs progress, until they have completed an entire draft.

Publishing

This part of the writing process is fun for our students and for us. I like to challenge teachers to find ways that reach beyond the traditional and solid forms of publication of students' work, including bulletin board displays and hallway features during the night of open house. The three most creative ideas that teachers have taught me over the years include the following (I apologize that I am not able to match the idea with the person who shared it with me).

Media Center Kiosks.   After students have written nonfiction works, have students create a display for their work in the corresponding section of your school media center. Other students can consult your students' reports for introductory information on issues about which they are seeking a book. For example, if your students have written biographies of famous Latino/Latina authors, their reports would be displayed near the biography section for schoolmates to consult. If they have written reports on environmental pollutants, their reports can be displayed in the vicinity of books devoted to biology, chemistry, and the environment. Your students will enjoy designing a poster or banner to hang in the media center to announce the display, and they will enjoy the fact that they have real readers for their work.

Cafeteria Color.   Ask students to transcribe their signed pieces of creative writing, including poems, memoirs, short essays, and so on, onto paper that has a colorful or otherwise interesting border. (If word processing with clip art is available, you might consider assigning several students the task of supervising the transcription of all poems and other short written pieces onto a computer, where they can be printed using unusual fonts and interesting paper.) Mount each of those pieces on a large sheet of construction paper, and then laminate the mounted paper. Ask a group of students to take them to the school cafeteria or the teachers' lounge, where they can be used as place mats.

Mark It for Market.   Have students transcribe their favorite sayings—perhaps from a story they have just read, onto one side of a piece of colorful paper that is cut so that it is approximately two inches wide and eight inches long. On the reverse side, have them write an original saying that imitates their favorite one in style, theme, or topic. Laminate these and have students use and even sell them as bookmarks.

On the subject of publishing student work, Cheryl Kopec Nahmias reminds us of an important lesson: Students are diligent writers when they have a real purpose and a real audience. Her idea for integrated literacy instruction follows:

> My middle school students engaged in a project where they wrote and published a book of children's stories for third graders in a nearby school. Knowing who their audience was and knowing that their published work would have to be read aloud and shared with teachers and students at the elementary school had an amazing effect on their writing. They became

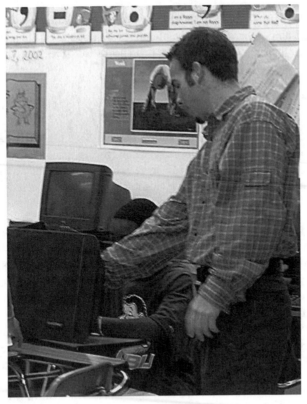

Student teacher Craig Bultman encourages a young writer.

much more intent on developing lively, error-free prose than they had ever been before. They investigated rules for writing dialogue to be sure that they were writing conversations well. They began to see the benefits of multiple drafts, and they drew connections between art (illustrations) and writing, as well as story-telling and writing. (June 6, 2002)

Writing Assignments, Assessments, and Evaluations

Personal Goals

In order to use a student-sensitive approach for teaching writing in middle school classrooms, we can build on three prongs of a simple yet effective writing framework that considers writing and students' personal goals, academic goals, and social goals. For most middle school students, the topic that is easiest to write about is the self. We can take advantage of middle school students' preoccupation with their physical, emotional, and social characteristics in myriad ways. We must remember, though, that students from some cultures and countries will be uncomfortable writing about themselves, and we need to have options available for them. For example, Japanese-American students may avoid writing about themselves due to a cultural belief that bringing attention to oneself is inappropriate.

Focused Freewriting. Have students keep a focused freewriting journal; they will write entries for one week about participation in your language arts class. The next week, they will reflect on and write about their participation in their mathematics, science, social studies, and other courses. At the end of two months, ask them to review all of their entries and write an "Autobiography of a Student." This activity may help middle school writers discover some of their personal strengths. It can easily be modified to become a focused freewriting journal about participation on a sports team, in a church activity, and so on.

This focused freewriting activity is more valid as a school-related assignment than the standard freewriting journal, since students tend to complete free-choice entries as if they are writing diaries. If you choose to have middle school students write in journals with no restrictions, be sure that they understand your legal responsibilities. If you read hints that the student is being abused, you must report that information to the proper authorities in your school. Hints that the student is involved in illegal activities are also subject to report.

Academic Goals

The majority of writing that middle school students are asked to do while in school is academic writing. This category includes activities that range from full-length research reports, to chapter summaries, to sentence-length explanations of problems or phenomena. When they learn to approach writing assignments with a metacognitive eye that enables them to think about what they are thinking, students can monitor their academic growth. They can learn to find gaps in their understanding and to prepare to fill those gaps. Following is a description of " 'T' It Up!" a popular writing activity that can be modified for many different purposes.

"T" It Up! This activity can be used when students are required to read and summarize an academic text in any subject area. This is how it works: After students have read the focal passage, have them draw a large T on the top half of a piece of paper, creating two columns and a cross bar. In the left-hand column, they are to write significant details from the passage that they have read. This might include highlighted words, words in topic headings, names that are introduced, and so on.

In the corresponding spaces in the right-hand column, students jot down what they know, based on the reading material and their own experience, about each item that is listed in the left-hand column. They can number the items in the left-hand column in terms of importance, or arrange them chronologically, and so on, depending on the nature of the assignment. The chart then provides structure for summary writing, which students complete on the bottom half of the same page, so that they can check their information as they compose.

By creating the T-chart, students are able to see immediately where gaps in their understanding exist. In this sense, creating the chart and writing the summary that follows both use writing as a metacognitive tool, for academic purposes. (I was introduced to the T-chart by

Jeff Golub, in *Activities for an Interactive Classroom* (pp. 63–65); Golub recommended using the T-chart to generate descriptive writing.)

Social Goals

Middle school students are usually eager to learn more about the social dimensions of writing and to experiment with writing to achieve social goals. Activities that encourage social interaction are likely to encourage students to expand their writing repertoire and to check their own surface features so that their messages are not only correct but easily read and interpreted by their friends. An activity that engages students in writing to achieve social goals is the Friendly Advice activity.

Friendly Advice.   Ask students how many of them have ever read a Dear Abby–type column in a newspaper or on the Web. After they answer and discuss some characteristics of advice columns, tell them that each of them will soon have a part-time job as a Dear Teen advice columnist. They will be expected to perform their job at the beginning and ending of class for the next few days. Have students brainstorm a class list of the kinds of light problems and frustrations that they, as young adolescents, are facing at the time. A volunteer should record this list on the board or overhead. (As the teacher, you might start the list by suggesting items like these: lack of transportation to the mall, too many chores on the weekend, not enough allowance money, and younger sisters and brothers who follow me around. You might also find it necessary to emphasize that this is not the place for extremely personal items such as parental alcoholism, violence, and so on; you will have an important impact on setting a light tone for this activity.)

Explain that the brainstorm list is to be used merely as a prompt for their individual thinking. Once their minds are primed, distribute three (or more, if you wish) 3×5-inch note cards and a corresponding number of envelopes to each student. Instruct students to write a single question on a card; the question should reflect a "light problem or frustration" for which they want advice from a peer. They will then sign the question with a clever, problem-related line—"badly bugged by brothers in Boston," for example—copy that same signature line onto the outside of the envelope (so that they can identify each of their envelopes on a later day), and then seal the question in the envelope. They should then repeat the process for the other two cards.

After approximately ten minutes, ask students to drop their three sealed and signed envelopes into the "I Need Help!" class box. The next day, on arriving to class, every student draws one envelope from the box and spends the first five minutes of class writing a response to the enclosed question, using the flip side of the note card (so that the question and answer are kept together). The answer-writer, like the question-writer, signs with a creative nom de plume and returns the card to the envelope. The answer-writer then puts the envelope in the class "Hope That Helps!" box. During the final ten to fifteen minutes of class, allow students to come to the box one at a time, so that they can find their envelope. They can take their card to their desk and read their classmate's advice. Students should be encouraged to share particularly useful or entertaining questions and advice aloud. (This activity is a modified version of one introduced by teacher Brenda Clark in *Motivating Writing in Middle School* [1996, p. 4].)

Assessment and Evaluation of Writing

As a beginning teacher, I approached evaluation of students' writing from two extreme positions. Some days, I read their work with an arrogant passion for marking and correcting mistakes, suggesting better word choices, more powerful sentence structures, stronger conclusions, and so on. Other days, I read with eager enthusiasm, praising students' attempts to express ideas in creative ways, even when they were not completely successful, remarking on students' unique insights, voice, style. That vacillation created constant confusion among my students. One day, a student asked, "Are you going to be hard or easy on us when you grade this one?" A day later, one queried, "Do you care more about what we say or whether we break any rules when we write this paper?" Those questions prompted me to examine my practice. What I found was that my evaluation of writing was detached from the instructional goals that I set for my writing lessons.

Questions about the evaluation of writing send us back to questions about writing instruction in integrated literacy settings and take several forms, including these:

- What are our instructional goals, and how can we measure students' growth toward them, as writers and as thinkers?
- What do we look for as evidence that our students are developing the skills and talents that are the explicit focus of the writing lessons that we implemented?
- How can we determine whether or not students are able to transfer writing skills across disciplines and problems, using writing as a mode for generating thinking, as well as a vehicle for extending, clarifying, and finally crystallizing their thoughts?
- Do we evaluate writing that is done for personal and social goals differently than we treat writing done for academic purposes, and if so, how?
- What signs indicate increases in students' confidence and pleasure when they assume roles as writers?
- At which stages of the writing process will I give evaluative feedback, and will I grade items individually or require a writing folder or portfolio, evaluating and assigning a single grade for it?

As the preceding discussion suggests, much of the evaluation of writing occurs formatively, when peers respond to their classmates' work and when the teacher leans across the desk during a writing chat to praise a student for a particularly powerful sentence, for example. In this sense, evaluation of writing should be constant, and commensurate with evaluation of the quality of our students' thinking. However, as beginning teachers, it is helpful to explore at least two other specific forms of evaluation that you may want to use: rubrics for immediate feedback and portfolios for making evaluations of students' growth as writers over the course of a grading period, a term, or a year.

Using Rubrics to Clarify Expectations and Provide Immediate Feedback

As this list demonstrates, we must be clear about the purposes for writing and the audience that students will address when we ask them to engage in writing assignments. It implies, too, that we must either specify a required form and style or accept students' choices about how they approach assignments. Frequently, we tell students what we have "counted" when we return their papers with evaluative marks and grades on them. However, we can be clearer about our expectations, and thus more helpful to our student writers, if we provide them with evaluation rubrics at the time that we announce the writing assignment. One of the most effective uses of rubrics that I have observed involved the student writer filling out an evaluation of her piece of writing, using a rubric prepared by the teacher; the teacher using the same rubric; and then the two sitting together to compare their evaluations. This situation sparked serious and specific discussion of the writer's work (see Figure 5.6). Please note, too, that the rubrics included here are merely samples; your instruction will be enhanced when you design rubrics with your specific instruction, goals, and students in mind.

FIGURE 5.6   Who Am I? An Autobiographical Snapshot: A Sample Writing Assignment with Sample Evaluation Rubrics

Please note: This sample writing activity and evaluative rubric represent student-sensitive writing assignments that stimulate writing for personal goals. The rubric should be altered for each assignment, with differences apparent particularly when the purpose for writing is academic or social.

Who Am I? An Autobiographical Snapshot

Place in the curriculum and instructional goals

Students have read and studied Cynthia Rylant's visually and verbally stunning *Something Permanent* (1994), a collection of poems that Rylant wrote as complements to the Depression-era photographs by Walker Evans that also appear in the book. They are ready to write their own poems but will create verbal pictures of themselves, captured at one particular point in their lives, so they can write autobiographical snapshots.

Students will use exploratory writing to learn more about themselves, in terms of how their lives have been shaped by their experiences, and then will use expressive writing to share what they have learned with an audience of their peers.

Lesson Activities

Prewriting: Students will first create a life map by graphically rendering the events, people, and places that have had an influence on who they are at present. Students should begin the maps by drawing a single point in a left-hand corner of the paper, and from that point, add a line that travels toward the present. They will then add and label no fewer than five points along the line, points that signify the important events, people, and places along their life route, from the beginning to the present. They will fully explicate each of these points in a key that they write and insert alongside the map.

In small groups, students will discuss their maps. Each will ask group members for input regarding which of the highlighted points might provide the most interesting, entertaining, or poignant snapshot of the student. This map, complete with exploratory writing, serves as a guide for their composition of the autobiographical snapshot.

Writing: Students return to Rylant's book and either select a poem to use as a structural model, or create their own poem, using the form that seems most appropriate to them. Since this is an example of writing toward a personal goal, I do not recommend that you impose a particular form on the poems that students compose.

FIGURE 5.6 Continued

Revising, Polishing, and Publishing: Upon completion of the poems, students return to their small groups, where they share drafts of their autobiographical snapshots with their peers. They should then return to their desks to revise and polish their poems, based on audience input, and then move to a computer, if available, to produce a formal copy for display. If you find that students are interested in this project, you might extend it by asking them to add actual photographs, taken from the period of life that is the focus of the verbal snapshot, to their poems, if possible, and then create a photography and poetry gallery in the classroom.

Evaluative Rubric

Remember that each rubric needs to reflect the instructional goals and the activity itself, so that evaluation is fair and can serve as a continuation of the lesson.

For this lesson, I would recommend the use of two rubrics: a self-evaluation form, which gives attention to process and product, and a reader-evaluation form, which allows the reader to tell the writer whether or not the poem works for that reader.

Self-Evaluation: Please put "yes" or "no" in the blanks beside the numbers, and then finish the statements or add any comments that you would like to share.

1. _____ I recalled significant people, places, and events and was able to note them on my life map.
2. _____ Peers' ideas influenced my decision about which point I would use for my snapshot.
3. _____ I chose this one of Rylant's poems to use as a model: _____
   OR
   _____ I chose to develop my own form for my poem because _____.
4. _____ I include details in my poem that make the snapshot of me clear and easy to see.
5. _____ I wanted my poem to be _____ (funny, serious, sad, etc.).
6. _____ I am pleased with the quality of the snapshot that I created.

Reader's Evaluation Rubric

My name:

Name of person whose poem I am evaluating:

1. _____ The autobiographical snapshot gives me a clear, interesting picture of one part of the life of the person whom it is about.
2. _____ I think that the poet wanted me to feel _____ (happy, sad, entertained, etc.) when I read the poem, because _____.
3. The best word(s) and line(s) are these: _____ and _____.
4. _____ The poem kept my attention and made me want to know more about the subject.
5. _____ If it were my poem, I would be happy with it.
   OR
   _____ If it were my poem, I would probably keep working on this part.

Note that these rubrics give evaluative feedback to the writer; as the teacher, you can use the second rubric when responding to the poem, but you are also likely to have to add a grade. In that case, you might add to the reader's rubric a sixth slot for the grade. You would need to be clear, before students turn in their final copies, about how accountable they would be for mechanical surface features such as spelling and punctuation.

Using Writing Portfolios to Demonstrate Growth over Time

The term *writing portfolio* has become ubiquitous, and its overuse brings confusion for the beginning teacher who hopes to use *portfolios* as part of the writing workshop and language arts curriculum. The term currently may refer to a loose conglomeration of unfinished and finished drafts that students compile and stuff into a manila folder. It may mean a carefully chosen collection of best works or performance pieces that foreground a writer's range across a variety of forms, or emphasizes his artistic abilities in a single genre. It can designate the body of artifacts and evaluative information, including in-class examinations and standardized test results, spelling quizzes, and vocabulary puzzles as often as samples of journalistic, narrative, or dramatic writing that a teacher compiles as evidence of the student's work and growth during a term or year. It can even refer to the packet of student work that the teacher of sixth grade language arts passes along to the teacher of seventh grade language arts in late May or the set of documents that the state collects to assess student writing in a school.

Depending on which definition you adopt, the portfolio can be a central feature of the writing workshop and literacy curriculum. It will have significant implications for the way that you plan, organize, and implement instruction, and the way that you evaluate student work and the effectiveness of your teaching. My advice for beginning teachers, and all who want to try to incorporate writing portfolios for the first time, is to start with a very specific plan for answering these key questions:

- What is the purpose of having students develop writing portfolios? (Am I more interested in seeing their growth or seeing their best products?)
- What will be included in the portfolio? (all drafts of writing assignments? polished drafts of a few that represent various types of writing?)
- Who will decide what is included and what is omitted? (the teacher? the student writer? a peer group?)
- Will individual artifacts be evaluated before they are inserted into the portfolio, and if so, can the writer revise them, before including them in the portfolio? Will that revision effort be reflected in a grade?
- How will the writer introduce the contents of the portfolio to the teacher/reader? (with a letter to the reader that gives some information about each artifact? an essay in which the writer describes herself as a writer? in a writing chat?)
- How will the total portfolio be evaluated and graded, if at all?
- What will be the due date for the portfolio, and when will I need to review them?
- Can I design a rubric to guide my review and evaluation of the portfolios?
- How much time am I able to commit to reading and evaluating students' portfolios?
- Where will the portfolios go when I am finished with them?

The answers that you bring to these ten questions will shape your writing workshop and literacy curriculum.

When a Test Requires Writing

Students are often asked to write test answers that demonstrate their knowledge of subject matter. Here are some examples of that kind of test question: A social studies teacher asks eighth graders to write an essay to compare and contrast the Mississippi River with the Colorado River; a mathematics teacher asks students to explain how they solved an algebraic equation; a science teacher asks students to write the steps of the scientific method and to comment on each. In each of these cases, the students will be given credit for their knowledge of the subject matter (rivers, equations, methods) only if they can write well enough to convey that knowledge. Do you see how easy it might be to confuse a student's skill as a writer with his knowledge of the subject? How often have the young adolescent students with whom we work received low grades on content-area tests as a result of their inability to write clear, convincing answers? This problem is especially acute when we, and our colleagues across the curriculum, teach English language learners. We must not make the mistake of confusing lack of fluency in written English with lack of subject matter knowledge. We should not give a student a low grade on a test of her knowledge if she has limited ability to demonstrate her knowledge due to the nature of the test item. One way to avoid this confusion is to create evaluations that do not rely on asking every student to write essays or paragraphs on the same questions, with the expectation that all essays should be similar.

The issue of using writing as a medium through which we test knowledge of subject matter is one that we have to help colleagues across the curriculum understand and one that we have to face within our language arts classes, too. In *Lighting Fires: How the Passionate Teacher Engages Adolescent Writers* (2001), Joseph Tsujimoto, who teaches eighth graders and is a poet, reflects and comments on his practices:

> Traditional timed writings generally test students' understanding of what they've read and their ability to communicate their knowledge clearly. Usually all students are given the same questions to answer or the same passages to interpret. Most often they are required to complete the exams within a class period. Their writings, then, under the illusion of fairness, are compared against each other and are ranked or grouped for grading.
>
> In the past, I have assigned such exams myself too often. And, too often, the results drove me to distraction ("After *all* we've been through?!"). Not only were most of the writings repetitive from paper to paper—and tritely so, often regurgitating what had been said in class discussion, but most were also immensely boring, couched in the stalest expressions, and lacked genuine conviction. Where was their sense of poetry and grace? Or humor? Or their sense of *human* talk? . . .
>
> But why complain, I would ask myself. The questions were not the students', and rarely were the questions I concocted for them of striking interest. . . .
>
> And what of the writings themselves? How meaningful might they be to the students? How important? How close to their hearts and their understanding of the world? Might they have worked things out—memories, vague feelings, questionable values—broadening their consciousness or modifying their vision *had they been given the opportunity*? Might they have made sense of the ways people and society operate—creating order, form, and meaning where none existed before—*had they been allowed to write on what they wanted*? (p. 170–171)

Tsujimoto's (2001) answer to requiring students to write test answers that "drove him to distraction" has been to have students write "open exams" in which the teacher dictates only a general question or statement that is related to the literature or other work that has been studied. Students must first decide how to frame their responses and then how to develop them appropriately and with passion. Tsujimoto gives the example of an open exam question that he assigned after teaching *To Kill a Mockingbird*: "Write a paper in response to *To Kill a Mockingbird*" (p. 169). Aware that the students struggle with the ambiguities of such an assignment, he then provides more specific options, such as these:

> You may write another function paper, especially if you feel you want more practice with this type of writing. Here are some topics: What is the function of Part One of *TKM*? What is the function of Scout, Jem, Dill, Boo, or Atticus? What is the function of any passage that you find significant? (p. 171)

He also offers his students the option of following the lead of other students who have written responses to the novel. He reads aloud examples that demonstrate a broad range of responses; one writer compares characters in the novel to people in her life; another explores the issue of racial prejudice from the personal level; one experiments with point of view by writing a short story response; another attacks the stereotypes presented in the novel and on a popular television show (pp. 172–183).

Like Tsujimoto, we need to reflect on our practices as they relate to the use of writing to test subject matter knowledge; our practices should reflect our goals for students' learning and our pedagogical principles. If we are committed to teaching writing to help students discover and use their own voices, even our tests should allow them some freedoms to use those voices.

When Students' Writing Is What Is Tested

Another issue related to writing and testing relates to situations in which students' skills as writers are tested; the subject matter, in these situations, becomes secondary, while the writer's ability to construct clear, logical, well-supported arguments, descriptions, narratives, or explanations is of primary concern. In recent years, tests of students' writing have entered the arena of state-level standardized testing. In Florida, for example, eighth graders, like their fourth and tenth grade counterparts, take FCAT Writes as part of the battery of tests included in the Florida Comprehensive Assessment Test (FCAT). For all eighth graders in the state, with some exceptions for students who are in full-time ESL classes and special education programs, this means responding to a randomly assigned expository or persuasive writing prompt in a 45-minute time period. Examples of the prompts that have been used as samples across the state include these: "Everyone has chores. Explain how you do one of your chores" (expository), and "Convince the PTA at your school that watching television does not have a bad effect on your grades" (persuasive). Essays are evaluated holistically with a scale of 0 (lowest) to 6 (highest) by readers who are trained to look for four features: a main idea, support for the main idea, absence of extraneous details, and adherence to conventions of standard English grammar, usage, and mechanics.

All beginning and veteran teachers need to be aware of the kinds of writing tests that their students will be expected to take and pass. In Florida, eighth graders who fail to score a 3 or above on the FCAT Writes are in jeopardy of having to repeat the eighth grade, because the writing assessment is part of the formula used to determine whether or not a student can be promoted. For our students' sakes, then, we must become familiar with the ways that writing is tested, and prepare students for performing well on that kind of test of writing. Teachers whose students are typically successful assure us that their regular writing curriculum does more to prepare their students to do well on the standardized test than any kind of specialized instruction that is tailored specifically to the test. I would recommend, however, that we give students practice responding to the kinds of prompts that they will encounter on the standardized assessments. This recommendation is particularly strong for those of us who tend to have students engage in creative writing that takes many forms and that veers away from formulaic expository or persuasive essays.

A Picture Is Worth a Thousand Words Project

Let's look at one group of middle school writers to see what we can expect from students who are engaged in a well-designed and meaningful writing project that is characteristic of a student-sensitive integrated literacy pedagogy. Veteran middle school teacher Jan Graham provided me with an example of what middle school students are capable of accomplishing when we expect them to be writers in her "A Picture Is Worth a Thousand Words" project.

Jan Graham, who teaches sixth and seventh graders, has found that interdisciplinary thematic instruction provides her with the foundation from which she and her students can work as readers, writers, speakers, listeners, languagers, thinkers. Examples of the themes around which her interdisciplinary instruction is organized include these: "Exploring the Me I Am Learning to Be," "What's the Difference? Exploring Disabilities," and "Survival: Learning from Life's Rules, Rituals, and Regulations."

In order to explore the theme "Our Fragile World," Jan and her students read fiction and nonfiction about the environment. Then they organized a field trip to an area wildlife center, where they all spent the afternoon observing nature and taking photographs. Once the photographs were developed, students worked diligently to enhance their visual images with words by writing a poem, story, or memory statement to complement each of their own photographs. They carefully revised and polished their writing and then selected their favorite piece, which was bound into the class's *Our Fragile World* book of photography and words.

Preparation

To prepare for this project, Ms. Graham had to do some out-of-the-ordinary work. After getting approval for the project from the assistant principal for curriculum and soliciting the help of the Exceptional Student Education teacher with whom she co-teaches two classes, Ms. Graham invited a guest speaker from the local newspaper office to teach the class some photography skills and tricks. The students were enthusiastic because they knew that they would soon have an opportunity to apply the photography skills for themselves.

Next, Ms. Graham sought support for the project by applying for a mini-grant made available by the school system. The grant money helped with bus and lunch expenses for the field trip and for some of the costs of taking and developing photographs. Ms. Graham bargained with a local drugstore to discount disposable cameras and film developing costs. With the discounted prices, she was able to assign one camera to every group of four students. The students determined for themselves that the best way to share the cameras in the groups was to promise that each person would take no more than five photographs. At the end of the day, by group agreement, they would decide how to use their remaining frames. According to Ms. Graham, students not only cooperated, but when each group's photographs were developed, individuals demonstrated what teachers hope students will feel: ownership of their work and the pride that accompanies it.

Students as Photojournalists on Assignment

The day of the field trip was an exciting one; many of the students had never been to the wildlife area, even though it is approximately a 40-minute drive from the school. They were shocked to see that the river and its deep springs, on which they took a boat ride, were guarded by alligators and decorated with several species of ducks, birds, fish, turtles, and other wildlife. Despite their excitement at being there, the students did not forget their assignment. That day, they were not students but photojournalists, there to take photographs they would write about and include in the class book. What kind of writing did students—including several who have documented learning disabilities—accomplish, when they had ample preparation, a meaningful purpose, and a specific audience for whom to write? Here are some samples of the work that accompanied their photographs:

> A turtle as wide as an elephant sits on a log, where branches hang down like long, slithery snakes. I hope the turtle makes it to the other side. Mossy gray yarn tangles itself around the lush trees. *Nichole*

> The smooth wind blew on a sunny day. Water flowed gently and softly. Green plants swayed from side to side. Animals swam in the cold water so quietly. Birds flew gracefully in the air, like smooth paper airplanes. Dead and living trees made peace and got along with each other. Breathing animals talked to each other in their own way. All the animals and plants are beautiful and magnificent things of the earth. *Byron*

> My beautiful lily was looking at me.
> It was swinging left to right.
> It seemed like an angel come down from heaven. *Kelly*

Notice that Nichole's piece is almost a word collage, Byron's is a narrative listing, and Kelly employs simile. None of these pieces is a perfect work of art, yet each demonstrates the importance of providing students with an inviting topic to write about, allowing them to shape their individual identities as writers and thinkers.

Goals

The students' writing is evidence of their accomplishment. But it doesn't tell the whole story. Ms. Graham was careful to use objective measures to demonstrate growth during the year and found that her instructional goals produced these outcomes:

- 95 percent of the students produced at least one significant and complete piece of writing during each of the four major instructional units during the year, indicating improvement in their ability to state a main idea and support it with logical ideas and clear language.

- 67 percent of the students showed at least a one-point increase (on a six-point scale) in a practice round of the state's writing assessment by the end of the year.
- 95 percent of the students read, explored, and evaluated a theme from one of the novels studied during the year and completed a final evaluation of the novel.
- 90 percent of the students published a piece of writing, incorporating literary devices and writing traits studied during the year, and mounted their piece of writing with accompanying photographs for inclusion in the class photograph and words book.

In addition to these goal-related outcomes, Ms. Graham noted that the project addresses many of the state and school standards for language arts, particularly those that focus on developing literacy through reading, literature study, and writing. And most important of all, the project proved to the sixth and seventh graders that they don't have to pretend to be writers when they are in their language arts classes; they *are* writers.

The "A Picture Is Worth a Thousand Words" project provides strong evidence of the truth of one of the most important laws of teaching and learning: Students live up to (or down to) our expectations. As their teachers, our obligation to our students is to establish high expectations and to support and assist students as they strive to reach and go beyond them. Our job is to give them opportunities to prove to us, and to themselves, that they can be writers, that they can be people who express their ideas articulately, accurately, creatively, gladly.

Spontaneous Overflow of Writing

For many teachers, writing instruction is difficult because it demands that we take so many different stances: We allow students to make some choices but impose a few of our own; we encourage them to take risks but we mark mistakes; we are their coach but we are their judge. It is difficult, too, because we have to find ways to establish an environment in which students are comfortable spreading their ideas out in front of us and their peers. Veteran teacher Patricia Buckley speaks for many teachers when she states, "My biggest challenge is teaching writing."

And yet, despite its challenges, it is perhaps through writing that we learn more about the spontaneous overflow of our students' lives than through any of their other languaging activities. By offering our students creative and engaging assignments, authentic and helpful assessment and evaluation, and enthusiastic support as advocates for their work, we treat middle school students like people who write. And in the process, they become people who write.

Integrated Literacy Checklist

In this chapter, literacy skills in all of the language arts areas are integrated with the focus on writing.

Reading

Students are readers and evaluators of their own and their peers' texts in several activities: the Creative Genius and Read All about It! bulletin boards, message swap, pair-listing, Draft First, Polish Later, Autobiographical Snapshots, Tour of Ideas, and the peer response forms, as well as the Sentence Sense and Sentence Savvy activities.

Literature

Students are readers of literary texts, including the quotes on the "Writers for Adolescents on Writing" posters and the literary models used in the copy-change activity. They are also engaged in creating their own literary texts as they write stories, poems, newspaper reports, advertisements, scripts, autobiographical snapshots, research reports, and so on. Students also explore literary language in the Synesthesia activity.

Speaking/Listening/Language

Students spend a lot of time first as listeners and then as advice givers when the focus is on writing instruction. This role is most apparent in the Writing Chats, but it also is important as they voice their choices regarding form, topic, length, deadlines, respondents, and so on. Further, they listen to their own writing being read aloud in evaluative activities like the Read Aloud and to others during the oral "publication" of student writing. The Synesthesia activity and the Growing Up writing prompts incorporate speaking/listening/language as parts of the writing process as well.

Media

Students may choose to write for, about, or to the media when the focus is on authentic writing. The newspaper, with daily advice columns, will serve as a model for them when they engage in the Friendly Advice project. They are encouraged to use word processing and other available technologies both to produce and publish their writing. Students can also incorporate recorded music and movies into extensions of the Growing Up project.

Help for English Language Learners in the Activities Suggested and Examples Provided

All of the writing activities will help ELL students acquire language. By writing, they are able to control the speed of the language and thereby learn individual vocabulary words and pay attention to sentence structures and their deviations from the structures of their first language. Those activities that use graphics, including the peer response forms, graphic organizers, the acronym ARMS, and "T" It Up, will be particularly useful due to the visual support for language use that they provide. Those that include small group discussion and personal connections, such as the Synesthesia activity, the Tour of Ideas, and the Growing Up project, are also particularly helpful for ELLs.

The frequent use of small groups, peer responses, the self-evaluation list during the polishing stage, and the peer-review rubric will give ELL students language practice and will welcome them into classroom discourse as full participants.

NCTE/IRA Standards Highlighted in Chapter 5

Standard Number Four: Students adjust their use of spoken, written, and visual language (e.g., conventions, style, vocabulary) to communicate effectively with a variety of audiences and for different purposes.

Standard Number Three: Students employ a wide range of strategies as they write and use different writing process elements appropriately to communicate with different audiences for a variety of purposes.

Standard Number Six: Students apply knowledge of language structure, language conventions (e.g., spelling and punctuation), media techniques, figurative language, and genre to create, critique, and discuss print and nonprint texts.

Standard Number Seven: Students conduct research on issues and interests by generating ideas and questions and by posing problems. They gather, evaluate, and synthesize data from a variety of sources (e.g., print and nonprint texts, artifacts, people) to communicate their discoveries in ways that suit their purpose and audience.

Standard Number Eight: Students use a variety of technological and information resources (e.g., libraries, databases, computer networks, video) to gather and synthesize information and to create and communicate knowledge.

Standard Number Ten: Students whose first language is not English make use of their first language to develop competency in the English language arts and to develop understanding of content across the curriculum.

Standard Number Eleven: Students participate as knowledgeable, reflective, creative, and critical members of a variety of literacy communities.

Standard Number Twelve: Students use spoken, written, and visual language to accomplish their own purposes (e.g., for learning, enjoyment, persuasion, and the exchange of information). (Farstrup & Myers 1996, p. 3)

Works Cited

Atwell, N. (1998). *In the middle: Writing, reading, and learning with adolescents*, 2nd edition. Portsmouth, NH: Boynton/Cook.

Baines, L., and Kunkel, A. (2003). *Teaching adolescents to write: The unsubtle art of naked teaching*. Boston: Allyn and Bacon.

Calkins, L. M. (1986). *The art of teaching writing*. Portsmouth, NH: Heinemann.

Carroll, P. S. (2001). Authors' insights about the art of writing: Learning to notice, and other broad thrills. *English Journal*. 90 (3), 104–109.

Clark, B. (1996). Friendly advice. In J. Hutchinson (Ed.). *Standards consensus series: Motivating writing in middle school*. Urbana, IL: NCTE, pp. 4–5.

DiCamillo, K. (2000). *Because of Winn Dixie*. Cambridge, MA: Candlewick.

DiCamillo, K. (2001). *The tiger rising*. New York: Scholastic.

Golub, J. N. (1994). *Activities for an interactive classroom*. Urbana, IL: NCTE.

Irvin, J. L., Buehl, D. R., and Klemp, R. M. (2003). *Reading and the high school student: Strategies to enhance literacy*. Boston: Allyn and Bacon.

Keyes, D. (1997). Flowers for Algernon. In *Literature and integrated studies*: Grade Eight. Glenview, IL: Scott Foresman, pp. 485–512.

Mayher, J., Lester, N., and Pradl, G. (1983). *Learning to write: Writing to learn*. Upper Montclair, NJ: Boynton/Cook.

Milner, J. O., and Milner, L. F. M. (1999). *Bridging English*, 2nd edition. Upper Saddle River, NJ: Merrill of Prentice Hall.

Nahmias, C. K. (2002). Personal conversation, Tallahassee, Florida. June 6, 2002.

Noguchi, R. R. (1991). *Grammar and the teaching of writing: Limits and possibilities*. Urbana, IL: NCTE.

Romano, T. (1987). *Clearing the way: Working with teenage writers*. Portsmouth, NH: Heinemann.

Rylant, C. (1994). *Something permanent*. New York: Harcourt.

Steinbeck, J. (1937/1993). *Of mice and men*. New York: Penguin.

Tsujimoto, J. (2001). *Lighting fires: How the passionate teacher engages adolescent writers*. Portsmouth, NH: Boynton/Cook Heinemann.

Weaver, C. (1996). *Teaching grammar in context*. Portsmouth, NH: Boynton/Cook Heinemann.

Wilhelm, J. D. (1996). *Standards in practice grades 6-8*. Urbana, IL: NCTE.

6 Overflow of Oral Language: Listening, Speaking, and Languaging with a Purpose

Young adolescents involved in small group discussion.

I made many mistakes during my first several years of teaching English and language arts, but none caused me more trouble than this two-edged one: I assumed that a quiet class was a good class, *and* I believed that the way to get a group of young adolescents to be quiet was to be louder than they were. I had a lot to learn about classroom discourse—and classroom management. In the years since then, I have come to regard the opportunity to receive a daily dose of young adolescents' oral languaging as one of the most exciting and engaging aspects of working in the middle school setting. It is in their language that young adolescents are most likely to overflow.

Oral Language in an Integrated Literacy Pedagogy

A focus on students' oral language is an important aspect of an integrated literacy pedagogy, and the approaches that we consider in this chapter are consistent with the four core beliefs of the integrated literacy pedagogy:

Belief One: A focus on oral language encourages teachers to pay attention to students as individuals and as members of many groups, including their classes at school, the social cliques they join, the clubs they are in, and the teams on which they participate. When we focus on students' oral language, we have an opportunity to be refreshed and enchanted by who our students are as humans.

Belief Two: A focus on oral language allows teachers to consider our own students' strengths as languagers, as well as plan for their growth. By paying attention to our students' use of language in a variety of situations, not just in the sometimes stale formats of teacher-directed classroom discourse, we create opportunities to learn about how they use language to make sense of their world. When we pay close attention, we can also take advantage of opportunities to teach our students new ways to draw on their understandings and skills, too. Whether our classes include students who are English language learners, young adolescents who use low-prestige dialects, speakers of prestige dialects, or students from each of these groups, our focus on oral language allows us to work with them.

Belief Three: A focus on oral language requires that we expand traditional definitions of literacy. Although oral language has been valued by societies and communities as the original means of passing along stories and histories, written language forms have traditionally been more highly valued in classrooms. The multilingual nature of our communities today, though, demands that we give attention to oral language. Further, if our goal is to meet students where they are and then to lead them toward expertise as languagers, we need to bring all of the forms of oral language that are important to young adolescents into our classrooms. When young adolescents' production and reception of oral language are parts of our curriculum, we bring nontraditional resources into our classrooms for study, from television shows and popular songs, to storytelling sessions and pep rallies.

Belief Four: Oral language has not been as prominent a focus in the preparation of teachers of middle grades language arts programs as reading, literature, and writing instruction have been in the past several decades. For this reason, many beginning and veteran teachers feel less sure of themselves as they begin to make decisions about curricula, goals, activities, assessment, and evaluation of students' skills as listeners and speakers, as creators and consumers of oral language. We need to refer to professional standards to help guide our decisions about appropriate expectations, goals, and activities and to simultaneously make observations and collect data regarding our students' needs in order to inform our decisions and actions regarding oral language instruction.

Exploring Students' Oral Language Use and Development

In this chapter, we focus primarily on the language that adolescents receive as listeners and the language that they produce as speakers. Along the way, we examine two key aspects of languaging: We look first at the *power of language,* with an emphasis on strategies that encourage students to be precise and purposeful speakers and listeners. We look at how we can put language at the center of classroom inquiry and how we can configure the classroom in ways that promote informal language use for academic and social growth. Within that section, I sketch a speech unit, too, as a means of bringing a more formal focus to oral language use.

Second, we examine the *language of power*. (I have borrowed and paraphrased Constance Weaver's use of the terms *dialects of power* and *power of dialects* in *Teaching Grammar in Context* [1996, p. 229].) In this section, our emphasis is on what teachers need to know to integrate the study of dialects into oral language instruction. We also question our responses—as teachers and as humans—to students' and others' uses of low-prestige dialects. I do not attempt to discuss all of the academic and sociopolitical issues that swirl around the issue of dialects within and beyond school settings. However, I hope to demonstrate, in a discussion of dialects, that middle school students can and do appreciate the fact that they use regional, generational, economic, racial, and/or peer dialects. They know that there are occasions when they need to repudiate those dialects and use standard English, the dialect that the National Council of Teachers of English's Conference on College Composition and Communication labeled, in a 1988 policy statement, "The National Language Policy," as the "language of wider communication." The chapter ends with some suggestions for incorporating oral language activities into the classroom to promote awareness and appreciation of linguistic differences. These activities are designed to help students understand that dialects, even those that are not spoken at school by their teachers, are governed by rules, and that dialects present us with differences, not deficiencies. The chapter also ends with links to the integrated language arts, suggestions for English language learners, and highlights of the NCTE/IRA standards addressed in the chapter.

The Power of Language: Students as Speakers and Listeners

Young adolescents have, for the most part, an amazing facility with spoken language. They make meaning, or participate as languagers, in their home, neighborhood, clubs, church, sports teams, job settings, and school. They use specialized language among themselves to identify insiders and exclude outsiders. They learn to use the vocabulary of their hobbies, such as skateboarding and hip-hop music. They invent new generational pidgins to reflect their values and attitudes. They adopt phrases that are introduced by their idols. They code-switch when they can't find just the right word in one language or dialect and need to borrow a word or phrase from another one. They shift registers when talking among themselves and among adults. And all of this happens without formal instruction in language, without lessons on "proper" or "appropriate" or "correct" uses of spoken language. As neuroscientist Steven Pinker (2000) explains, language use is an "instinct": As humans, we are born with both the desire and the ability to communicate through oral language (with exceptions among those who suffer damage to the brain's language centers). Our job as teachers who choose a student-sensitive integrated literacy pedagogy is not to focus on the internal structures that hold our language together and that generate an infinite number of new sentences even with a finite number of words. Instead, it is to help students fine-tune and expand their innate abilities to use oral and written language so they can make sense of, and know, their world through their language.

Our challenge as teachers who want to help students become even more effective language users is to find ways to take advantage of students' enthusiasm for words. We can meet this challenge with a playful pedagogy that encourages experimentation and exploitation of the power of language and that instigates investigation and inspection of the language of power.

A Playful Pedagogy for Language Learning and Growth

Middle school students, as we saw in Chapter 2, are often preoccupied with how they appear to the rest of the world. Many resent being treated as if they are children but don't want to shoulder adult responsibilities. Some are desperate to demonstrate that they can be viewed as young adults. They need to understand that the first impression they give someone is often through the language that they use. Therefore, one of the most important lessons we can teach middle school students is that their oral language, like the clothes they wear, the music they prefer, the food they eat, the friends with whom they spend time, identifies them. That concept alone should be enough to convince our middle school students that practice in oral language use—in generating and receiving spoken language—is worth their time and effort. One approach that my colleagues and I have found especially helpful for introducing language study to young adolescents is to spend time engaged in word play on a daily basis. In addition to piquing their interest regarding the oddities of our language, word play encourages young adolescents to buy into the idea that their use of oral language is a significant issue in terms of how they will be perceived by the world.

Warming Up with Word Play

The top priority of the activities suggested in this section is fun. The purpose of these activities is not to provide a carefully sequenced study of language; instead, it is to heighten students' interest in the symbol system that they use and rely on almost constantly—their language. Through these activities and other short and fun word plays, our students can become conscious of the importance of their oral language, as well as aware of the power of language and more attuned to the language of power.

Activity One: Words Are Us!   One way that we can get young adolescents involved in language study, with a focus on improving their abilities to tap into the power of language, is to heighten their awareness of how words work in the world. A strategy that holds promise for increasing awareness is simply to start each class day, or one class each week, with a Words Are Us! activity. To set up this activity, take a few minutes to show students some words, phrases, and language structures that have intrigued or surprised you. Recently, for example, I spotted this sign at the football stadium on campus: "Visiting Team's Guests' Entrance." For an instantaneous word play, I merely wrote the words on the board, faced my class, and asked, "What part of speech is *guests'*, anyway?"

Another day, I heard a commentator say, "The family was stricken with grief," and wondered, "When do we use stricken, and when do we use *struck*?" I asked students to search for an answer, promising a reward (the right to wear the Language Person medal for the day). Within hours, an answer appeared on my desk. The student who submitted it explained the differences between the two words to his classmates the next day. When *recapitulate* came up in conversation, a student pointed out that, although we expect *re-* to mean "do again" (as in "review"), *recapitulate* has nothing to do with *capitulate*. This realization led the class on a scavenger hunt for words that begin with *re-* but for which *re-* does not mean to "do again" whatever follows. *Remove, remind, repeal,* and *regard* were suggested, and a debate about *revision* ensued.

For a more planned activity, I tape the National Public Radio's Sunday morning broadcast of BBC cricket match scores. I play a portion of the broadcast while students listen and jot down notes, then play it again, so that they can add more notes, if necessary. We work together to try to determine what *points* mean in that complicated sport. After you have modeled a few Words Are Us teasers for your students, ask them to sign their names to a schedule, committing themselves to lead the class in a five-minute Words Are Us activity on their day. This low-risk opportunity to lead the class in an oral discussion of a language feature or quirk is a wonderful way to get even reluctant students engaged in class work. The Words Are Us activity also invites English language learners to participate; it is an ideal opportunity for them to teach their classmates about some of the words from their home language. (Students who are too shy to speak to the whole class should not be forced; to do so would generate anxiety about using language orally, and thus run counter to your goal for the word play portion of class. You might ask them to share their Words Are Us finds with a small group or just with you.)

Activity Two: Is It English?   It is essential that your students know that you are interested in playing with language and inviting them to play, too. This activity is similar to the experiment that we did in Chapter 5 when exploring our instinctive knowledge of grammar: Write a sentence composed of nonsense, non-English words on the board, such as "Demy cormeded splor mirgy blook." Ask students simple questions about the sentence, such as "What action is happening in this sentence?" "Who or what is doing the action in this sentence?" Because they inherently understand the structure of English (if they are speakers of English), they will be able to answer, "Something is being 'cormeded' and 'Demy' is doing the 'cormeding.'" Discuss what their answers tell them about what they know about how the structure of English (which is its grammar) works, and praise them for their brilliance. Let them generate their own nonsense sentences. The room will be abuzz with the sounds of languaging.

Try the flip side of this activity, too: On the board, write a series of words that students will recognize as English words, but in an order that no speaker of English would use, such as "Ballgame rain the was because cancelled the of." Ask several volunteers to read the words as they appear, and listen with the class as they prove how difficult it is to ignore what they know the order *should* be in order to read the words in the order that they are given. Point out, when they suggest that they know these words but that the order is all wrong, how much they already know about their understanding of the grammar of our language. Again, praise them for their linguistic brilliance. (See "What Is Grammar, Anyway?" in Chapter 5, for an explanation of what students' responses to these sentences suggest about their intrinsic understanding of English grammar.)

Activity Three: Palindromes.   Palindromes provide fun word play for middle school students, and they work best when responses are both spoken and written. Here is how to do a simple activity using palindromes: Ask a volunteer to read each word or phrase in Column A, below, aloud. After each word or phrase, the volunteer should call on classmates who can use one word that means the same thing and that is spelled the same way when spelled forward and backward. (Give an example or two from the list to get them started.) Solutions are given in Column B.

Column A (prompts)	*Column B (solutions)*
Part of the body	(eye)
Midday	(noon)
A young dog	(pup)
Flat	(level)
A word for addressing a lady	(madam)
A kind of watercraft	(kayak)
A system for detecting aircraft, ships, etc.	(radar)
An action	(deed)
Pieces of music for one person	(solos)
Somebody's father	(dad)

After they have completed the list, see how many more palindromes they can generate, working in teams. A challenging variation is to have students work in teams to list words that mean different things when spelled forward and backward. An example is *meet* (which is *teem* when spelled backward).

Activity Four: Headliners.   Michael Pierce, a long-time teacher of English language learners, asks volunteers to read aloud these headlines. As they read, the class hears surprising things, and tunes in to what can happen when we are careless with the intricacies of language structure:

> Astronaut Takes Blame for Gas in Spacecraft!
> Safety Experts Say School Bus Passengers Should Be Belted
> Two Sisters Reunite after 18 Years in Checkout Lane
> Squad Helps Dog Bite Victim
> Red Tape Holds up New Bridge
> Enraged Cow Injures Farmer with an Ax

Students have a great time when they figure out the unintended meaning that is embedded in each of these headlines. At the same time, they build confidence in their knowledge of the (sometimes tricky) ways the English language works.

Oral Language Opportunities

While it is true that a great amount of language learning happens indirectly or incidentally, through our participation in language situations, we can structure our classes to promote more careful, thoughtful use of listening and speaking skills. The instructional formats listed in this section represent many of the ways that students participate as listeners and speakers. As you review the list, think about the demands each language opportunity places on students who are skilled and confident languagers, those who are self-conscious and less skilled, and those for whom English is not a first language.

Conversations.   You can ask students to participate in actual conversations instead of the usually teacher-directed discussions that are more characteristic of middle school classrooms. In conversations, information is exchanged without formal turn-taking. If your students are used to classroom formats in which they make all of their remarks to the teacher, you will want to take time to teach them, through demonstrations, how to participate in classroom conversations. Middle school students sometimes need to be taught how and when to listen to others and how and when to contribute their points so that the entire group hears and considers them. In some cases, depending on their interests and needs for information, it is also appropriate to encourage a subset of the class to break off from the entire class and engage in a smaller conversation group. Conversations are especially useful for you as a way to gauge what students already know about a topic before we begin more formal instruction.

Whole- and Small-Group Discussions.   Discussions are, of course, a natural activity for promoting oral language use in the classroom. Typically during discussions, you provide focus by asking a question or making a thought-provoking statement before calling on several members of the class to take turns answering or responding. The direction of a discussion is, in general, more defined than in conversations. When discussions are used in small-group situations, one person may be designated as a note taker, who shares written notes with the other members of the group following the discussion. Discussions are useful as a way to review and reinforce main points that have been previously introduced, to encourage participation in thinking about a new topic, and to assess students' understanding of a topic that has been presented earlier.

Lectures and Reports.   Students can practice their oral language in a more formal way by preparing lectures or oral reports and presenting them to a small group or the entire class. During a student's lecture, the class members are expected to listen and take notes. It is important to remember, if using the student lecture/oral report format, that middle schoolers often need to be prompted to take notes when someone other than you is giving a lecture or report, particularly if that person is a classmate. Though discredited by some teacher educators, lectures and reports remain a common feature of classroom life. Our students have seen them modeled in school, church, clubs, and other settings, and may enjoy taking responsibility for what is said about a topic as the lecturer/oral report presenter. Student lectures/oral reports are especially effective when used as a means of introducing new information about which few in the class have background knowledge; they are most effective, especially for English language learners in the audience, when paired with a set of written highlights or visual aids.

Summaries. You can call on students to participate as oral languagers by asking them to provide their classmates with summaries. They might summarize what was learned or done during the previous class period (if the "summary" occurs early in the class session), or they might reiterate main points from the day's lesson (if the summary occurs near the end of the class session). During a class session, students can also be called on to summarize the content of an assignment, and so on, while the rest of the class listens and takes notes. Students should be encouraged to highlight the key points of their summaries by writing them, in abbreviated form, on a board or overhead, where they can be used later in review and preview activities. This visual reinforcement will be particularly helpful for English language learners as well as for students who process information better by seeing it than by hearing it.

Announcements and Directions. We expect students to be tuned in as listeners at all times. In school settings, though, that expectation is unrealistic, since demands on listeners are constant. When we ask students to reflect on the times and ways that they are expected to listen during a typical school day, they are likely to note schoolwide announcements made over a loudspeaker or closed-circuit television as one listening challenge. Ask students to make suggestions about how the announcements could be made more effective, and then offer them opportunities to try their suggestions in your classroom. For example, if a student says that she would listen more if music accompanied the morning announcements, ask her to bring in a recording of music and to create an announcement. Then try it, using a microphone, in your class. If the results are positive, she might want to approach the principal with a recommendation for schoolwide implementation of announcements that are accompanied by music. We can also invite students to make public service announcements about group meetings, sports practices, lost books, and so on as part of our classroom routine to encourage them to use oral language clearly and purposefully.

Scripted Performances, Dramatizations, and Role Plays. Students can be encouraged to fine-tune their use of oral language by participating in scripted performances such as reading aloud or preparing a script and then dramatizing a short story, poem, or scene from a novel. Students can also use oral language by participating in role plays, which are more impromptu than the scripted dramatizations. In role plays, students might take on the personas of characters from a story that they have recently read, and pretend that those characters are in a situation or setting that does not occur in the story. They might add new characters, possibly from other stories that they have read in class, or slightly twist the plot of a story, and so on. The point with these oral language activities is that they allow students to try out, to adopt, someone else's voice momentarily. They also allow students to interpret language according to their own instincts, and thus open up conversations about the interpretive choices they made.

As these instructional formats indicate, it is not difficult to engage students in purposeful listening, speaking, and languaging with a focus on oral language, in the middle school classroom. There are also many instructional strategies and activities that formalize students' participation in listening, speaking, and using language. One of the most popular is the speech unit.

One Teacher's Speech Unit

We can devise many kinds of speech units, each with its own set of goals and outcomes. My favorite speech unit moves through five focal points: animal communication, nonverbal communication, study of the art of creating speeches, a small group speech activity, and a speech before the whole class. The unit begins with the study of communication in the animal world, and is designed to give students increasing levels of confidence so that by stage five, in which they present a speech as individuals, they will be able to perform well.

Animal Communication

One year, after viewing a film on animal behavior that I borrowed from the science teacher, a group of eighth graders and I went outside. In the school yard, I watched with delight as one group of students enthusiastically traced the path of a platoon of ants as they marched toward a jelly bean, while another group listened intently to blue jays and robins and recorded the differences in their songs, using a shorthand that they contrived on the spot. When we returned to the classroom, the first group wrote hypotheses about ant-to-ant communication in their journals. The second wrote descriptions of the artistic quality of each bird's song. From there, some chose to do research about animal communication for their science classes. This broad focus on forms of communication led us to consider nonverbal communication among humans.

Nonverbal Communication

The second stage in this speech unit is to focus on nonverbal communication among humans. You can use humor to introduce the idea of nonverbal messages by merely imitating and exaggerating the body language signals that your students send you in various situations. The notion of proximics, or the personal space that we like to establish around us when we converse with others, is an intriguing area for discussion that can be presented easily through role plays. For example, ask two students to role play a scene in which a player is being disciplined for poor performance by his soccer coach. How close does the coach stand to the player with whom he is unhappy? How does that closeness make the player feel? Now ask them to imagine that the coach is the player's dad. Does that shift create a change in the situation? Ask two more students to role play a scene in which one approaches the other and asks a mundane question, such as "What time is it?," from several different distances. Have the person making the inquiry ask first from a comfortable few feet away. Then have her move closer and closer to the listener, until the listener's personal space is violated.

The class audience should note that personal space is not the only issue here, but that the listener's body language communicates information, too. Does she back away as the inquirer moves closer? Does she cross her arms in front of her to create more distance? Does she look away from, or directly toward, the inquirer? These questions provoke thoughtful conversation among students who usually take body language for granted.

Ideally, your student population will include adolescents from a variety of races and cultures. Since body language, gestures, and informal rules regarding proximics are culturally defined, this activity sets up an opportunity to talk about differences in nonverbal communication that exist across cultures, and the consequences of misinterpreting those nonverbal signals. As a wrap-up of this activity, have students discuss these scenes in small groups, and require that everyone make at least one statement about the scenes. This requirement will provide subtle help for them when they are required to talk to the whole class, later in the unit.

Studying the Art of Creating Speeches

During the third stage of the speech unit, I recommend that you take some time to introduce students to several kinds of speeches, including persuasion, demonstration, and explanation (exposition). Throughout the year, collect videotapes of speeches from television news and other shows; go to the Web and have students listen to recordings of both Martin Luther King, Jr.'s "I Have a Dream" speech, and President John F. Kennedy's Inaugural "Ask Not What Your Country Can Do for You" speech. Look for a variety of both impassioned and uninspiring speakers. Ask high school students who have participated in speech contests to visit and demonstrate their skills, and discuss the choices they made while preparing their speeches. With each example that they hear, have students try to identify the following elements: (1) speaker's purpose, (2) type of appeal that the speaker makes (to the listeners' logic, emotion, sense of humor, and so on), (3) what the speaker seems to know about his or her audience, (4) organizational structure of the speech, and (5) the type of introduction and conclusion used. By learning to identify these elements in others' speeches, your students will be setting themselves up to know where and how to use them in their own speeches.

Giving a Persuasive Speech: A Small-Group Activity

Stage four is to move from study of to creation of formal speeches. Have students work in small groups to generate a topic for a two-minute persuasive speech. The topic should be of real interest to the students in the school, such as the homework policy or dress code. Students within each group co-author the group's speech, with attention to the fact that the audience will be their classmates. Each person in the group should contribute to the composition of the speech, writing it down on notecards if available. Then each member should take two minutes to present the co-authored speech to the group. After all have presented within the groups, one person per group is selected to give the speech to the entire class. It may be beneficial for students to engage in the co-authored speech process more than one time before moving on to the fifth and final stage, the individual speech to the class.

Individual Speeches before the Whole Class

I recommend that teachers ask students to give a demonstration speech—on a topic about which they are an expert—the first time they present a formal speech to the class. There are at least two reasons. During a demonstration speech, students are allowed to manipulate a prop; a student who is demonstrating the ways to tie various knots, for example, has a rope nearby. The student who demonstrates how to build a terrarium has soil, plants, and a glass aquarium on the table in front of her. Although some students will unconsciously distract their audience by handling the props too much, most are comforted by having something familiar within their grasp as they talk. The props also provide students with a graphic reminder of the focus of their speech, thus potentially preventing one of the biggest problems that students have when they deliver formal speeches: In their nervousness, they forget what they intended to say.

Have students sign a speech schedule, and announce that you will be evaluating their speeches, with an eye and ear toward elements such as the following, all of which would have been studied in the previous stage: voice quality (volume and pace), eye contact and posture, attention to the interests of the audience, effectiveness of organization of the speech, impact of the introduction, body, and conclusion, and appropriate use of language. Incorporate these elements into a rubric on which you write comments as each student delivers his or her speech. In order to increase the chances that students are as attentive and courteous to the seventh speaker of the day as they are to the first, ask a cluster of students to join you as evaluators of each speech. Rotate the members of the cluster so that everyone evaluates at least one speech and every speaker receives feedback from several classmates as well as from you. Student evaluators should use the same rubric that you use, sign their comments, and give them to you so you can review them before giving them to the speaker, along with your comments.

Veteran teacher Liza Bryant requires her seventh and eighth grade students to do a number of oral presentations before they do formal speeches. Her students make informal presentations within their groups, and they work as a group to make informal presentations to the class. She notes that the time they spend giving low-risk talks prepares them to speak with confidence and purpose when they participate in a more formal speech unit. I like her strategy of using informal group talk as a prelude to the formal speech unit. It respects our young adolescents, recognizing that when we ask them to stand before their peers to make a speech, we are asking them to make themselves vulnerable to a tough audience. By starting with informal talks in small groups, then having the entire group stand together to present to the class, we can teach students how to shed some of what Liza identifies as markers of their nervousness, including rushed sentences, low volume, stutters, and forgetfulness.

One last note about a speech unit: Often, preservice teachers ask, "Should I make a student give a speech in front of the class if he really doesn't want to or says he can't?" My answer is, simply, and without apology, "No." Young adolescents are sometimes so self-conscious that standing in front of the class, vulnerable to peers' observations that they are too fatskinnyuglytallshortwhitedarkrichpoor, can be more than a small problem. Instead of insisting, I would ask that student if he would be able to give his speech in a small group, or, if not to them, to me. I would also tell him that he is welcome to sit down to give the speech and to make it a "talk"; I have seen students' comfort level increase when I merely encourage them to "sit at a desk and tell me your talk." When they sit behind a desk, a host of worries, from stains on a shirt, to waist sizes, old shoes, and protruding ribs, are not as readily visible to the audience. In a student-sensitive classroom, students should feel free to tell you if they have a particular concern regarding performing in front of the entire class, knowing that you will treat their worry gently.

Teacher Mark Shapiro is caught making a silly pun.

The Language of Power: Dialects in Spoken
and Written Language

The topic of dialects—their place in the classroom and beyond—is controversial among teachers of English and language arts because the way we speak denotes who we are, where we are from, what our values are. Students who come to us speaking various dialects, such as Black English vernacular (also called American Black English or ABE, African American vernacular or AAV, and Ebonics), Appalachian mountain dialect, or the hybrid of English and Spanish known as Spanglish are at a disadvantage in several intersecting ways. If the dialect that they speak or write deviates from the prestige dialect that is valued by the dominant culture, they risk identifying themselves, or having themselves perceived as, less educated, less cultivated, somehow less worthy than those who use proper English. Language then further alienates the nonnative or nonstandard speaker from the dominant culture. Yet if those same students learn the language that is taught at school and begin to use the prestige dialects in their homes and neighborhoods, they risk separating themselves from their families and community. Language then pushes them away from the support system and the people who matter most to them. As Suarez-Orozco and Suarez-Orozco (2001) note, for English language learners, "learning to speak standard English is not only a way of communicating; it also becomes an important symbolic act of identifying with the dominant culture" (p. 104). This acquisition of English, in its spoken and written forms, becomes a marker that they are different from those in their family and community who rely on another language. Ironically, then, the success that English language learners experience with acquiring "standard English," or the "language of wider communication" (see Chapter 5), often becomes a force that alienates them from their own ethnic group. The issue of *contexts* for language use, and the related issue of *appropriateness,* are issues that students should explore as young adolescents. Because of the academic and social implications of students' ability to harness the power of language and to understand the language of power, they are essential issues for the integrated literacy pedagogy.

Dialects: Different, Not Deficient

As teachers, we must be aware of the fact that our students' language is part of their identity and to remember the "deep affective roots" that support the communicative role of language (Suarez-Orozco & Suarez-Orozco, 2001, p. 106). The March 2001 issue of *English Journal* was devoted to language issues. In that issue, several teachers spoke out about dialects. Their words suggest that they are aware of the matrix of issues that surround the topic of dialects.

Gary Young, for example, realized that his high school students were embarrassed by their rural Southern dialect, which they saw portrayed on television and in movies as a marker for ignorance and even racism. He was aware that research indicates that use of nonstandard dialects has a "measurable negative effect at job interviews," an impact on "teacher expectations," a correlation with the number of "special education referrals," and an impact on the "overall quality of education." He knew that he should teach his adolescent students to use standard English—for their own good (Young, 2001, p. 21). However, he first had to acknowledge that his previous lessons on the grammar and mechanics of correct English emerged from a model that he terms "Southern shame." He explains, "In my mind, Southern English, East Texas English, wasn't just different, it was inferior, and part of a good education was getting rid of it. Well, that would have to change" (p. 21). The instructional change that Young implemented was simple yet powerful: He shifted the language instruction focus away from issues of correct and incorrect to discussion and practice with appropriate and inappropriate usage, within specific contexts. Young concludes that:

> Standard English is not inherently superior to other dialects; it's just more widely accepted and carries more prestige. People who speak other dialects probably aren't stupid and probably aren't ignorant; they're just unconvinced. And we're not going to convince them with shame and browbeating. They have to understand why it's in their best interest to learn Standard English and when it's appropriate to use it. (p. 21)

Young's attention to the issues of context and appropriateness are indicative of a student-sensitive, integrated literacy pedagogy.

Sara Dalmas Jonsberg, in "What's a White Teacher to Do about Black English?," realized that some of her students were ashamed whenever they slipped into their native dialect, Black English, in the classroom. Jonsberg has become committed to a pedagogy in which she treats bidialectalism as a form of bilingualism. She values bidialectalism as a rich contribution to classroom discourse: "If we are going to celebrate diversity in our classrooms, we must learn to be respectful not just of various literatures, but of the various knowledges, rooted in various languages, that our students bring with them into the classroom" (Jonsberg, 2001, p. 52). She advocates an approach in which language use is a choice that students must learn to make in regard to different contexts, and to recognize the political realities that have elevated standard English to the position of prestige dialect:

> [Students] can . . . understand how the larger culture has come to value one dialect over another. They can learn that "good" English has to do with politics and power more than with aesthetics or immutable rules. They can learn to be critical of a tradition that uses language implicitly to measure a speaker's morality and social value—when, for example, variations are described as "corrupt" or "defective" or "broken." (p. 52)

These teachers understand that dialects are different, not deficient, forms of language. I believe that our challenge is to teach young adolescents to use standard English, or what I refer to as the "power dialect," but also to teach them to respect and value not only their own dialects, but those of their classmates, neighbors, and members of society at large.

Teaching Respect for Dialects

For the lessons that deal with building respect for various dialects, our living example as we receive and respond to language variations will be more compelling than our words. And yet there are lessons about dialects that will reinforce the affective nature of acceptance of others' dialects. We need to emphasize that every dialect is rule governed and show students proof. One brief example regarding BEV is to write two sentences on the board: "He be working at the university" and "He working at the university." Speakers of BEV will be able to distinguish between the two sentences, using a rule that dictates that the copula *be* is used when referring to continuing (past, present, future) action, while the copula is omitted when the action is temporary. In these sentences, the first implies that he has worked, and will continue to work, for a long time at the university. In the second, he is working there only for the moment. We need to learn more about the dialects spoken by our students so that we can build our bank of examples of the rules. We need to demonstrate often the fact that "no dialect allows its speakers to cut corners at will" (Pinker, 2000, p. 177).

Can we expect middle school students to understand and appreciate the power of language, and the language of power, within the context of society? Can we expect them to learn to distinguish between times when one derivation of the standard language is appropriate and times when it is not? Absolutely. Martha Story, teacher of elementary, middle, and high school students, encourages us to recognize students' ability to make language use choices:

> Most students realize that situations in which they can use the nonstandard forms are in general conversations and informal discussions. They seem to understand that there are times to join in with the nonstandard use, and times when they should use formal forms. (June 6, 2002)

Cheryl Kopec Nahmias states that her students in one school, all of whom were African American, "preferred Black English in their speaking, but they were pretty adept at switching to standard English if they needed to change for different audiences." She continues by describing the balance she aimed toward:

> We had many conversations about the benefits of both dialects, and the advantages and disadvantages of using Black English or standard English in various contexts. I was more focused on enforcing standard English in my students' expository writing and I tended to provide contexts, such as formal debates, in which they would write out their speeches and then deliver them orally, using standard English. In creative writing, I was less concerned about enforcing the use of standard English because, quite frankly, their poetry and dialogues were often much better when written in the dialect they were more comfortable speaking. Their expressiveness in Black English was incredible. There was a musicality and humor that could never be captured in standard English forms. (June 6, 2002)

Teacher Althoria Taylor remarks on students' language competence:

> It always amazes me when students are able to be bilingual [bidialectal] successfully, when the student who walks the halls and communicates with classmates in his home language then comes into the classroom and proudly spouts formal standard English. Middle school students know how to use the right language at the right time. Sometimes, our job is just to remind them that the scene they just left—the hallway, for example—has changed to the classroom. That reminder is often enough—they switch language styles on the spot. (June 6, 2002)

These teachers have learned what beginning teachers will find: Students have an affinity for using language, and they enjoy demonstrating their language acrobatics. Our job is to tap into their spontaneous overflow of language energy and include it in our language instruction. The lesson set that follows is one example of how we can engage students in the study of dialects, with a focus on appropriateness, contexts, and appreciation for differences. The ideas begin with a project that encourages students to see themselves as speakers of a generational dialect. We then move into a consideration of features of African American vernacular English (AAVE), or BEV, as a means of helping students discover the rule-governed nature of dialects that differ from the prestige dialect.

Dialects among Us: A Sample Lesson Set

One of the intimidating aspects of teaching oral language, with a focus on dialects, is that we run the risk of insulting or embarrassing some of our students by pointing out how their utterances differ from the majority of their classmates'. We must therefore be diligent in assessing students' understanding of one crucial distinction: To speak a dialect is to speak with differences, not with deficiencies. Once they are comfortable with examining differences, without disparaging them, we can begin to focus on the fact that speakers of dialects follow specific rules that are associated with the dialect, just as speakers of standard English do.

Since middle school students are typically self-conscious, we don't want to draw attention to their oral use of language in a way that might embarrass them into reticence or silence.

One solution that is useful for us as we work with young adolescents is to have them engage in a spoken dialects project that will help them realize that we are all speakers of generational dialects. A generational dialects project honors students as individuals and as members of their age group; it focuses on their personal interests in words; it encourages them to see that literacies change over time, and it allows us, their teachers, to draw on professional standards for teaching language within particular contexts and for particular purposes. Young adolescents enjoy comparing the words, phrases, and syntax that they use with those that their parents' and grandparents' generations used when they were preteens and young teens. This kind of project has the added benefit of reinforcing the fact that language is like a living organism that changes and grows, instead of like a dead artifact that can be placed on a shelf to be studied.

Introductory Generational Dialect Project.   This project is designed to increase students' awareness that language changes and that it is better to think of spoken utterances in terms of whether they are appropriate or inappropriate, given a certain context and audience, than to try to determine if the use of language is good or bad, right or wrong.

Here is how to conduct this simple project:

The in-class phase, part one:
1. Ask your students to work in small groups to generate a list of their favorite sayings and terms (omitting any that would make their grandmothers blush) and then to create a glossary for these sayings and terms.
2. Have each group report on its list and glossary definitions, and create a class list. Display the list on an overhead transparency, a reserved place on the bulletin board, or a computer file that is designated for the project.
3. Ask the class to work together to identify ten of the terms or sayings that are of greatest interest and then to categorize those words by function. For example, they might categorize *ill* and *bad* as "a word that describes something that is good," and they might categorize *hip-hop* and *rap* as "a popular kind of music and style."
4. Ask each student to write the top ten terms, by category, and add the student-generated glossary definitions (or provide a copy of the list for them). This sheet of terms will become an important tool for the out-of-class phase of this project.

The out-of-class phase, part one:
1. Have students arrange to talk with an adult who is of their parents' generation and an adult who is older than their parents, perhaps of their grandparents' generation. (Ask colleagues to submit to your students' inquiries if any students are unable to find an adult who will cooperate with them during this project.) Emphasize to students that they are now dialect researchers and that they will get the best results if they interview people whose ages differ widely.
2. Have the students use the class-generated top-ten list as a resource for their interviews. They will ask questions related to the categories of words and phrases that they identified as important for their generation, and record adults' and older adults' responses regarding which words they used for the same function.

For example, imagine that the first word on the class-generated top-ten terms list is *ill*. Students can start the conversation about how words have changed by telling the adults: "When my friends and I say, 'That game is ill,' we mean it is really good." Then they should ask the adults and older adults whom they are interviewing, "What words did you use to describe something that is really good when you were a teenager? What words do you use today?" When they get to the item related to *hip-hop,* the student might ask, "What words were used to name the popular music when you were a teenager? What words describe the music you like best today?" After each answer, the students should write down the adults' responses. They might prefer to keep one page for answers from "parents' generation" and one for adults from an "older generation."

3. After collecting their data, students will organize it and analyze it on a chart that you provide. The organization can occur outside of class this way: Distribute to students two copies of a chart, and tell them that their job is to fill in the chart with the information that they have gathered. The simple chart should have three columns, labeled Student, Adult, Older Adult. It should be placed on a single piece of paper, with numbers one through ten down the side. The students' top-ten list words should appear in the first column. In the second column, students should add the corresponding terms that the adults used as teens and use today. The student should then repeat that process in the Older Adult column. For example, when the student receives the chart, the top two entries will look like this:

Student	Adult (age =)	Older Adult (age =)
a. ill		
b. hip-hop		

When the student fills in the chart, the first two entries will look like this:

Student	Adult (age = 35)	Older Adult (age = 70)
a. ill	cool/good	keen/nifty
b. hip-hop	rock 'n' roll/rock	big band/easy listening

The in-class phase, part two:

1. With their completed charts in hand, students should return to their small groups, compare results, and create a master chart for the group. It will be interesting to see how many terms that correspond to their contemporary terms emerge.

2. While they are in small groups, ask them to discuss these questions: "Can you say which terms that appear on the group's chart are right and which ones are wrong? Why or why not?"

3. Gather the small groups together for a whole-class discussion about the organic nature of language, and the danger of judging people based on whether or not their language sounds right or wrong to us. Review the notion of appropriateness by highlighting that what is right in one situation (or one time period) is likely to be different for another situation (or time period) but that different does not mean wrong.

The most obvious difference that students will find when they listen across generations will be in diction—the words themselves. This finding provides a useful context for introducing the notion of slang words as one marker of a speaker's dialect. For more on the distinction between dialect and slang, see "It's Just Slang, Isn't It?" in *Spreading the Word: Language and Dialect in America* by John McWhorter (2000, pp. 17–26).

Oral Histories.   This generational dialect (or generational slang) project might be used as a prelude to a more formal and time-consuming oral history project. Oral histories require that students become researchers, similar to the role they play in the generational dialect project. The goal is to have students talk to members of their family and community to seek information. Each class of students might decide whether they want to focus on a particular issue or to canvas a neighborhood to find out as much as they can about its people, in general. For example, all of the student researchers in one class might ask people in the community to respond to one question, such as "What was discrimination like in this neighborhood in the 1960s?" All of the student researchers in another class might, on the other hand, decide to work one-on-one with individuals in the community and ask a series of questions to their one person. For example, they might identify one elderly resident of their neighborhood and ask her several questions, such as "What is your strongest memory associated with your neighborhood? How long have you been living here? Do you know your neighbors? What are they like? What would you change about your neighborhood if you could? How would you describe it to other people who have never lived here?"

Oral histories are usually conducted by a student gaining permission to tape record those who agree to have their voices and answers to interview questions recorded. The student might then transcribe the words spoken by the person interviewed, and arrange them into a written account of the person and the interview. Whether students transcribe the tapes to prepare written accounts, or merely label the taped interviews, the class will be able to generate a class document of the oral histories. Ideas to tap when conducting oral histories include questions such as these:

- How did you refer to your parents when you were my age?
- What did you call your teachers when you were my age?
- Do you remember which subjects you took in school? What were they called?
- When you were my age and you talked with your friends, what did you usually talk about?
- What words did you use to describe dancing? kissing? getting ready to take a test?
- What were some of the activities that you did with your friends?
- Did you have any pets? What did you call them?
- What were your friends' names and nicknames?

Exploring the Rules of Various Dialects: Using African American English Vernacular as an Example.

During the generational dialect project and/or the oral histories project, students collect and study evidence that suggests that language changes, that definitions of right and wrong have little basis, and that dialects can be "different" without being deficient. A positive next step may be for them to test what they now know in terms of their assumptions about a commonly used dialect, Black English vernacular (BEV). The ideas for teaching BEV have their basis in "Linguistic and Sociolinguistic Requisites for Teaching English," by sociolinguist and educator Walt Wolfram (1998).

Wolfram has used the following sequence of exercises with preservice teachers and fourth graders, with a similar goal: to reinforce an understanding of the "intricate, intrinsic basis of patterning" (1998, p. 92) that is present in BEV and to demonstrate "how all varieties of languages must be respected for their intrinsic patterning" (p. 94).

Wolfram begins his activity by asking students to read pairs of sentences and to place a check mark beside those that use the verb *be* appropriately. Pairs include these samples:

1. ___a. They usually be happy when they come home.
   ___b. They be happy right now.
2. ___a. Juan be coming to school right now.
   ___b. Gloria always be coming to school.
3. ___a. My foot be broken from the accident.
   ___b. Sometimes my foot be hurting.

(Answers 1. A; 2. B; 3. B)

Wolfram then asks students to volunteer their answers and records them. For us as teachers it is important to know that Wolfram explains that even when young children participate in this activity, those who are speakers of BEV are more likely to choose the correct sentence in each pair. He explains that speakers of BEV innately understand that "*be* typically is used to indicate a regularly occurring activity" (Wolfram, 1998, p. 94).

Once students have figured out the rule for the use of *be,* ask them to apply it to another set of sentences, marking which ones use *be* properly. Here are some sample sentences, modeled after those that Wolfram uses (1998, p. 94):

1. ___ The girls always be giggling during class.
2. ___ The girls don't be giggling right now.
3. ___ Sometimes, the students be ready for recess.
4. ___ Right now, the football players be warming up.
5. ___ Teachers always be giving homework.

(Answers: 1. Yes; 2. No; 3. No; 4. No; 5. Yes)

An essential part of this focus on BEV is to talk with students about the implications. You might ask them to finish statements like these in order to assess their understanding:

1. The rules that determine how speakers of BEV use *be* show me that BEV _____.
2. Since BEV has rules and consistent patterns built into it, I know that when people speak in BEV, they _____.
3. When someone speaks in a dialect that is different from the one I use, I will not make the mistake of thinking _____.

Integrated Literacy Checklist

In this chapter, literacy skills in all of the language arts areas are integrated in the focus on oral language. The following sections provide reminders about activities described within the chapter and brief suggestions about other related language activities.

Reading

Comparison of Authors' Language Style or Language Use: Students are encouraged, when studying language, to consider which styles and structures appeal to them. Invite them to spend time with texts, and determine which styles create a barrier that keeps them outside of the text.

Study of Famous Speeches: Students can read copies of famous speeches and identify rhetorical patterns such as repetition. An example is, "I have a dream that . . . I have a dream that . . . ." Another kind of rhetorical pattern that involves repetition is "chiasmus." An example is, "Ask not what your country can do for you; ask what you can do for your country." Attention to these kinds of patterns may help students identify and describe the features that make the speeches effective and memorable.

Writing and Reading Speeches: Students are encouraged to write out their own formal speeches and then to serve as readers for their classmates prior to the days for giving speeches.

Literature

Dialects in Literature: The study of dialects should include samples of dialect excerpted from literary sources. These excerpts should be read aloud and discussed in terms of the author's purpose for writing with dialects, as well as the impact of that stylistic choice.

Language Standards in Literature: Literature provides models for proper use of the grammar and mechanics of standard English, as well as counterexamples, those that prove that rules are not always followed.

Writing

Writing Is Not Merely Talk Made Visible: A simultaneous focus on speaking and writing as meaning-making activities allows students to better understand the differences between the two modes of communication.

Generational Dialects Project and Oral Histories: These activities may have written components that emerge from notes taken during conversations with adults and from audiotaped interviews with participants.

Media

Famous Speeches: Students will mine these speeches, many of which are available in spoken versions on the Web and in electronic encyclopedias, for examples of stylistically effective features.

Animal Communication Movies: Movies that introduce information about how animals communicate within their own species can enhance a speech unit.

Nonverbal Communication: Videotaping students as they demonstrate body language, gestures, and personal space increases their ability to analyze and evaluate both the body language and listeners' responses to it.

Words Are Us!: There are myriad examples of word puzzles and language games on the Web. Many are appropriate for the five-minute Words Are Us activity that is recommended as a regular class feature.

Help for English Language Learners

Words Are Us!: This activity allows ELL students to choose a topic, to become the class expert on that topic, and to practice speaking as an expert in front of the class. Examples like Michael Pierce's headlines and the palindrome activity help ELL students discover, with their native-speaking classmates, that English can be a tricky and funny language.

Classroom Conversations and Discussions: These invite ELL students to participate at their own pace and comfort level as meaning makers in a low-risk environments.

Summaries, Lectures, and Reports: When supported with written highlights or notes, help ELL students match oral and written language in their minds.

Scripted Performances and Dramatizations: These allow ELL students an opportunity to practice reading written language aloud and to hear themselves speak English aloud for a group.

Speech Unit: Again, ELL students have an opportunity to test their languaging with the support of a structured assignment. They might choose culturally or linguistically relevant topics that allow them to speak as the class expert.

Dialects: The emphasis on dialects as different, not deficient, in the generational dialect project, oral histories project, and AAEV lessons will give students who are not ELLs an opportunity to reevaluate assumptions they have made regarding the intelligence of ELL students and may engender a greater amount of respect for linguistic differences among all students.

NCTE/IRA Standards

Standard Number One: Students read a wide range of print and nonprint texts to build an understanding of texts, of themselves, and of the cultures of the United States and the world; to acquire new information; to respond to the needs and demands of society and the workplace; and for personal fulfillment. Among these texts are fiction and nonfiction, classic, and contemporary works.

Standard Number Three: Students apply a wide range of strategies to comprehend, interpret, evaluate, and appreciate texts. They draw on their prior experience, their interactions with other readers and writers, their knowledge of word meaning and of other texts, their word identification strategies, and their understanding of textual features (e.g., sound–letter correspondence, sentence structure, context, graphics).

Standard Number Four: Students adjust their use of spoken, written, and visual language (e.g., conventions, style, vocabulary) to communicate effectively with a variety of audiences and for different purposes.

Standard Number Six: Students apply knowledge of language structure, language conventions (e.g., spelling and punctuation), media techniques, figurative language, and genre to create, critique, and discuss print and nonprint texts.

Standard Number Nine: Students develop an understanding of and respect for diversity in language use, patterns, and dialects across cultures, ethnic groups, geographic regions, and social roles.

Standard Number Ten: Students whose first language is not English make use of their first language to develop competency in the English language arts and to develop understanding of content across the curriculum.

Standard Number Eleven: Students participate as knowledgeable, reflective, creative, and critical members of a variety of literacy communities.

Standard Number Twelve: Students use spoken, written, and visual language to accomplish their own purposes (e.g., for learning, enjoyment, persuasion, and the exchange of information).

Works Cited

Blachowicz, C., and Fisher, P. J. (2002). *Teaching vocabulary in all classrooms,* 2nd edition. Upper Saddle River, NJ: Merrill Prentice Hall.

Jonsberg, S. D. (2001). What's a (white) teacher to do about Black English? *English Journal 90*(4): 51–53.

McWhorter, J. (2000). *Spreading the word: Language and dialect in America.* Portsmouth, NH: Heinemann.

National Council of Teachers of English, Conference on College Composition and Communication (1988). *The national language policy* (position statement). Urbana, IL: NCTE.

Nahmias, C. K. (2002). Personal conversation. Tallahassee, Florida, June 6, 2002.

Pinker, Steven. (2000). *The language instinct: How the mind creates language.* New York: Perennial Classics of HarperCollins.

Suarez-Orozco, C., and Suarez-Orozco, M. M. (2001). *Children of immigration.* Cambridge: Harvard University Press.

Taylor, A. (2002). Personal conversation. Tallahassee, Florida, June 6, 2002.

Weaver, C. (1996). *Teaching grammar in context.* Portsmouth, NH: Boynton/Cook Heinemann.

Wolfram, W. (1998). Linguistic and sociolinguistic requisites for teaching language. In John S. Simmons and Lawrence Baines (Eds.). *Language study in middle school, high school, and beyond: Views on enhancing the study of language.* Newark, DE: International Reading Association.

Young, G. (2001). Shame on whom? *English Journal 90*(4): 20–22.

7 Overflowing with Competing Messages: Critiquing Popular Media

Two students considering media connections for their upcoming presentation.

Recently, I had the opportunity to observe Michael, a veteran teacher, as he worked with a small group of at-risk seventh graders in the computer lab at a local school. Michael, who was volunteering his time, had agreed to try to help the students, each of whom had standardized test scores that were significantly below grade level. As far as the classroom teacher could tell, the eight lowest-scoring students could not read at all. She had tried to help them, but because she had twenty students in her class who could read, in addition to the eight who could not, she decided that her time was better spent with the twenty who could read. When Michael went to the classroom the first day, he was asked to take the eight lowest-scoring students to the media center and "do anything" to try to help them learn to read. The students, who referred to themselves as "the dummies" (lack of school success was not new to any of them), had no expectations that they would pass seventh grade.

After talking with the group of eight for about a half hour, Michael asked each to tell him what they liked to think about, talk about with their friends, do in their free time. One student, whom I will call Jay, spoke up quickly, "I am a hip-hop singer." Jay's friends chimed in, saying, "He is. He knows everything about hip-hop. Just ask him anything about any song. About styles, too. He knows everything." Michael said he wasn't sure what "hip-hop" means. Jay offered to show him "on the Net." Within minutes, Jay, who was at risk of failing seventh grade due to extremely low test scores and poor performance in classes, was navigating Web sites to collect and share information about his favorite hip-hop artist with Michael.

A wily teacher, Michael was curious about whether or not Jay could actually read the information on the Web, especially since Jay's classroom teacher had assured Michael that Jay was a nonreader. To our amazement, Jay not only could read the information aloud, but he could reword, interpret, and even evaluate it for Michael's benefit. Jay was even able to pronounce difficult vocabulary words such as *debut* and *visionary* correctly and to explain accurately what they meant in context. Clearly, Jay was a reader—although he preferred to read only when it suited his own purposes, limiting himself to topics that were of interest to him and that gave him status among his friends. For the next few weeks, Michael worked to help Jay develop not only his already substantial reading skills but also to recognize the benefits of participation in class as a reader and thinker to progress in school.

I have given a lot of thought to what happened with Jay in that situation. It raises a host of questions, including these, which begin with a focus on Jay's situation and then expand to address media in the classrooms in a more general way:

■ What would have happened to Jay if he had not been pulled aside and sent to the library with Michael, a teacher who tapped into his interests and asked Jay to use those interests to demonstrate his skills as a languager?

■ How many opportunities to help students develop their skills do we miss, merely because students are not always eager to play by our rules as their teachers?

■ How might we design lessons that do a better job of taking advantage of students' interest in popular culture and their affinity for using technology to help them grow as learners?

■ How often do we fail to recognize or understand our students' areas of expertise and assume, falsely, that they are not thinkers?

■ What are other areas of media that are important in the literacy development of young adolescent students?

Questions like these and others that are sure to emerge as we work with today's middle school students should help guide us as we consider ways of incorporating attention to media and technology into our classrooms. The National Council of Teachers of English refers to this newest area of subject matter as "mediacy." Through integrating media studies into our classrooms, we have an opportunity to try dishes that often are more exotic than the traditional print-based fare of the language arts classroom. When we include media on our menus, there is a chance that even reluctant readers and writers like Jay will share meals with us.

Media Study in an Integrated Literacy Pedagogy

Young adolescents are beginning to explore the world on their own terms. Unlike children, who are often told how to act and what to think, young adolescents draw on multiple sources of information as they make decisions for themselves. (This is true not only in school settings like the one where Jay is negotiating the world. Remember Krista's typical day, as described in Chapter 1?) While the lessons that they learn from their families will provide them with the foundation for the values systems that they begin to develop as young adolescents, middle school students are also vulnerable to other sources of influence. For example, a 12-year-old girl might choose to wear the kind of revealing clothes that a popular singer wears, even if doing so upsets her parents, because she believes that she will be more popular, accepted, or impressive if she imitates the popular singer. A 14-year-old boy might decide that making ugly remarks about women is cool because he hears his favorite movie star making statements that degrade women. An 11-year-old girl might decide that she is way too fat and force herself to lose weight based on her media-constructed image of the perfect female body. Her 13-year-old classmate might decide that he cannot participate in the math club since a popular television show depicts smart students as nerds. As these examples indicate, it is particularly appropriate and important that we help our young adolescent students become careful, critical consumers of media. A curricular emphasis on media is complementary to the four major beliefs that serve as the foundation for an integrated literacy pedagogy.

Belief One: In studying the influence of media, we can ask students to respond as individuals and as groups and to examine their behavior in both roles. In fact, it is at this point in the curriculum that one of the most interesting paradoxes of adolescence can be brought to the surface for careful examination: Young adolescents want to be thought of as unique individuals, yet they also crave group membership, and often submerge their individuality beneath a group identity.

Belief Two: Media study provides an ideal opportunity to zero in on the topics and themes that are of interest to our own students and then to move with them through layers of sophistication as they study those topics and themes. As Jay's story demonstrates, students who are interested in a topic find ways to explore it; if they have access to the Internet, they are likely to be able to teach us, their teachers, not only about the topic but also about how to dig deeper to uncover more information. We can then help them learn to think about that information with critical minds and to transfer those critical skills to other reading and thinking tasks as well.

Belief Three: Adding media study to the middle school language arts curriculum guarantees a definition of literacy that is broader than the traditional one, that limits literacy to "the skills required to read and write to communicate." When we include media study in the curriculum, we encourage students to continue to develop their skills as languagers who make sense of and know their world through formally taught and learned means (identifying main and inferred ideas, writing expository essays, analyzing poetic lines, dramatizing scenes, for example). But when we include media study in the curriculum, we also encourage students to consider how much they learn without being directly taught, with particular attention to the messages regarding how they should dress, what they should like, how they should behave, and what they should think.

Belief Four: Media studies have not traditionally been a part of the language arts curriculum. For most of the twentieth century, our curriculum was based on the "tripod" of reading, writing, and literature study. Our instincts and observations regarding the media influences that are most pervasive among our students provide an essential resource for us as we begin to formulate media-related goals and teaching/learning activities. We can pair our situated knowledge and understanding with the more general professional standards that delineate what is appropriate for middle school students to know as media consumers and media makers.

Teaching Media Issues

We must recognize the impact that television, movies and videos, magazines, music, and the Internet has on shaping young adolescents. Our biggest challenge and goal are to help our students to become thoughtful consumers, not vulnerable targets, of mass media. A secondary goal will be to assist young adolescents as they learn to be makers of media, to shape its messages by contributing their own knowledge, understanding, and perspectives.

Experts disagree on what should be included in a comprehensive definition of *media* (Downes & Miller, 1998, p. 1). In this chapter, we first focus on the following branches of media and the impact they have among young adolescent consumers: television and movies/videos, popular music, magazines, advertising, and the Internet and the World Wide Web. Next, with an eye toward the overarching goal of developing students' literacies so that they will be able to make sense of their world, we explore ways to help our students make nutritious choices when they consume mass media.

In the first section, we focus on critical viewing of television, movies, and video through the Camera's Eye project; we consider activities that promote critical experiences with popular music, such as the Creating Sound Tracks project; and we explore the potential of activities that promote sagacious use of the Internet and Web such as the E-Log project and the Technology in Adolescent Literature project. The chapter ends with examples of preservice teachers' lessons on the competing and confusing messages of mass media and with lists of ideas for integrating media across the language arts, suggestions for English language learners, and highlights of the NCTE/IRA standards that are addressed in the chapter.

Media and Media-Generated Definitions of Adolescence

Concerns Regarding Television and Movies/Videos

It is common knowledge that we increase our chances of reaching our students when we bring elements of their world—their favorite television shows and movies, their music, their magazines, their idols—into the classroom. However, we must remember that it is not enough to bring artifacts into the room; we must help students learn to read the media of their world with critical eyes and ears. Sara Shandler (1999) shows us why. Sara was 17 when she began *Ophelia Speaks: Adolescent Girls Write about Their Search for Self* with this candid self-assessment:

> I was a media-fed child. I can't remember a time when the television wasn't my favorite baby-sitter, my most reliable companion, my preferred role model. *The Cosby Show*, *Growing Pains* . . . jumped out of the fluorescent tube and planted expectations in my preadolescent mind. Every Thursday, in health class, the After-School Special offered a "realistic" view of the years to come. . . . Then, after years of preparation, of longing to talk on the phone, go out with my friends, and wear mascara, I finally became a teenager.
>
> Adolescence is not what I thought it would be. Happy endings aren't inserted conveniently before the last commercial break. The peer pressure isn't unrelenting . . . the first loves aren't thrillingly perfect. But, more unsettling than the unforeseen tedium, my face isn't blemish-proof and my stomach isn't immune to bloating. I was fed a cookie-cutter standard of beauty, and I do not invariably meet the media's image of perfect. As a media baby, I'm a disappointment. (p. 3)

Shandler's acknowledgment that she was a "disappointment" as a "media baby" points an accusing finger at the unhealthy influence that media images can have on the development and self-image of today's adolescent females; her words have implications for the development of adolescent males, as well. No teacher, and probably no parent, would have been able to shield Sara, or other young adolescents, from images of unattainable perfection that she absorbed while she gobbled up a diet high in mass media. But as teachers of literacy, we can help adolescents learn when and how they are being manipulated by television shows and movies, magazines, popular music, and the Web. Armed with an understanding of the their position as consumers, our preteens and teens can learn to avoid being vulnerable to manipulation, even when they are marked as easy targets.

Victor C. Strasburger, in *Adolescents and the Media: Medical and Psychological Impact* (1995), cites a 1993 Nielsen media study that indicates that the average American teen watches twenty-two hours of television per week, not including videocassette movies or video games, and that television viewing is the most popular leisure activity of teens (p. 2). Televisions are ubiquitous in America: 98 percent of our homes have at least one television, which is more than the percentage of homes with indoor plumbing.

What are the problems that are most obvious when considering the possible effect of television viewing on teens? Strasburger explains that TV gives teens " 'scripts' about how adults are supposed to act; it teaches them about gender roles, conflict resolution, patterns of courtship and sexual gratification, and methods of coping with stress" (Strasburger, 1995, pp. 7–8). The problem is that fictitious depictions of relationships, problems, and resolutions are unrealistic. Nevertheless, teens see the characters as role models:

> What is observed may be imitated, or it may simply influence a child's beliefs about the world. Modeling may be a crucial factor in teenagers' decisions about when and how to begin consuming alcohol, for example. Sports and rock stars frequently appear in beer and wine ads, and the underlying messages are clear: "Real men" drink beer; beer drinkers have more fun, more friends, and are sexier. (Strasburger, 1995, p. 8)

David Hamburg (1994) criticizes television's portrayal of sexuality: "Television provides young people with guidance about how to be sexy, but not much about how to be sexually responsible" (Hamburg, 1994, p. 192). Strasburger (1995) supports Hamburg's contention when he cites a 1988 study by S. Steenland, which indicates that adolescent girls may be led to believe the following by watching television shows:

- Girls' looks are more important than their brains.
- Intelligent girls are social misfits.
- Teen girls are more passive than teen boys.
- Teen girls are obsessed with shopping, grooming, and dating, and are incapable of having serious conversations about academic or career interests.
- Almost all teen girls are middle class or wealthy. (p. 11)

Strasburger also draws attention to the portrayal of violence as an extreme and serious example of how television fails to reflect reality. Television violence is "happy violence, characterized by being clean and fast, with few tragic consequences and with no real connection to criminal statistics or realities" (1995, p. 14). The American Psychological Association points out that over 1,000 studies show media violence as "one *cause* of real-life violence," and that teens see 10,000 murders, rapes and aggravated assaults per year on television (pp. 19 and 21). Many studies suggest a strong correlation between seeing and committing violent acts. For example, in a study of more than 1,500 adolescent males, Nelson found that those who viewed excessive amounts of violent TV committed a greater number of antisocial, criminal, and misdemeanor acts than did light TV viewers. Nelson also found that aggressiveness in sports and use of foul language were explicitly associated with high television exposure (p. 30). These troubling statistics are certainly a cause for adults to think about the viewing habits of adolescents, and they provide an almost frantic call for lessons that encourage critical thinking about media images.

Research into the effects that viewing an inordinate amount of television have on adolescents (and into what would constitute an inordinate amount and for whom) is difficult to conduct. The difficulty is due, in part, to the fact that there are few adolescents in the United States who could be included in a control group of nonviewers, as well as to other environmental variables that cannot easily be teased out and considered independently. Nevertheless, common sense suggests that television has a potentially overwhelming impact on how adolescents conceptualize adulthood. This point of view is not, however, universally accepted. Herbert Gans rejects it in *Popular and High Culture: An Analysis and Evaluation of Taste* (1999). Gans insists that those who claim that television violence breeds actual violent behavior are blowing evidence out of proportion. He argues that if the formula were correct, an increase in violence would have resulted in proportion to an increase in the availability of mass media. Further, he suggests that the formula fails to account for the fact that females and nonpoor adolescents are seldom perpetrators of violent behavior. Like the poor and males who are more likely among teens to perpetrate criminal behavior, females and nonpoor teens are also viewers of violence on television and in movies. Gans does allow, however, that children and poorly educated adults who have not learned to discount television as unreal and who make extensive use of mass media "may be more affected by the media than the rest of the population" (p. 51).

In *Channel Surfing: Race Talk and the Destruction of Today's Youth* (1997), social critic Henry Giroux insists that youth, who live in an "electronically mediated culture," have been recast by society as a collective "menace" (pp. 5–6). According to Giroux, the demonization and trivialization of youth in dominant representational media are intentional acts on the part of the adults who control media production. For example, television advertisements such as those for Calvin Klein's jeans, which portray youth with the dark circles and emaciated figures of so-called heroin chic, reinforce the idea that youth are misguided menaces and cannot be trusted or taken seriously by society. Popular contemporary movies portray adolescents as "groveling dimwits" or as violent thugs, without any insights into the reasons that the youth live in a society in which they have learned to act like animals. Popular television and music are also tools used by adults to retain their superiority over youth, according to Giroux:

> Television sitcoms such as *Friends* portray young people as shallow, unmotivated, navelgazing slackers intent on making do without the slightest interest in a larger social and political world. . . . These white middle-class youth are defined largely through their roles as conspicuous consumers, their political indifference, and their intense lack of motivation to engage a world beyond their own self-indulgent interests. On the other hand, represented through a celluloid haze of drugs, crime, and sex, black youth are viewed as menacing and dangerous. (p. 73)

Giroux forcibly reminds us that it is adults who have control of media. It is, therefore, adults who define youth, through the popular media, while young people themselves are not given much say in how they are presented to the world. When teens live down to adults' lowest expectations, adults have no one to blame but themselves. Teens' allegiance to particular television shows fluctuate from year to year: Reality television such as *Survivor*, full-length animated programs like *The Simpsons*, music videos of MTV and VH-1, and afternoon and evening soap operas (*The Young and the Restless* and *Dawson's Creek*) are likely to attract different segments of teen audiences. Regardless of their immediate favorites or longstanding choices, however, adolescents need to learn to view television and movies through critical lenses.

Do you believe that teens' interpretations of what television and popular movies suggest to young adolescents—regarding sexual activity, violence, reality, or cool behavior—are not your concern as a teacher of language arts and multiple literacies? Think again. Our job includes paying attention to the language source that typical students turn to for hours every day. Therefore, we are obliged to turn our thoughts and some of our class time to television and movies and their messages.

Concerns Regarding Music

It is possible that teens spend even more time listening to music than they spend in front of television and movie screens. Much of the time that they spend in front of televisions is spent watching music videos. Music is important in the socialization of young adolescents. Members of peer groups often are drawn together because of interest in similar kinds of music, or they build an interest in similar kinds of music as part of their group's evolving definition. Some teens use music as an antiestablishment symbol.

Strasburger (1995) cites one study of over 2,700 adolescents, aged 14 to 16, that indicates that average teens in the southeast United States listen to music approximately forty hours each week (p. 82), or almost twice as much time as they spend watching television or playing computer games. He finds that, aside from heavy metal and gangsta rap, most contemporary rock music "is surprisingly mainstream in its value orientation," with romantic love as the primary theme, despite the fact that the treatment of love has become more physical and graphic in recent years (p. 89).

Jeffrey J. Arnett, a professor of human development and family studies, paints a slightly different picture, noting that today's adolescents are drawn to a variety of musical types, including the "harsh, dark sound . . . with themes of alienation and anger" of heavy metal, the "brighter, lighter sound" of hard rock, and pop songs that "concern mainly boy-girl and hedonistic themes—sex, angry love, lost love, desired love, partying, and more sex" (Arnett, 1995, p. 41). We also know that teens are drawn to the aggressively insistent lyrics and beat of rap, the storytelling of country music, and the uplifting messages of contemporary Christian bands.

David Elkind uses a 15-year-old female's journal entry to denote the kinds of mixed and confusing messages that teens hear when they are drawn to popular music:

> This song was about sex. The song was saying basically "come over to my house so we can do it!" This represents sex as being o.k. Later I heard "Let's Wait Awhile" by Janet Jackson. Which basically says, "Let's not rush into it." It's kind of hard as a teenager to decide which is right. The [song saying sex was ok] . . . seemed happy with a carefree attitude. Janet sounded sad and depressed. Even though I know it's better to "wait awhile" the other song was more appealing. It seemed harmless. They talk about [sex] like "come over and have ice cream. . . ." I really know which is the right way, but sometimes the way the media talks [sic] about it you really begin to wonder. (Elkind, 1998, p. 132)

This young female is a step ahead of many teens whose diet includes a lot of popular music, because she has stopped to contrast and evaluate competing messages and the means by which they are transmitted. She demonstrates in her journal a critical skill that we need to encourage in all of our middle school students: We must teach them to question the portrayal of youth, adults, sexual activity, drug use, violence, love, lust, anger, hatred, and all other attitudes and behaviors.

Baines, Strehle, and Bell (1999) note that over $12 billion was spent on music on 1995 and that teenagers aged 15 to 19 comprised the largest group of customers. They add an ominous note that teachers need to consider: While songs that glorify human denigration and prurience, such as rap group 2 Live Crew's "Hey, We Want Some Pussy" and "NWA" (Niggers with Attitude), have faced challenges in courts, they have continued to sell well in music stores (p. 166). Today, MTV, VH-1, and countless individual music videos have fueled stronger interest in the sexual and violent undertones of some lyrics, often making visually explicit an idea that may be more subtly suggested in the lyrics.

Concerns Regarding Magazines

Recently, I had the opportunity to watch as a computer graphic artist altered a 5×7-inch photograph to make a man's foot look smaller and his leg more shapely. More dramatically, in the same photograph she removed a branch from one tree and attached it to another tree. Her purpose was to give the photographic image balance. I wish that every young adolescent could watch as that artist changed a person's appearance and rearranged Mother Nature's limbs with a quick swipe of the mouse. Young adolescents long to emulate the bodies, clothes, style, and joie de vivre of the people whose pictures appear in teen-targeted magazines. Sadly, many become so caught up in the beautiful photographic images that they fail to realize that the clothes are pinned into flawless fits, the faces are retouched, the look of happiness is often a forced and compensated smile. Our students trust that they see the real world in teen magazines, and it becomes the world they desire for themselves.

In 1995, I conducted a study of the topics, themes, images, and advertisements in popular magazines that are marketed for teens. As expected, I found that most of the teen-marketed magazines are devoted to fashion and beauty, music, and sports (with a surge in the popularity of magazines about skateboarding, BMX bicycles, and professional wrestling that I had not seen earlier). What did surprise me, though, was the disrespect that many of the magazines showed toward their readers. I suspect that the attitude adopted is calculated to resonate with readers who want to be cool and young and fresh. As a teacher and a human, I found the attitude irritating, belittling, and bothersome. *Rolling Stone*, which is popular in middle and high school libraries provides a potent example. Its issues contain requisite articles on rock music and musicians. But one issue I read also had a feature on Garry Shandling's television show, in which Shandling referred to his co-workers as "f . . . ing idiots" (ellipsis added) (Martel, 1994, p. 66). This jolt was followed in the same issue by a review of Oliver Stone's *Natural Born Killers* in which the reviewer referred to the movie as a "surreal splatterfest" that Stone had "puked up" after "ingesting every media-hyped crime story from Bobbitt to Buttafucco to Menendez and Simpson" (Travers, 1994, p. 83). This critic's disparagement of popular news media struck an ironic tone for me.

In the beauty and fashion magazines, then as now, the focus is on how to make one's body tiny and toned and skin blemish free, how to get a guy's attention, and how to cultivate friendships and drop losers. Advertisements support the hypotheses of the articles by suggesting that a person is worthless unless she is beautiful, that beauty must be extremely narrowly defined, and that only those who are beautiful deserve to reach their goals and find contentment. Happily, today's young adolescent females can also choose magazines and zines (electronic magazines, discussed in the next section) that focus on health and fitness, community participation and volunteerism, and other issues that do not necessarily involve advice on how to count calories, apply mascara, or add another male to their lives.

As teachers, we need to know what our students are reading and to keep in mind the impact it can have on our students. Consider the haunting words of 17-year-old Jessica Bulman in her miniature reflection, "Catalogues": "Searching through catalogues, you wish you could order the bodies not the clothes" (in Shandler, 1999, p. 5). This confession should serve to remind us of the necessity of teaching teens to look carefully and critically at the visual and verbal information presented in magazines and in advertisements of all types.

Concerns Regarding Advertising

In *The Rise and Fall of the American Teenager*, Thomas Hine discusses how advertisers and advertisements manipulate contemporary youth:

> The distance between spontaneous expression and large-scale commercial exploitation has never been shorter. Creators of youth fashion, such as Nike, go so far as to send scouts to the ghetto to take pictures of what young people are wearing on the street and writing on the walls. Nike seeks to reflect the latest sensibilities, both in its products and its advertising. The company feeds the imagery right back to those who created it, offering them something they cannot afford as a way of affirming themselves. (1999, p. 280)

Many child and adolescent development experts are concerned with the demeaning way that adolescents are portrayed and the debasing messages they are sent about who and what adults expect them to be. Elkind (1998) contends that the media, particularly television and advertising, have contributed heavily to the decline of parental authority in the families of our society. He says that advertisers have quickly recognized and taken advantage of what he refers to as "parental impotence" (Elkind, 1998, p. 130) and notes that:

> [W]e have advertising campaigns directed at teenagers who have become a niche market (and who have a large proportion of disposable income because they are not usually asked to contribute to family finances). Much of this advertising uses sexual innuendo to motivate young people to purchase products. The more such advertising permeates the media, the more powerless parents feel to combat it, and the process feeds upon itself. (p. 131)

The problems that young adolescents have with advertising are related to their intellectual and psychosocial development. Many are not yet able to distinguish between idealistic and actual portrayals of reality. Young males who envy the muscular bodies in body building magazines are willing to believe advertisers' claims that they can achieve that kind of form by taking medically questionable supplements, "Hydroxycut" and "Ripped Fuel" among them.

Several years ago, I taught a 12-year-old whose life was permanently altered because she believed her 17-year-old boyfriend when he crooned, "I will always love you," before he talked her out of her clothes and into unprotected sex that resulted in pregnancy. This girl was vulnerable to her boyfriend's lies, and he was evidently eager to take advantage of her psychosocial and intellectual immaturity. She, and many young adolescents, are similarly susceptible to advertisers' ploys, promises, temptations, seductions. As literacy teachers, we can approach advertising and its impact from an academic stance, and as humans, we can approach it from a stance of wiser experience.

We need to consider questions like these when contemplating whether or not we can take time for teaching about print and nonprint advertising in our curricula:

- Do our students realize that the purposes of advertising are to get their attention and then to get them to respond?
- Do they understand that advertisers are considered successful when they can stimulate consumers' senses long enough to cause the consumer to associate pleasure with the product?
- Do they realize that advertisers try to appeal to their sense of sight by showing images of glamorous people and exotic scenery? that they want to create memorable ads by appealing to the sense of sound, with the noise of a truck grinding up a steep mountain or of babies giggling? that they appeal to the sense of taste and smell by drawing viewers into actors' reactions to scents of body lotions and detergents and to flavors like burgers and fries or homemade ice cream since television does not reproduce actual taste or smell?
- Do young adolescents know that advertisers will use authority figures ("I am not a doctor, but I play one on T.V.") and friend figures (including celebrities, the guy next door, and even cartoon animals) to convince them to trust the advertisers' judgment about their products?
- Do our students know to listen for words like "superiority," "quality," "beauty," "efficiency," "novelty," "stability," "reliability," "utility," "simplicity," and "safety," or derivations of these, as indicators that the advertiser is trying to show them how well the product competes with similar products?
- Are our students aware that the overall goal of advertising is to cause them to buy the advertised product, whether they need it or not?

If we answer no to any of these we have uncovered an area that we can explore with our students, in the name of literacy and human development.

Concerns Regarding the Internet and the World Wide Web

According to the U.S. Department of Education's National Center for Educational Statistics, slightly over 50 percent of the 2.4 million public school classrooms in the nation had Internet connections in the fall of 1999, a percentage that had increased from only 3 percent in 1994 (Heide and Henderson, 2001, p. 7). What might Internet connections, which link computers, mean for us in the literacy setting?

Here are a few possibilities:

- Students can participate in individualized instruction that addresses their skill levels, interests, and learning modality strengths.

- Students can conduct simulations and authentic inquiries into topics and resources to which they would not have had access in 1990.
- Students can improve their social skills and self-esteem by working collaboratively to create multimedia presentations.
- Students can communicate directly with groups of business people, preservice teachers, scientists, writers, artists, and other electronic classroom guests.
- Students' audiences extend well beyond the classroom.
- Students' opportunities to assume the role of teacher increases.

With Internet access, our students can participate in electronic conversations with any person in the world who is also wired to the Internet. That is great news. And it is scary. It demands that, as teachers, we accept the daunting responsibility of helping students discriminate between useful information and trash. In scanning the Web for sites that appeal to young adolescents, I found links to over 100 zine titles. To locate these, I went to the search engine, google.com, and typed the key search words, "teen zines." This search produced a long list of zines, with links to each, that are catalogued on the dmoz.com Web site. Google also led me to several public libraries that have teen-oriented Web sites where zine lists are posted. For example, the Dwight Foster Public Library in Fort Atkinson, Wisconsin, has a "Teen Web Center" at www.fort.lib.wi.us/zines.htm. The site provides links to these zines, among a dozen choices: *Cyberteens*, which has a forum, art, games, a serial novel, and a chat room where teens can go to give each other feedback; *TeenVoices*, which challenges the mainstream media image of girls by presenting teen females' original writing and artwork; and *The InSite*, for teens who want to change their worlds. In addition to these choices, I found that some zine sites have a fairly narrow focus; subgroups of adolescents that they cater to include orchestra members and music lovers, gay and lesbian youth, those interested in various sports, members of racial and/or ethnic minority groups, and those with particular hobbies such as collecting comic books or playing board games. While much of the material on these sites is interesting and of high quality, there are, of course, instances where the teen contributors are profane and give bad advice. Students certainly need to learn how to watch their diets whenever they are traveling in cyberspace. On one site, for example, young females were exchanging ideas for how to hide food so they could remain anorexic even when hospitalized and forced to eat. As with music and magazines, we need to know as much as possible about what students are actually tuning in to on the Internet. We should not sacrifice their trust and spy on them, but through open conversations, we need to be bold about asking them to teach us what does and does not appeal to them. Again, we are reminded that we will meet our overarching goal of helping students learn to make sense of their world only if we understand as much as possible about them and their world.

Offering Young Adolescents Nutritious Media Diets

When we examine these media branches with our teacherly perspectives, we can find many ways to empower our students as consumers, to teach them to monitor their diets and eat nutritious foods. Let's look briefly at three of these branches—television and movies/videos, music, and the Internet—as we consider more specifically some ways that we might integrate media into our middle school literacy curricula.

Promoting Critical Viewing of Television and Movies/Videos

All news regarding young adolescents' consumption of television and movies/videos is not bad, of course. John Golden in *Reading in the Dark* (2001) and Alan B. Teasley and Ann Wilder in *Reel Conversations: Reading Films with Young Adults* (1997) argue eloquently that students can learn to "read" popular movies (in their more accessible video format) and then transfer their critical literacy skills to print texts. They offer practical ideas and encouragement for teachers to incorporate film study into the literacy curriculum, with reminders that students must learn not only to comprehend but also to critically analyze what they view.

The Camera's Eye.   Golden (2001) begins his book by introducing students to some of the key film terminology and cinematic effects. He introduces the vocabulary of film through activities in which students experiment with cinematic terminology and effects by holding rolled-up pieces of plain paper to their eyes and using them as simple cameras. For example, with their cameras in place, students can learn about long-shot framing, in which the character or object appears small or at a distance. They also learn about close-shot framing, in which the "object or subject takes up nearly 80 percent of the screen space and therefore appears to be very large" (p. 5). After they see these effects through their paper cameras, students and their teacher discuss the implications of these two framing devices. Students realize, for example, that the long shot allows the viewer to look at an entire scene, not just one focal character or object, whereas the close shot forces the viewer to look only at the object that the camera has in the frame, excluding the bigger context.

Similarly, Golden teaches his students about camera angles by having them adjust their paper cameras to view something from different positions. A position below the object creates a low-angle effect, while a position in which the camera person stands above and looks down on an object creates a high-angle effect. With these simulations, students are able to conclude that the low-angle effect causes the object to look big and powerful and can exaggerate strength and size. The high-angle effect, on the other hand, causes the object to look smaller, weaker, perhaps powerless.

The significance of these discoveries is that they give students new eyes for watching how a film or television director subtly manipulates the viewer—how framing, camera angle, music, other sounds, focus, and lighting affect the viewer's experience with the film or television show. In this way, they teach the students to view movies and television with critical lenses.

Golden's students then learn to transfer their skills for analysis of visual scenes to their reading of print texts. Golden offers a lesson on characterization to demonstrate how students learn to transfer critical literacy skills from the film medium to print texts. He begins teaching characterization by showing short clips of the Shekhar Kapur film, *Elizabeth* (1998), and then asking students to describe, in writing, the young queen in terms of her attitude, appearance, behavior, conversation, and feelings (in Golden, 2001, pp. 61–63). When students read a short story or novel, they are reminded to visualize the characters and to try to determine what they are like by describing their attitude, appearance, behavior, conversation, and feelings.

Those of you who are beginning teachers might ask, "Should I show a movie/video version of a play, story, or novel after we have read it, or before?" You might worry that introducing a work of literature by using a film version will spoil the literary experience. I think that you will find, however, that using a film to introduce a story enhances reading. It gives the reader schemata on which to build when she approaches the text and some visual ideas about time, place, and characters. She may consciously choose to keep or reject these images as she compares them with what occurs in her mind's eye as she reads. I agree with Teasley and Wilder and with Golden, who recommend the use of excerpts instead of entire movie texts when the teaching/learning goals deal primarily with the print text and the use of full-length movies when the goals revolve around film study.

Promoting Critical Experiences with Music

Connecting Books and Music.   Like television and popular movies, which can be incorporated into the classroom to promote critical thinking and to build skills in literary analysis, music offers many possibilities for the middle school integrated literacy curriculum. Music may be useful as a hook that draws a young adolescent into literature. If you suspect that some of your students will read books if the books address popular music, or promote the idea that teens can become musicians, ask them to form a literature circle or book club (see Chapter 5) to read a novel as a group. As they discuss the book itself, they should track the author's development of ideas related to music or musicians by creating a chart with four columns (one narrow and three wide): Under column one, one group member records the page number on which any music-related reference is found; under column two, a group member writes out the quote about music or musicians; under column three, a group member writes a brief explanation of how that quote connects with other parts of the story; under column four, a group member writes about the significance of the quote beyond the story itself. After the music-themed literature circle has completed the book and its tracking chart, the students should study the chart and try to draw some conclusions regarding the author's attitude toward music and musicians. The group might then be asked to present their findings to the class as a panel of experts on the music motif in a novel.

Several authors who write for adolescents have written books that feature characters who are interested in music or in becoming musicians. A tiny sample includes these: Virginia Euwer Wolff (1991) (*The Mozart Season*), Sue Ellen Bridgers (1987) (*Notes for Another Life*), Karen Hesse (1997) (*Out of the Dust*), Christopher Paul Curtis (1995) (*The Watsons Go to Birmingham—1963*), Marie G. Lee (1992) (*Finding My Voice*), Anne C. LeMieux (1995) (*Do Angels Sing the Blues?*), Francesca Lia Block (1989) (*Weetzie Bat*), David Klass (2001) (*You Don't Know Me*), and James Haskins (1993) (*Black Music in America: A History Through Its People*). With or without the literature circle approach, these books are capable of prompting conversation among adolescent readers about the place of music in the lives of young adolescents.

Creating Sound Tracks.   Another literary connection for music is to ask students to create a five- to eight-song "sound track," for the stories, novels, and plays that they read in or out of class and to write a brief rationale for each song on the sound track. For this activity, students should work in groups. First they will brainstorm to create a list of songs that, in their opinions, relate to or in some way connect with the story, novel, or play as a whole. From this list, they will choose the story's "theme song." Next, they will divide the story into parts: the beginning, the conflict, the climax, and the resolution. They will return to their original list of story-related songs to see if those will work to accompany each of the parts of the story. (At this point, they may need to add more songs to their brainstormed list.) Students should work together until they can list song titles that accompany each of the major parts of the story. If they are enjoying themselves in their role as music matchers, they might also choose to designate a song to represent each main character. Ideally, the students in the group will be able to collaborate, outside of class, to create an audiotape or CD of the songs that they have listed for their sound track. Each group member could be responsible for recording one song and bringing the recording to class, where the songs can be compiled onto a tape or CD. (Any student who does not have access to recording equipment might have another job within the group, such as in-class editor of the compilation.)

To do a good job with this activity, students must first understand the literary work on the literal level, and they must also comprehend which scenes and characters are significant in the development of the story. Once they have completed this activity, some students might choose to create (or "burn") a CD for themselves and to illustrate a cover. Be sure to ask for a copy to use when you introduce the literary text in the future!

A simpler alternative is to ask students to identify a popular song that illuminates or complements a poem that they have read in class and to copy down and illustrate the two texts on a poster with a note on how the song and the poem compare.

One beginning teacher took the literature and popular music idea a step in a slightly different direction: He recorded a collection of snippets from songs that were popular among his students and used them in a pretest review of *Romeo and Juliet*. Some of the songs dealt with misunderstandings; others dealt with play-related topics such as friendship, loyalty, love, and deception. He conducted the musical review by playing a song snippet and then asking volunteers to decide which character(s) would sing the lines. After the class came to consensus on the question about character(s), he asked other volunteers to try to pinpoint the scene during which the lines from the song would be played and explain why. The teacher reported that students hummed their way through the *Romeo and Juliet* examination.

The Music of Reviews.   Another benefit of bringing students' music into the classroom is that it provides a quick route to conversation with our students about the ways they make sense of their world and about what they value. Students might conduct a survey to determine which songs are most popular in their class, grade, or school. They can work in small groups to create legitimate survey questions, and pilot test them in the language arts class, looking for glitches. Once the group irons out any glitches, members can take copies of the survey throughout the school, asking for students' responses and recording them carefully in a survey notebook. Group members might conduct the survey over a period of four days (being sure that they do not ask anyone to respond more than once). On the fifth day, group members should bring their survey responses to class and work individually, at first, to chart their results, creating a list of the top ten songs that emerged from the responses to the survey that they gathered. Once all individual data have been analyzed, members will report to their groups, where they prepare a compilation of all the survey results and create a chart of the top ten songs, according to their sample of the school population. Ideally, students will be able to bring in recordings and listen to the lyrics of the songs at the top of the group's list. Groups might then make oral reports of their results to the class, aided by charts. They could also discuss questions such as "Why are one group's results different from, or the same as, another group's?" "What do our lists of the most popular songs at our school seem to say about our school and about us?"

Students could also work in groups or as a whole class to analyze the most popular songs. They might, for example, compare and contrast messages that the popular songs promote through the lyrics and sound. To extend the project further, they could return to their groups to develop a scale for rating each of the most popular songs, using group-designated criteria for their rankings. For example, a group that is concerned with wholesome content of the song might use a scale in which 1 means "No way I would want my mother or little sister to hear this!" and 5 indicates "This is a terrific song that I think everyone would enjoy." Another group might develop a scale that ranks the song in terms of its energy: it rates a 1 if "This is so dull that I almost fell asleep by the second stanza" and a 5 if "I couldn't stop dancing to this even after the last note played."

The benefits of analysis of song texts are many. Like film analysis, students learn critical skills that they can transfer to other reading tasks when they learn to evaluate music. Also, they learn how to make distinctions that are socially valuable: Students who hear lyrics without really listening to them may uncover some ugly and objectionable realities as they learn to read lyrics and sound critically. They may begin to think more carefully about the messages that are presented as they practice listening attentively to words and word patterns. They should be urged to move beyond comprehending the lyrics and sound to evaluating those messages in terms of the recording artists' intentions and motivations, and their own values orientation. Our students will be empowered as consumers of music when they learn to listen with their minds as well as their ears.

Promoting Sagacious Use of the Internet

E-Habit Logs. One way that we can encourage students to count their electronic calories and to make healthy choices is to track their use of electronic communications, such as email and Web surfing, and to log their trends and habits. They might keep a log of their email activity for one week and on the following Monday answer a series of questions like these:

- How many times were you on-line each day last week?
- What was your purpose for being on-line each time?
- With whom were you communicating or to whom were you sending messages most often?
- What is the general content of most of your messages—are you sharing jokes, asking questions, making social plans, for example?
- Would you be pleased, embarrassed, or nonchalant if your parents, grandparents, teachers, or other adults saw the messages you have sent and received in the last week?
- How would you describe the literary style of the messages that you write on email?
- How does your e-writing compare and contrast with the writing that you do on paper?

After writing their responses, students could engage in a metacognitive review of their responses and write a paragraph-long reflection on their habits as electronic communications consumers. You might then encourage them to share their metacognitive reviews and reflections with the class as a means of generating a discussion about how today's young adolescents use the Internet. There is one serious drawback to this activity: Students who do not have access at home to the Internet or to email will feel left out. To avoid that situation, you might choose to simply restrict the electronic log and reflection assignment to the communications that students initiate and the messages that they receive while at school, using the school computers. In that case, you will need to plan for extra time during which students will be able to work on the Internet and engage in emailing. You might even discuss the project with your colleagues across the curriculum, and plan the log and reflection assignment for a week when your students will be using the Internet in another class, as well as in your own class.

Technology in Adolescent Literature.   We can also encourage students to track references to email and other electronic technologies that they find in contemporary books for young adults, as a gauge of how well literature reflects reality. Caroline B. Cooney's *Tune in Anytime* (1999) provides a light-hearted look at how one young teen turns to technology, including television and the Internet, while her family is falling apart around her. Todd Strasser's painful *Give a Boy a Gun* (2000), in contrast, shows how students can use email for quick, coded, harmful communications. You might encourage students who are both avid readers and technology buffs to work as a club to read and write reviews of contemporary adolescent novels in which technology is featured. At the end of a grading period, the students in the reading/technology club could present a panel discussion about the books and the technology trends that they identify in them.

Various Purposeful Applications.   What can we expect middle school students to do with electronic media to develop their critical literacies? Here are a few of the computer applications and selected tasks that will become more common as computers become more accessible and teachers gain experience and success with integrating them into the classroom:

Databases: to seek and locate information for research, to perform comparison and contrast of trends

Desktop publishing: to create newspapers, magazines, greeting cards, bulletin boards

Email: to enhance communication among students and others within and beyond the school, county, country; to create interest groups with listserves

Graphics utilities: to create illustrations for fiction and nonfiction, graphic organizers, Web page design

Multimedia platforms: to create portable presentations, to organize resources, to enhance or create Web pages

Simulations: to engage in exploratory thinking; to develop fantasy and science fiction stories, as well as those set in the past

Word processing: to draft, revise, polish, and publish writing; to create posters and banners; to make handouts for reports and speeches

World Wide Web: to communicate beyond the classroom, to engage in research, to publish student work, to create and engage in Web Quests and in ThinkQuest competitions (see Heide & Henderson, 2001, pp. 157 and 163, for details).

Heide and Henderson (2001) offer teachers sound advice regarding our responsibility and obligation where electronic learning is concerned:

> Learning about the highly technological environment in which we live is critical to today's students. They will need to function comfortably in it and make intelligent decisions about the relationships among humans, technology, and the natural environment. In our society, important decision-making positions are held and will continue to be held by those who have developed the skills of obtaining, evaluating, and generating information. Parents and society expect educational institutions to prepare students for the world in which they will live. Although we cannot be certain about the exact nature of their adult world, we can predict that technology will continue to play a central role. Our students already live in a world of technology; our education system must now reflect their world and adequately prepare them for this reality. (p. 7)

Dealing with the Overflow of Competing Messages and Media Confusion.   Some of the most interesting and pleasurable lessons I have ever taught or observed have involved exploration of media messages. I remember, for example, the satire on a teen magazine that one beginning teacher, Kate, developed. The cover blurbs on her magazine had quotes that stated the real intentions of the articles inside: "I Really Hate Talking to Dull Guys," "Yuck—Look at Her: Why You'll Never See Me Eating a Doughnut," and "I'm Faking It When I Pretend to Be Her Friend." The blurbs and photos that Kate used on the cover of her magazine reflected what she found to be shallowness in much of the content of popular teen magazines. And I remember preservice teacher Brittny's reality television project. Adolescents served as a panel that was charged with making recommendations to networks regarding the best audiences for existing reality shows. Her student panels viewed clips of actual television shows: In one, a man was to choose his bride from a group of five women who were competing for him; in another, a group of young adults competed for money by doing dangerous and disgusting things like bungee jumping into a canyon and eating fly larvae; in the last example, young adults merely had to live together in a swanky apartment, being videotaped constantly, until they got sick of each other. The adolescent panel made some surprisingly astute and mature recommendations and predicted that the reality television genre will have a short life.

Students undoubtedly gravitate toward assignments that involve television shows, print advertisements, teen magazines, and music. Our challenge is to help them learn, as consumers, that their overflow of enthusiasm for media should flow through channels of critical thinking, not into gutters.

Integrated Literacy Checklist

In this chapter, literacy skills in all of the language arts areas are integrated in the focus on media literacy.

Reading

In each of the film and music activities suggested, students learn to read symbols other than alphabetic print. They learn to read the messages of framing decisions and camera angles, for example.

Students create and conduct a survey and read and interpret their classmates' responses to questions about favorite songs. Then they use those responses to generate an analysis of the data.

The definition of reading is appropriately expanded when we consider the media, although more traditional definitions also apply when students receive email, navigate Web sites for research information, and so on.

Literature

Students learn to read films as if they are reading literature; they learn to transfer their critical reading and interpretation of film to print texts.

Students write descriptions of how literary elements are developed in print texts after analyzing films for those same elements (characterization was the example used above).

Students choose, compare, and contrast popular songs with canonical and contemporary poems, commenting on the common themes, forms, audiences, purposes, and so on.

Students describe literary scenes by choosing music that could be paired with the literature and writing rationales for their choices.

Students track the fictitious use of media and the importance of music in novels written for adolescents.

Students create sound tracks for literary works and write rationales for their choices.

Writing

Students describe, in writing, the effects of various cinematic effects on the viewer and the impact of the film or television show.

Students track the fictitious use of media in novels of young people and write descriptions of what they find.

Students track their own use of electronic communications and write conclusions about their content and habits.

Students create and analyze surveys about favorite songs and write about the results of their data analysis.

Listening, Speaking, and Languaging

Students study films and television shows, as well as televised advertisements, with attention to the language used by individual characters, the music and sounds added, and the impact of those on the overall effect of the movie, television show, or advertisement.

Students attend to the language of advertising to become aware of how advertisers try to entice consumers.

Students listen to and interpret music to make sense of lyrics and sounds and then, in some cases, compare and contrast the music to literary texts.

Students listen to music to select songs that could be used on a sound track for a literary piece.

Help for English Language Learners

This chapter should be particularly helpful for those who teach English language learners. In *Fifty Strategies for Teaching English Language Learners* (2000), Adrienne L. Herrell recommends that we incorporate video clips, overhead projector transparencies, VCRs, audiotapes, and other media as often as possible when we teach. Although she warns that ELL students might be tempted to download reports from the Internet and therefore need explicit instruction in how to cite Internet resources, she articulates many reasons for using multimedia instruction. Her words suggest a strong fit with an integrated literacy pedagogy:

> Multimedia presentations in the classroom support students in conveying information to their peers. The use of visuals of many types helps students and teachers to connect vocabulary and meaning, making their reports more interesting. The use of the computer, VCR, and other technology in the classroom is appealing to students and serves as motivation to be more innovative in completing assignments. The use of the Internet in the classroom introduces some challenges, however. Just as in researching from more traditional materials, students will need instruction in giving credit and citing sources. They may be tempted to simply download reports from the Internet; therefore, specific guidelines will need to be set and monitored in the classroom setting. (p. 138)

Each of the activities and goals of this chapter addresses the needs of English language learners by allowing students to practice building literacies with symbols that are not limited to spoken and written language.

The activities also encourage English language learners to express their own reactions to films, television shows, and music and allow those students to assume the role of expert with their own interpretations and conclusions.

Because videotaped television shows and movies and audiotaped music can be replayed, ELL students who need to hear these again, for the sake of clarity or comprehension, can easily repeat them.

NCTE/IRA Standards

Standard Six: Students conduct research on issues and interests by generating ideas and questions and by posing problems. They gather, evaluate, and synthesize data from a variety of sources (e.g., print and nonprint texts, artifacts, people) to communicate their discoveries in ways that suit their purpose and audience.

Standard Seven: Students use a variety of technological and information resources (e.g., libraries, databases, computer networks, video) to gather and synthesize information and to create and communicate knowledge.

According to Andrew Garrison, director, the NCTE Commission on Media has considered a range of issues related to media use, including such trends as distance learning, the ubiquity of advertising within school environments and in school-targeted media, insufficiency of teacher training in technology, and global advances in educational technology and school implementation (www.NCTE.org, report available April, 2002).

Works Cited

Arnett, J. J. (1995). *Metalheads: Heavy metal music and adolescent alienation*. Boulder, CO: Westview Press of HarperCollins.

Baines, L., Strehle, E., and Bell, S. (1999). Music and musicians' effects on adolescents. In P. S. Carroll (Ed.). *Using literature to help troubled teenagers cope with societal issues*. Westport, CT: Greenwood, 162–179.

Block, F. L. (1989). *Weetzie Bat*. New York: Harper.

Bridgers, S. E. (1981). *Notes for another life*. New York: Harper.

Bridgers, S. E. (1987). *Permanent connections*. New York: Harper.

Cooney, C. B. (1999). *Tune in anytime*. New York: Scholastic.

Curtis, C. P. (1995). *The Watsons Go to Birmingham—1963*. New York: Bantam.

Downes, B., and Miller, S. (1998). *Media studies*. Lincolnwood, IL: NTC/Contemporary.

Elkind, D. (1998). *All grown up and no place to go*, revised edition. Reading, MA: Addison-Wesley.

Gans, H. J. (1999). *Popular culture and high culture: An analysis and evaluation of taste*. New York: Basic Books of Perseus.

Giroux, H. (1997). *Channel surfing: Race talk and the destruction of today's youth*. New York: St. Martin's Press.

Golden, J. (2001). *Reading in the dark: Using film as a tool in the English classroom*. Urbana, IL: NCTE.

Hamburg, D. (1994). *Today's children: Creating a future for a generation in crisis*. New York: Times Books of Random House.

Haskins, J. (1993). *Black music in America: A history through its people*. New York: HarperCollins.

Heide, A., and Henderson, D. (2001). *Active learning in the digital classroom*. Portsmouth, NH: Heinemann.

Herrell, A. L. (2000). *Fifty strategies for teaching English language learners*. Upper Saddle River, NJ: Merrill of Prentice Hall.

Hesse, K. (1997). *Out of the dust*. New York: Scholastic.

Hine, T. (1999). *The rise and fall of the American teenager*. New York: Avon.

Klass, D. (2001). *You don't know me*. New York: Farrar, Straus & Giroux.

Lee, M. G. (1992). *Finding my voice*. New York: Houghton Mifflin.

LeMieux, A. C. (1995). *Do angels sing the blues?* New York: Avon.

Martel, J. (1994). Garry Shandling. *Rolling Stone*. September, pp. 66–73.

Shandler, S. (1999). *Ophelia speaks: Adolescent girls write about their search for self*. New York: Harper-Perennial.

Strasburger, V. C. (1995). Adolescents and the media: Medical and psychological impact. (Volume 33 in *Developmental clinical psychology and psychiatry*, A. Kazdin, series editor). Thousand Oaks, CA: Sage Publications.

Strasser, T. (2000). *Give a boy a gun*. New York: Simon & Schuster.

Teasley, A. B., and Wilder, A. (1997). *Reel conversations: Reading films with young adults*. Portsmouth, NH: Boynton/Cook.

Travers, D. (1994). Movies: Blood from a stone. *Rolling Stone*. September, 83–87.

Wolff, V. E. (1991). *The Mozart season*. New York: Scholastic.

CHAPTER

8

Integrated Literacy across the Curriculum

A student preparing to write an essay about U.S. relations with Israel in his language arts class.

When Susan Nelson Wood was teaching language arts to seventh and eighth graders at Estill County Middle School in rural Kentucky, she learned the value of interdisciplinary thinking and instruction, and the power of teaching and learning literature when it is juxtaposed with life. She explains what experience taught her:

> I remember how I used to try to teach the "required" works from our class anthology, but with faint results. For example, Jack London's "The Story of an Eyewitness" never worked until

the day after we had a 2 A.M. tremor along the New Madrid fault. Kids came to the school hungry to talk, to tell their stories, and to find out what really happened when the earth seemed to stand up, shake off, and settle back down. They had heard people talking, and seen news about the fault on the morning television shows, and some had read about it in the local paper. I couldn't move to London's story fast enough, that day, and they loved reading and discussing it; they were enthusiastic about giving their own "eyewitness" accounts, and about discovering how a writer described a situation that was similar to one that they had just experienced.

From that experience, I learned to use more prereading strategies, such as focused freewriting: "What do you know about . . . ?" and to have students do research using local and national newspapers and televised news to create informative brochures about nonfiction events that are embedded in fiction. After the New Madrid fault, my students created brochures on faults in the southeast, and on earthquake preparedness for Kentucky.

What Susan demonstrates is a willingness on the part of a teacher of language arts to move beyond the boundaries of our traditional subject matter so that we can work with students at the points where literacy matters. Susan was able to recognize and take advantage of the opportunity to use Jack London's short story as a curricular anchor for interdisciplinary lessons. In our own classrooms and schools, we can look for similar opportunities and enlist the support of our colleagues who are teaching classes in social studies, science, mathematics, and other areas. Following are two sample lesson sets, both designed to encourage the use of literature as a curricular anchor in an integrated literacy classroom, with implications and recommendations for reinforcing literacy across the curriculum.

Integrated Literacy with Interdisciplinary Connections: An Instructional Framework

Integrated Literacy with Interdisciplinary Reinforcement

In its "Position Paper on Middle Level Curriculum: A Work in Progress" (May 2002), the National Middle School Association (NMSA) recognizes the importance of interdisciplinary teaching and learning for young adolescents. After stating its assumptions about the social and intellectual nature of learning and the need for environments that promote learning and growth, the NMSA recommends "the following conditions should be evident" (in middle schools):

- All areas of knowledge and skill are viewed as important and are integrated throughout the student's school experience.
- Students explore integrated themes that engage them in serious and rigorous study.
- Curriculum is developed by careful and continuing study of students, social trends and issues, and research-supported school practices.
- Flexible learning groups are based on students' needs and interests.
- Active collaborative self-directed learning is used.
- A variety of educational materials, resources, and instructional strategies are used.
- Staff development promotes and supports developmentally responsive practices.

- The staff is organized in ways that encourage ongoing collaboration.
- All staff help plan and participate in long-term professional growth opportunities. (NMSA, 2002)

Interdisciplinary Team Instruction

These recommendations encourage a pedagogy that includes interdisciplinary team planning, instruction, and evaluation of students' learning. The interdisciplinary focus can be woven into the fabric of the integrated literacy pedagogy because it is consistent with the four core beliefs that serve as the foundation for that pedagogy.

Belief One: In interdisciplinary team structures, students are recognized as individual learners with unique strengths and needs, yet emphasis is placed on the individual's membership in the interdisciplinary team's learning community. Middle school teams typically create logos and names for themselves and then make banners, pins, and even t-shirts that promote their team. An individual student is less likely to be lost in the cracks emotionally, socially, or academically in a school in which she is a team member because she will spend her days with the same group of students—a smaller group than the population of her entire school or her entire grade. She will also spend the entire day with teachers who talk to each other about the concerns they have regarding students. If even one notices that she is having difficulty, that teacher will bring it to the attention of his colleagues, who will work together to try to assist her.

Belief Two: The interdisciplinary team concept allows teachers to work with students to determine which themes will be studied across disciplines. This feature of interdisciplinary teaming honors the fact that young adolescents learn more when they have an interest in the topic and when they are given some choice. Further, the interdisciplinary team organization allows each student to be viewed as a multifaceted thinker. Without any input from other teachers, I might draw the conclusion that a student who has great difficulty writing essays in my language arts class is "just not too bright." However, within the interdisciplinary team organization, I might learn from that student's science teacher that he shows flashes of brilliance as a scientific thinker. The information about how students perform across the curriculum gives us valuable insights to who they are, and who they can become, as learners and thinkers.

Belief Three: The interdisciplinary team organization promotes the use of broad definitions of literacy. The fact that a team of teachers is involved with each student's learning improves the chances that the student will have opportunities to use many different media for learning. Also, teachers in interdisciplinary team structures often agree to rearrange class schedules to accommodate their colleagues' instructional needs. For example, imagine that you have just taught the adventure-survival novel *Hatchet* (1987) by Gary Paulsen in your language arts class. You want students to understand what the frozen tundra is really like, so you work with the science teacher to select a National Geographic film that features the region. The science teacher and you agree to combine your class periods for one day to show the entire film in one sitting. While your follow-up lessons require that students return to the novel and choose a passage to which they will add authentic geological details, the science teacher's follow-up lessons might require that students conduct research into the geology of glaciers. These different instructional activities, in which different definitions of literacy are implied, emerge from a shared, media-enhanced experience that is typical of interdisciplinary instruction.

Belief Four: As noted above, the interdisciplinary teaming organization is recommended by the National Middle School Association. The organizational scheme is also highly recommended by the Carnegie Council on Adolescent Development in its initial report on the education of young adolescents, *Turning Points: Preparing American Youth for the 21st Century* (1989). The Carnegie Council advocates interdisciplinary team teaching as an approach in which "teams of teachers and students . . . work together to achieve academic and personal goals for students." The council also recommends:

> Teachers share responsibility for the same students and can share problems together, often before they reach the crisis stage; teachers report that classroom discipline problems are dramatically reduced through teaming. This community of learning nurtures bonds between teacher and student that are the building blocks of the education of the young adolescent. (p. 38).

As professional teachers, we can use our instincts in addressing the needs of our students, but we benefit too when we draw on the observations, knowledge, concerns, and insights of colleagues who also work with our students. The interdisciplinary team organization is a fine fit within the integrated literacy pedagogy.

Literature-Based Integrated Literacy Units and Interdisciplinary Instruction Possibilities. In the sections that follow, we consider a curricular framework for organizing integrated literacy instruction around two adolescent novels, *April and the Dragon Lady* and *Freak the Mighty*. We also consider possibilities for coordinating our focus on literacy lessons with the goals and content of our colleagues' mathematics, science, and social studies lessons through an interdisciplinary team organization. My goal is that the framework, which combines an integrated literacy pedagogy with an interdisciplinary perspective, will help teachers conceptualize a scheme for organizing literature-based thematic units around almost any book.

This framework may be especially helpful for teachers who are beginning to make gradual moves toward an integrated literacy orientation. It provides, through planning reminders, an uncomplicated structure for listing activities in which language skills are seamlessly integrated and a section where tie-ins for interdisciplinary teaming and for technological enhancement are suggested. I encourage you to modify and transfer the activities to the young adult books that are favorites among your own students.

These lessons may also be helpful for those of you who are eager to collaborate with your colleagues to develop interdisciplinary reinforcement of teaching goals and student learning. Encourage your colleagues to try a few of the reading, writing, and oral language activities described here within the context of their own classrooms. Some may be reluctant, fearing that they will be expected to grade for grammar if they have students write or to create a rubric for speaking if they ask students to give oral reports in their classes. Share with them your ideas for assessing and evaluating literacy growth, and also share the responsibility for evaluating students in terms of their growth. Everyone can benefit. By reinforcing what you do as a teacher of language arts, your colleagues will be helping students make connections across their subjects and from school to life. Before we examine the two literature-based models for integrated literacy instruction that is reinforced through interdisciplinary team instruction, let's look carefully at the notion of interdisciplinary team organization itself.

Interdisciplinary Team Organization

Some of you work in, or will work in, middle schools that actually function on the junior high school model: Teachers are grouped into subject area departments; they have few opportunities to meet with teachers of other subject areas; students move through six or seven different classes daily; and there are no explicit academic connections made between those classes. Others of you, though, work or will be hired to work in schools that have adopted and incorporated middle school philosophies and practices. One of the key characteristics of today's middle schools is the use of interdisciplinary team organization. In this structure, three to five teachers who specialize in different subject areas usually work together to be sure that the academic, social, and personal needs of their students are met.

The teachers on the team share the same roster of students. Their collaborative work might take one of several forms, including these three: (1) It might be limited to discussions about specific students on their team, with a focus on strategies that seem to help students overcome academic and other problems. (2) It might be much more extensive to include a shared planning period during which the team teachers exchange instructional objectives, standards being addressed, and lesson plans. Team teachers work together to identify ways that individual teachers' lessons can support and reinforce what students are learning in all of the other teachers' classes. With this organization, the teachers who share a group of students are likely to develop and teach at least one thematic unit together each year. The unit might culminate in a field trip or performance that involves all of the students and each of the teachers on the team. These teachers are not, however, likely to design and implement thematic units across the disciplines for the entire school year. (3) In the most developed forms of interdisciplinary team organization, teachers collaboratively plan and implement units of instruction. In this format, all of the teachers work together to develop an agreed-on and carefully articulated set of goals. The activities that they design reinforce the themes or topics of the instructional unit. In this configuration, the connections between what students learn in their mathematics, social studies, science, and language arts classes are made explicit and are continually reinforced. The team of teachers assesses and evaluates students' progress collaboratively and works together to assign grades. Most of today's middle schools employ some form of interdisciplinary team organization, but few use interdisciplinary team instruction across the school during an entire year.

In *The Exemplary Middle School* (2003), Paul George and the late William Alexander, authorities on the structures, philosophies, challenges, and accomplishments of middle schools, approach interdisciplinary team instruction from a realistic stance. They explain interdisciplinary team organization as the following:

> [A] way of organizing the faculty so that a group of teachers shares (1) the same group of students; (2) the responsibility for planning, teaching, and evaluating curriculum and instruc-

tion in more than one academic area; (3) the same schedule; and (4) the same area of the building. (p. 305)

George and Alexander draw on their studies of middle schools across the country to conclude that interdisciplinary team organization is a "critical element of the exemplary middle school" (p. 305). They recognize that it takes an enormous commitment of time, energy, and collaboration among administrators and teachers to implement and sustain this kind of organization. The benefits of working in an interdisciplinary team organization, however, are compelling:

> Almost immediately, teachers on the team realize the power inherent in their acting together. Time between classes becomes more closely supervised, as teachers begin to use the phrase "our students" more frequently. Teachers almost always report that the job becomes more satisfying and more productive. Students begin to notice that they are in classes with others who have the same teachers at the same and different times of the day. Students observe that teachers . . . begin to share the same academic and behavioral expectations. (p. 306)

Regardless of the kind of organization that is in place in the schools in which you work or will soon work, you will realize benefits if you are willing to discuss your instructional goals, plans, assessments, and evaluations with colleagues who specialize in the other subjects. Once you have established yourself as a teacher with clear goals, high expectations, and challenging lessons, you will be able to ask your colleagues to work with you for the benefit of the students whom you teach.

Literacy and languaging at the heart of middle school learning.

In the following discussion of models for integrated literacy instruction with interdisciplinary connections, let's assume this about the middle school in which you currently find yourself or where you will find yourself in the future: It is filled with teachers who are eager to collaborate as team members, but it does not yet use a fully developed interdisciplinary team organization. Your planning period is not at the same time as the other teachers who have your students, so you will not have the opportunity to design lessons together. You will, however, be able to let your colleagues know what you are doing in your classes and suggest ways that they might reinforce the integrated literacy goals that you are working toward. In this common situation, one teacher has to initiate discussions about how the teachers can ensure that there are explicit connections across the subjects. One teacher has to introduce a theme, topic, or focus to colleagues across the disciplines. Who better to take the lead than you, the language arts teacher?

Teaching *April and the Dragon Lady*

April and the Dragon Lady (1994), by Lensey Namioka, is a funny and moving novel about a clash of cultures and an adolescent's attempts to grow up in spite of the clash. April, a high school junior, is suffering from anomie. She is torn between the pressures of finding her niche among friends as a normal American teen and living up to the expectations and demands of her traditional Chinese grandmother. From the surface, April's life seems average; she participates in the school geology club, the Rock Hounds. She has a boyfriend, Steve, with whom she eats French fries and goes to movies, and a best friend, Judy, with whom she talks about her aspirations. April also has an older brother, Harry, with whom she quarrels, and a father who does not understand her.

Yet April's life is not ordinary because her family is not ordinary. April's father seems detached, especially since the death of April's mother, and her brother exalts in the special treatment he gets as the male child. April realizes that her grandmother, the "Dragon Lady," is a cunning and manipulative woman who insists on seeing the world from one perspective—that of the old Chinese ways. April respects her grandmother and does not want to upset the matriarch, but she wants to be an American teen, too. The grandmother pulls several stunts to command the family's attention: She wanders away and is presumed to be lost on a mountain; she chooses to abandon a party thrown in her honor; she poses as a homeless person. And April has no doubt that her grandmother does not approve of two things that the teen holds dear: her Anglo boyfriend and her desire to study geology at a college that is far from her Seattle home.

Interdisciplinary Instruction

The topics and themes of this novel are well suited for consideration in middle schools because they allow a gradual progression from attention to concrete details to attention to abstract ones. They nudge young adolescents into formal operational thought. The following activities suggest ways in which you might help students make personal connections with the text and extend those personal connections to focus on their families, their schools, and their communities.

Yin and Yang: Oppositions. One of the key issues in *April and the Dragon Lady* seems to be the protagonist's ability to reconcile differences, even oppositions, when they become obstacles for her. An example is her grandmother's insistence on the Chinese traditions concerning the protected and elevated role of males in a household. The Dragon Lady's views stand in opposition to April's desire—based on American influences—to see that her brother shares responsibilities for caring for their grandmother. The Yin and Yang activity focuses on the existence of opposites within the novel and extends into a consideration of how students handle the conflicting pressures in their own lives. Here is how to set it up:

Stage One: Announce to students that they will be creating a list of the oppositions that the main character, April, has to deal with in the novel (or a specified portion of it). They will have to determine, based on evidence from the book, how she handles each conflict. Have them divide a page of paper lengthwise into three columns. The first column is headed "Conflicts"; under the heading, students write conflicting pairs of words or phrases, such as reliable/unreliable and contented/discontented. The second column is headed "Resolved or Continuing." Under it, students write an indication of how April dealt with the conflict, along with the page number on which they find evidence to support their decision. The third column is headed "My Opinion"; under this heading, the student-reader comments on the way the conflict was handled, on the conflict itself, or on how he or she would have resolved it given the context of the story. This column is where the student's own reading of the novel is brought to the level of response and connection. Students should continue the list throughout the reading and study of the novel (or the specified portion), adding to it as needed.

When their lists are complete, have students gather into small collaborative groups and share their findings and opinions with group members. The third column responses, in particular, since they require divergent thinking, should provoke interesting discussion. If interest in the activity is high, you might ask each group to contribute to a master list of oppositions.

Stage Two: In the second stage of this activity, students create a list of oppositions with which they personally deal as young adolescents. Explain that in Chinese philosophy, yin represents those forces that are negative and dark, and yang represents those that are positive and bright. Then ask students to list the oppositions that they feel in their lives and to place them under one of two columns on a sheet of paper, one headed "Yin" and the other "Yang." After they have created personal Yin-Yang lists, give students one white and one black sheet of construction paper that you have cut to resemble the interlocking, swirling Yin-Yang symbol. They should transfer words from their list of oppositions onto the appropriate side of the symbol. If students wish to have them displayed, the artistic symbols of their oppositions can become class decorations. Some may also want to discuss or write a journal entry about their lives in terms of how they deal with the oppositions. Others might choose to write about Namioka's dedication of the book: "To the memory of my mother, who was all yang."

Stereotypes and Cultural Identity. Other key issues in this novel are stereotypes and cultural identities. Young adolescence is a particularly important time for students to explore these issues because preteens are typically developing their own sense of values, and they have an intense interest in the opinions of others. An activity that focuses on these themes may be conducted in three stages.

Stage One: During the first stage, have students write journal entries about how they have been stereotyped or about how they have relied on stereotypes to judge others. If students do not wish to write about their personal experiences, they might feel comfortable writing about the stereotyping that someone else, either real or fictitious, has endured or perpetrated. Students' discussion of personal examples can be the foundation for consideration of the use of stereotypes in television and magazine advertisements and in popular television dramas and situation comedies.

Stage Two: Following the introductory discussion, allow students to form teams as investigative student-researchers. Charge each team with collecting and evaluating evidence that represents the amount and nature of stereotyping in a particular print or visual medium. The investigators will need to support their conclusions with evidence and present their findings to the rest of the class in oral reports. If time allows and interest is high, students may wish to model their reports on an investigative television show such as *60 Minutes* or *Dateline* and videotape their presentations. Audience members will critique the effectiveness of each group's presentation, in terms of information presented and quality of presentation style.

Stage Three: During the third stage, have students search the novel for evidence of how the Chinese and Chinese-American characters demonstrate their personal and cultural identities. Ask students to prepare a sheet of paper by dividing it into four squares, labeled "language," "attitudes," "beliefs," and "values." In each square, students jot down evidence from the book of how a character's identity is associated with or controlled by his or her culture. Students should cite page numbers for future reference. Discussion of the contents of the squares should occur in small groups. Then students can write journal entries, essays, poems, or stories about their own cultural identities.

Rock Hounds.   April is an active member of a school geology club, the Rock Hounds. Students can explore Namioka's attention to rocks from several different angles, including these:

- Find textual evidence that supports their answers to the questions, "How is the jade bracelet used as a symbol in the novel? What does it represent to Grandma? to April?" This focus on symbols helps nudge young adolescent students from concrete toward abstract thinking.
- Conduct research on the symbolic meaning of different precious gems, such as rubies and diamonds. Students may wish to start by investigating the story that is associated with their birthstones. (Commercial greeting card companies frequently have calendars on which the birthstone and its symbolic meaning are listed.) They may write and present a brief report of their findings to a small group, arranged so that no one else in the group has their birth month. They may also choose a creative response in which they write a fable that is centered on the symbolic meaning of the birthstone. Reading

other fables with an eye on the patterns and elements that are characteristic of fables may help students prepare for this writing option. If several students choose this option, a class booklet of the fables could be prepared and displayed. Ideally, it would have at least one story for each of the twelve months and birthstones.

■ Prepare a word puzzle in which less-known meanings of words that are also the names of rocks could be used as clues. For example, besides its popular definition as a particular kind and color of gem stone, *jade* refers to a worn-out, worthless, or vicious horse and also to a type of gun tackle. The puzzles could be exchanged among classmates, and those who are able to stump their classmates might win a prize—a polished piece of quartz, for example.

Integrated Literacy Activities Checklist

Reading

Students read the novel, silently or aloud, in class or away from school.

Some students will read several legends to serve as models before they write their own.

Students read, as peer editors, others' compositions and respond to them orally and in writing.

Writing

Students write reports, stories, legends, puzzles, lists of oppositions, cultural identity squares, and so on.

Students write evaluations of the effectiveness of peers' investigative reports and also write evaluative comments when they serve as peer editors.

Students should write a self-evaluation of their growth as a learner and thinker at the end of the unit or study of the novel.

Listening, Speaking, and Languaging

Students are involved in discussion at the beginning of each activity.

Students may give oral presentations of gem reports, stories, legends, yin-yang artwork, and so on.

Students present television show–type investigative reports in which they have videotaped themselves.

Students must listen as participants during discussions of each activity, and contribute to the building of criteria related to the activities.

Students listen and respond to others' unique ideas when reports, legends, stories, cultural identity squares, yin-yang art, word puzzles, and so on are presented.

As members of a television audience, students must listen to their classmates' investigative reports and evaluate those reports.

Suggestions for Interdisciplinary Tie-Ins and Technology Enhancement

Science

Lessons might give attention to the health-related topics of aging and/or diabetes.

Students might work with the science teacher(s) to plan a field trip to a local rock formation after conducting research on the types of rocks and minerals that are indigenous to the geographic area.

The impact of the eruption of Mt. St. Helen's (part of the Cascades volcanic chain that is featured in the setting of the novel) could be studied, with attention to destruction of flora and fauna and the rebuilding that has occurred since May 1980.

Mathematics

Lessons might focus on word problems that involve distances to be traveled, incorporating the notion of how far Grandma could be expected to walk when traveling up Mt. Rainier for a particular amount of time as opposed to how far she could be expected to walk when she wandered around town.

Lessons may have students use maps to measure or graphs to plot the distances April would have to travel to go from Seattle to various colleges in other states.

Social Studies

Lessons could focus on comparing the demographics of students' home town with those of Seattle.

Research could focus on the reasons for high concentrations of Chinese Americans in particular cities such as Seattle and San Francisco and could extend to consideration of the other ethnic population centers in other cities as well.

Lessons might continue to focus on stereotypes associated with people of various cultural, ethnic, social, economic, and educational backgrounds.

Technology

Lessons may involve the use of the World Wide Web for information on the demographics of cities and for information on cultural organizations within cities.

Lessons could require the use of CD-ROMs as sources of information on Chinese traditions and language; video cameras, recorders, and monitors could be used for presentation of television-type investigative reports.

Teaching *Freak the Mighty*

Freak the Mighty (1993), by former middle school teacher Rodman Philbrick, is a delightful and poignant book about Kevin, or "Freak," a kid whose body never grows but whose brain cannot be stopped, and Max, or "Mighty," a kid whose body seems to never stop growing but whose intelligence is slow in developing. This odd pair, who together become "Freak the Mighty," are inseparable friends. Kevin rides everywhere from his perch on top of

Max's shoulders; from that position, he not only navigates but also teaches Max his own vocabulary words (which are defined in the novel's glossary) and hard-to-believe stories. When Max's father, a convict, gets out of jail and kidnaps his son, Kevin ("Freak") out-smarts Max's father and becomes a hero. Soon, though, Kevin's physical condition grows critical. Although Kevin had convinced his friend that doctors were going to turn him into the world's first human robot, his body finally quits. Kevin leaves Max—and others whose lives he touches—a legacy of strength, humor, and confidence.

Interdisciplinary Instruction

A New and Improved Ending.   In one of the closing episodes of the book, Kevin's mother, "the Fair Gwen," hosts a thirteenth birthday party for her son. It is during the party that Kevin has a seizure and must be taken to the hospital. He dies a few days later. Until this point, some readers may have been convinced, as was Max, that Kevin's condition would be changed by an operation, one that Kevin claimed would make him the world's first human robot.

Ask students to rewrite the end of the book, imagining that Kevin does have the oper-ation and does receive robotic parts. They should add an adventure that is consistent with the novel in terms of setting, characters, language, and tone. One example to offer students is the addition of an episode in which Max and "the new and improved" (p. 150) robotic Kevin face "Killer Kane," Max's criminal father, again. Another would be an episode in which Kevin uses his new body along with his new computer to become the academic and the athletic hero of his junior high school, with Max as his advisor.

Some may wish to dramatize and videotape their episode additions to show to the class. This activity would allow those readers who are uncomfortable with the fact that Kevin dies in the novel to provide classmates with a humorous and/or suspenseful alternative. It also encourages students to pay close attention to the original text in drawing on the settings, characters, language, and tone of the novel. Students can compare and contrast their new end-ings with Rodman's sequel, *Max the Mighty* (1998), and with the movie version, *The Mighty* (1998), now available on videotape.

Glossary Creation.   In an activity that will encourage students to make personal connec-tions with literature, they could be required to create a glossary, much like "Freak's Dictio-nary" on pages 161–169 (Philbrick, 1993), in which they identify, define, and create an illustration for the terms that they use in unique ways. They might prepare the glossary for the benefit of a hopelessly out-of-touch teacher, a parent, or even a younger sibling. Each could select a few entries to share orally with the class. Then the class could work together to compile, word process, print, develop a cover for, and publish its own glossary and title it "On Our Own Terms." It will be important that students study "Freak's Dictionary" and discuss its style and the kinds of words that are included before they begin collecting words for their own glossaries. This project could be introduced when students first begin reading the novel and could continue, with a minimum number of entries required each week, until the study of the novel and the unit in which it is included are completed. This activity, which lends itself to either individual or small-group work, gives students an impetus for answering the question "Who am I?" in terms of the language they use.

Disabilities: Facts and Fiction.   After students have read the 160-page novel, many will have questions about the physical condition from which Kevin suffered and other disabilities. Their curiosity may provide a good opportunity for inviting a guest or a panel of guest speakers to talk with middle school students about various physical and mental disabilities. The guests might be a blend of health-care professionals and people with disabilities who are eager to help others understand their problems—and the ways in which those with disabilities are also like those without disabilities. Students should prepare for the visit of the guest(s) by conducting research about the particular disabilities the speakers will address and using the research notes to write specific questions that they wish to ask the guest(s). Library resources, CD-ROM encyclopedias, and various World Wide Web sites could be used as research resources. You might choose to contact local organizations, such as the area Advocacy Center for Persons with Disabilities, Easter Seal Society, the Council for the Blind in your state, the Special Olympics leaders in your town or state, and other area health-care organizations and social services about appropriate sources of information for student research, as well as for the names of possible speakers.

Following the guest speaker's presentation, have students work in collaborative groups to create either a factual report or a fictitious but fact-based story about a day in the life of someone with a particular disability. A related activity would have students reading biographies of famous people with disabilities; a biography of contemporary physicist/philosopher Stephen Hawking would certainly appeal to Kevin and those middle school readers who share the character's enthusiasm for science.

Students would also be likely to benefit from conducting similar research regarding the programs designed to meet the needs of students with disabilities that are in place in their school system. The culminating step of this project, instead of composing a written report or an article, could be an oral presentation of the information during a meeting of the school's PTO/PTA or to students in one of the middle school's feeder schools.

Through projects related to this novel, students will learn to use literature as a way to view life in a mirror, under a microscope, or through a telescope (see Chapter 4). They will also increase their awareness and understanding of disabilities, and some may choose to pursue volunteer work in programs that serve children with special needs as a result of their literary encounter.

Integrated Literacy Activities Checklist

Reading
Students read the novel (individually and silently or—in parts— aloud, as a class).

Students read research information about disabilities in order to prepare for a guest speaker interview.

Students may read a biography, such as one of Stephen Hawking.

Students read and serve as editors for others' reports and stories/episode additions.

Students read "Freak's Dictionary" with an eye for the style of the entries, and they read their own and classmates' glossary terms to suggest entries for the class glossary.

Writing

Students write additional episodes, using the author's style as a model.

Students write reports and/or stories based on facts they compile by taking notes from various resources.

Students write their own individual and class glossary.

Students may be asked to write evaluative comments when classmates give oral presentations related to the book.

Listening, Speaking, and Languaging

Students read aloud or dramatize their additional episodes in which Kevin has a robotic body.

Students interview guest speakers with/about people with disabilities and/or representatives from the school system's various programs for students with special needs.

Students orally present their reports or stories about those with disabilities to classmates and/or to younger students.

Students give oral presentations (with visual aids) of personal glossary terms, modeled after "Freak's Dictionary," to the class.

Students listen as audience members when classmates read or dramatize an added episode.

Students listen as they interview the guest speaker(s); they are audience members who must listen closely so they can ask pertinent questions of the speaker.

Students listen to questions of classmates as they present glossary terms and listen as audience members suggest classmates' best terms—those that should be included in the class glossary.

Suggestions for Interdisciplinary Tie-Ins and Technology Enhancement

Science

Lessons and/or assignments might focus on degenerative diseases or on the current state of robotics.

Mathematics

Lessons might focus on proportions, weights, and measurements, using problems related to the differences in Kevin's and Max's height, weight, need for calories, and so on.

Social Studies

Lessons might lead toward a survey of the services provided to people with disabilities in the area.

Students might focus on legal issues concerning people with disabilities, including building accessibility, parking privileges, and discrimination.

Technology

Teachers and students might use a computer network to conduct research and to gather information for the reports related to the study of the novel.

Students can use CD-ROM encyclopedias as reference resources.

Students can videotape their stories and oral report presentations.

Students can use word processors to prepare their reports and stories.

Sharing Effective Literacy Instruction with Colleagues across the Curriculum

Arthur Applebee (2002) synthesizes recent research conducted by the federally funded Center on English Learning and Achievement (CELA) to suggest "six approaches to curriculum and instruction that can be productive starting points for schools seeking to improve reading, writing, and language achievement for all students" (p. 30). He summarizes the findings of a series of studies that have focused on identifying "what features of curriculum, instruction, and assessment make the most difference in literacy learning, from kindergarten through grade twelve" (p. 30). The schools studied represent a "diverse body of effective schools, with a particular emphasis on schools that serve traditionally underachieving populations—children of the poor and of linguistic and ethnic minorities" (p. 30). The six approaches to literacy learning do not promise success if applied independently, but "taken together they can have a significant effect on what students know and are able to do" (p. 30).

What does the research base tell us about effective literacy teaching and learning that we should share with our colleagues across the curriculum? Let's look at the six approaches that Applebee identifies as characteristics of effective literacy programs, with an eye toward interdisciplinary implications.

Engage Students in Higher-Order Talk and Writing about the Disciplines of English

In effective classrooms, students do not merely echo words and ideas that are presented in textbooks or by their teachers. Instead, they learn to use the critical language of the discipline to think for themselves. Instead of reading about someone's feminist interpretation of a work of literature, for example, students use the tools of feminist literary criticism to analyze a text. Then they draw their own conclusions. Critical thinking is more highly valued in these classrooms than is consensus. Applebee describes this approach as an example of one that promotes teaching students to "work *within* the tradition" of literary criticism, instead of merely "learning *about* the tradition" as outside observers of others' conclusions (2002, p. 31). Often, too, students in effective literacy learning environments generate a collection of different informed conclusions.

We can help our colleagues across the curriculum find ways to engage their students in the traditions of their subjects, too. For example, instead of only reading about the work of environmental scientists, which keeps them in observers' roles, middle school students might learn to use some basic tools of environmental research. Then they can design and conduct an environmental study themselves. In this way, they will be learning about the discipline as participants. The conclusions they draw from their environmental project will be informed by their role as scientists.

Ensure the Cohesiveness of Curriculum and Instruction

Applebee refers to the English/language arts curriculum as "something of a hodgepodge, trying to deal with everything that involves the use of language in any way" (2002, p. 31). While he acknowledges that effective classes approach literacy from many angles, he notes that "the most effective classrooms at all grade levels keep a clear focus on the disciplines underlying their subject and develop a web of discipline-based interconnections among the activities that students do" (p. 31). In other words, successful classes are characterized by recognizable interconnections. Instruction is presented in ways that allow students to recall and apply previous lessons and acquire the skills and knowledge that they will draw on in upcoming lessons. Connections between yesterday's and today's discussions are emphasized, for example. Students learn to transfer the reading skills that they develop in their language arts classes to reading assignments that they are given in their social studies classes. Connections within the language arts class, between classes, and from school to home and life outside of school are emphasized in literacy settings.

Our colleagues across the curriculum can find ways to ensure that they provide interconnections for students in their classes, too. Instead of teaching decimals as though they are isolated and independent building blocks for learning mathematics, for example, the mathematics teacher might find ways to emphasize ways that decimals and fractions, which students have already studied, are similar. In other words, she could bring to students' attention the "rich layers of possible links by inviting constant comparison, contrast, and revisiting of related ideas and experiences" (2002, p. 32).

Use Diverse Perspectives to Deepen Discussion and Enhance Learning

Applebee notes that diversity takes many forms. In classrooms, these forms are often manifest as differences in language, culture, race, physical abilities, family and community affiliation, and socioeconomic standing. His findings point to the fact that teachers in effective classrooms value diversity when they encourage students to gather evidence, articulate their own ideas, and insist that others learn to listen respectfully to "others."

Across the curriculum, teachers need to recognize that students come into their classes with differences. We need to help our colleagues understand that differences color students' perceptions of their teacher and of the subject matter, as well as influence their level of willingness to take risks, to participate fully as members of the class. We might encourage them to engage in self-evaluation, with an eye toward any subtle or explicit messages that they might send about what and who is valued in their classrooms, so that they can gauge their own performance regarding diversity. As Applebee notes, "The important thing is to recognize and cultivate the importance of multiple perspectives in enriching students' understandings"

(2002, p. 33). Attitudes that reflect this approach to literacy development should certainly not be limited to the language arts classroom.

Align Curriculum with Assessment

Instead of feeling condemned by the imposition of state standards and state tests, teachers in effective literacy programs have used them as "a lever to reexamine their own curriculum" (2002, p. 33). Applebee notes that the new standardized tests place a premium on "higher-order disciplinary knowledge and literacy skills" (p. 33). A curriculum that promotes integrated thinking, the kind of thinking that is described in the section on pages 224 and 225 will work toward both high test scores and, more important, high levels of literacy growth among students.

We need to be sure that our colleagues across the curriculum recognize that today's standards and standardized tests are not the same as they were in the past. We need to encourage them to integrate writing and reading as modes of critical thinking in their classrooms, as support for what we are trying to accomplish in ours. When students learn about the Civil War in their social studies class, for example, our colleagues might tend to give them a unit test with multiple choice and short answer questions that are intended to evaluate how much factual information the students have retained. We could recommend to this colleague that he consider asking students to continue learning through an alternative evaluation. He might ask them to role play scenes in which officers from the Confederate and Union armies confront each other. He might arrange for panel discussions in which "politicians" representing both sides discuss their stances. He might have students pose as family members who are writing letters from home to their distant sons, fathers, and other loved ones during the war. These activities will promote critical thinking about issues related to the Civil War, as opposed to rote memorization of information related to the war.

Scaffold Skills and Strategies Needed for New and Difficult Tasks

The success of this approach depends on teachers' commitment to focusing on the underlying structures of the discipline, and to identifying what students need to know and be able to do before asking them to complete complex tasks and engage in critical and complex thinking. In effective classrooms, scaffolding, or providing carefully sequenced support for new learning, is targeted at "the difficult parts of a particular task" (2002, p. 33). The connections established through scaffolding of instruction should be brought to the surface, where they are obvious and thus useful to students.

We can introduce the notion of scaffolding instruction to our colleagues in other subject areas much as we introduce the notion of cohesiveness in the curriculum (see page 225). We can help colleagues examine their lesson plans with an eye toward places in which they introduce new information or skills. At those places, we can recommend that they add scaffolding to assist them. For example, the science teacher whose lesson focused on metamorphic rocks yesterday might be ready to move to sedimentary rocks today. She can find ways to build on and connect what students learned about metamorphic rocks when she introduces sedimentary rocks. She will focus on making connections during what is usually, for students, the most difficult part of the lesson on sedimentary rocks. In effect, she sets up students to understand new material by supporting them with previously learned material. The main point is that we make the connections within and between lesson topics and context explicit so that students can incorporate those connections into their thinking.

Provide Special Help to Struggling Readers and Writers

Students who are poor readers and writers have difficulty in language arts classrooms, but teachers in effective literacy settings find ways to involve these students in discussions and other languaging activities while simultaneously helping them improve their basic literacy skills.

We can help our colleagues across the curriculum understand that if a student cannot read her health textbook, for example, she will not have a chance of understanding its content without intervention from her health teacher. We can share some of the strategies that we use in our language arts classrooms when we identify struggling readers and writers, including these: rewriting parts of the text for them; one-on-one conferences to check comprehension of concepts that are presented orally; tape recording portions of the textbook for students to follow as they read; adding simple written highlights of main points during lectures and in-class reading of texts; assigning reading and writing partners from the peer group; providing alternative (sometimes oral) evaluations so that students are tested on their content knowledge and understanding, not penalized for their inability to articulate their ideas.

Our colleagues across the curriculum focus their attention on mathematical formulas, historical events, health issues, biology, and so on, but they share our overarching aim, literacy. We are obligated to help our colleagues understand that, regardless of the subject they teach, our goal is a shared one: We all want students to learn to make sense of their world.

Integrated literacy theories, research, and teaching approaches offer little to teachers who insist on situating themselves as the central authority on all matters that emerge in the English/language arts classes. They offer little for teachers who believe that language is a set of facts that is learned best in sequences and fragments and who believe that a quiet classroom is always a good classroom. They offer little for teachers who ignore the fact that students' lives happen outside of, as well as inside, the walls of our classrooms, and those who teach their subjects while ignoring their students.

In other words, the integrated literacy pedagogy that I recommend throughout this book would not have worked for the teacher I was many years ago. I was one of those teachers who equated quiet classes with productive ones and who valued finished products but offered little instruction on writing and thinking processes. But I was fortunate; colleagues and students helped me learn.

Given the realities of a school's culture and resources, of class sizes and standardized testing, I found that my own deliberate move toward an integrated literacy pedagogy would have to be gradual. I suspect that many of you are in a similar situation today. I urge teachers at the middle grades level to begin taking steps toward instruction that focuses on students as active language users and learners. The first step is to ask ourselves what we are willing to do to help students learn to use language to make sense of their world in ways that will help them understand and navigate adolescence and eventually will carry them into adulthood.

Works Cited

Applebee, A. N. (2002). Engaging students in the disciplines of English: What are effective schools doing? *English Journal 91*(6): 30–36.

Carnegie Council on Adolescent Development. (1989). *Turning points: Preparing American youth for the 21st century.* New York: Carnegie Council on Adolescent Development, Carnegie Corporation.

George, P. S., and Alexander, W. M. (2003). *The exemplary middle school,* 3rd edition. Belmont, CA: Thomson/Wadsworth.

Namioka, L. (1994). *April and the dragon lady.* San Diego: Browndeer of Harcourt Brace.

National Middle School Association. (2003). The position paper of National Middle School Association middle level curriculum: A work in progress. http://www.nmsa.org, May 15, 2003.

Paulsen, G. (1987). *Hatchet.* New York: Laurel Leaf.

Philbrick, R. (1993). *Freak the mighty.* New York: Scholastic Point Signature.

Philbrick, R. (1998). *Max the mighty.* New York: Scholastic Point Signature.

Video

The Mighty (1998). Peter Chelson (director). Miramax Films.

APPENDIX

Professional Standards and Positions

The preface and twelve standards for English language arts instruction as established through the collaborative efforts of the National Council of Teachers of English (NCTE) and the International Reading Association (IRA) (1996) are reproduced here. Notice, in the highlighted sections, how often the notion of a broad definition of literacy and an integrated approach to literacy instruction are explicitly stated or implied.

National Council of Teachers of English/International Reading Association Standards for the English Language Arts (1996)

The vision guiding these standards is that all students must have the opportunities and resources to develop the language skills they need to pursue life's goals and to participate fully as informed, productive members of society. These standards assume that literacy growth begins before children enter school as they experience and experiment with literacy activities—reading and writing, and associating spoken words with their graphic representations. **Recognizing this fact, these standards encourage the development of curriculum and instruction that make productive use of the emerging literacy abilities that children bring to school. Furthermore, the standards provide ample room for the innovation and creativity essential to teaching and learning. They are not prescriptions for particular curriculum or instruction.**

Although we present these standards as a list, we want to emphasize that they are not distinct and separable; they are, in fact, interrelated and should be considered as a whole.

1. Students **read a wide range of print and nonprint texts to build an understanding of texts, of themselves, and of the cultures of the United States and the world;** to acquire new information; to respond to the needs and demands of society and the workplace; and for personal fulfillment. Among these texts are fiction and nonfiction, classic and contemporary works.
2. Students read a wide range of literature from many periods in many genres to **build an understanding of the many dimensions (e.g., philosophical, ethical, aesthetic) of human experience.**
3. Students apply a wide range of strategies to comprehend, interpret, evaluate, and appreciate texts. They **draw on their prior experience, their interactions with other readers and writers, their knowledge of word meaning and of other texts, their word identification strategies, and their understanding of textual features** (e.g., sound–letter correspondence, sentence structure, context, graphics).

4. Students **adjust their use of spoken, written, and visual language** (e.g., conventions, style, vocabulary) **to communicate effectively with a variety of audiences and for different purposes.**

5. Students employ a wide range of strategies as they write and **use different writing process elements appropriately to communicate with different audiences for a variety of purposes.**

6. Students apply knowledge of language structure, language conventions (e.g., spelling and punctuation), media techniques, figurative language, and genre to **create, critique, and discuss print and nonprint texts.**

7. Students **conduct research on issues and interests by generating ideas and questions and by posing problems. They gather, evaluate, and synthesize data from a variety of sources (e.g., print and nonprint texts, artifacts, people)** to communicate their discoveries in ways that suit their purpose and audience.

8. Students **use a variety of technological and information resources** (e.g., libraries, databases, computer networks, video) to gather and synthesize information and **to create and communicate knowledge.**

9. Students develop **an understanding of and respect for diversity in language** use, patterns, and dialects across cultures, ethnic groups, geographic regions, and social roles.

10. Students whose first language is not English **make use of their first language to develop competency in the English language arts and to develop understanding of content across the curriculum.**

11. Students participate as knowledgeable, reflective, creative, and critical **members of a variety of literacy communities.**

12. Students use spoken, written, and visual language to accomplish their own purposes (e.g., for learning, enjoyment, persuasion, and the exchange of information). (Farstrup and Myers for NCTE/IRA, 1996, p. 3)

Position Paper of the National Middle School Association
Middle Level Curriculum: A Work in Progress (2002)

Like the National Council of Teachers of English and the International Reading Association, the National Middle School Association (NMSA) supports a pedagogy that can be identified as an integrated literacy stance. Following are the five points of the NMSA statement on curriculum for the middle grades. Again, I have highlighted points of conceptual support for language arts instruction that explicitly call for or imply the benefits of an integrated literacy stance.

1. We believe learning experiences for young adolescents should:
   - **Address their varied intellectual, physical, social, emotional, and moral development;**
   - **Help them make sense of themselves and the world about them;**
   - **Be highly integrated and connected to life;**
   - **Include their questions, needs, developmental issues, and ideas;**

- **Involve them in rich and significant knowledge about the world;**
- Open doors to new ideas that evoke curiosity, the desire to explore, and, at times, awe and wonder;
- Challenge students and encourage them to take maximum advantage of educational opportunities;
- Develop caring, responsible, and ethical citizens who practice democratic principles.

2. Further, we advocate learning experiences which:
- **Value the dignity and diversity of all individuals;**
- **Allow students to learn and express themselves in a variety of ways;**
- **Use the full range of communication skills and technologies in purposeful contexts;**
- **Engage students in problem solving through a variety of relevant experiential learning opportunities;**
- **Involve students in meaningful service that encourages them to make a difference in the world around them;**
- Involve students in setting goals, planning, and assessing their own learning;
- Include continuous, authentic, and appropriate assessment of students' progress in academic achievement and the acquisition of desired behavioral attributes.

3. Such learning experiences, which must be accessible to all students, require environments in which:
- **Challenging content in partnership with appropriate learning strategies becomes the key to significant learning;**
- Students and staff are safe, cared for, understood, trusted, and respected;
- Each young adolescent can experience success;
- Faculty is empowered and supported in creating developmentally responsive curriculum and instructional approaches;
- Staff are positive role models;
- **The family is actively involved in students' educational endeavors;**
- **The learning community expands beyond the school.**

4. Because of these convictions, we believe the following conditions should be evident:
- **All areas of knowledge and skill are viewed as important and are integrated throughout the student's school experience;**
- **Students explore integrated themes which engage them in serious and rigorous study;**
- Curriculum is developed by **careful and continuing study of students, social trends and issues, and research-supported school practices;**
- Flexible learning groups are based on students' needs and interests;
- Active collaborative, self-directed learning is used;
- A variety of educational materials, resources, and instructional strategies are used;
- Staff development promotes and supports developmentally responsive practices;
- The staff is organized in ways that encourage ongoing collaboration;
- All staff help plan and participate in long-term professional growth opportunities.

5. Because of these convictions, we believe the following conditions should be phased out:

- The curriculum consists of separate subjects and skills taught and tested in isolation from one another;
- Content is judged to be more important than the process by which it is learned;
- Students are labeled and tracked into rigid ability groups;
- Lecturing, rote learning, and drill are used excessively;
- Textbooks and worksheets dominate;
- Faculty is organized by departments;
- Staff development efforts are short term and nonproductive. (NMSA, 2002)

Works Cited

Farstrup, A. E., and Myers, M. (Eds.). (1996). *Standards for the English language arts*. Urbana, IL and Newark, DE: NCTE and IRA.

National Middle School Association. (2003). The position paper of National Middle School Association Middle level curriculum: A work in progress. http://www.nmsa.org, May 15, 2003.

INDEX